Israel

COVENANT PEOPLE
COVENANT LAND

Seymour Rossel

UNION OF AMERICAN HEBREW CONGREGATIONS

New York, New York

Feldman Library

THE FELDMAN LIBRARY FUND was created in 1974 through a gift from the Milton and Sally Feldman Foundation. The Feldman Library Fund, which provides for the publication by the UAHC of selected outstanding Jewish books and texts, memorializes Sally Feldman, who in her lifetime devoted herself to Jewish youth and Jewish learning. Herself an orphan and brought up in an orphanage, she dedicated her efforts to helping Jewish young people get the educational opportunities she had not enjoyed.

In loving memory of my beloved wife Sally
"She was my life, and she is gone;
She was my riches, and I am a pauper."

"Many daughters have done valiantly, but thou excellest them all."

Milton E. Feldman

For sharing a life of devotion to our people—
For sharing a life of study and of teaching—
For sharing a life of work and pleasure—
For loving and for friendship—
For caring and for wisdom—
For Karen—
Forever.

Acknowledgments

The Talmud reminds us that the finest teachings are those taught in the name of one's teachers. Those who taught me about Israel and Covenant are many and their words may be found throughout this work. Special thanks are due to David Altshuler, Martin Buber, Eugene B. Borowitz, Melvin Glatzer, Manuel Gold, Cyrus Gordon, Yehoshafat Harkabi, Jacob Neusner, Marc Silverman, and particularly Morris Sugarman.

Many fine suggestions were made by the readers chosen by the Union of American Hebrew Congregations to review this work in its first draft, and by Aron Hirt-Manheimer, Steven Schnur, and Daniel Syme.

The excellent production of this volume is the work of Stuart Benick.

To all these, and to the many behind the scenes who lent their hands to strengthen mine, I express my grateful thanks.

Seymour Rossel
Chappaqua, New York
Chanukah, 5785

Contents

CONTENTS

ISRAEL:
Covenant People,
Covenant Land

Introduction
THE COVENANT, THE JEWS, AND THE LAND

The pilot announces, "We are about to land at Ben-Gurion Airport." The airplane touches ground beside the city of Lydda (Lod) where, in the first and second centuries, the Sanhedrin, the Jewish Court of Elders, met. Here, Rabbis Tarfon, Joshua ben Levi, Ishmael, Yohanan ben Zakkai, Eliezer ben Hyrcanus, and Akiba held conversations that would be recorded in the Mishnah and the Talmud. The fields they walked are now cemented over to form your runway.

You board a taxi for Jerusalem. As the taxi moves up the highway into the Judean Hills, you experience a different period of history. Along the highway, rusting, are the skeleton-like remains of trucks and armored cars. Once they were part of caravans trying to bring food and supplies into Jerusalem while it was surrounded by Arab armies. Now they are a constant reminder of the great struggle for Israel's independence that took place in 1948. You pass them in freedom. Nothing stands between you and Jerusalem to keep you from reaching the Holy City.

At the Western Wall, giant stones, cut by hand from solid rock, are all that remain of the great wall that once encircled the Temple in days of old. Looking up at them, you feel the power of the ancients, the glory that was Israel in the days of Solomon and the kings. Outside the city wall is a new kind of glory—tall buildings, a modern city. At the Western Wall, you have a special feeling about being Jewish. You pray where Jewish royalty and peasants, pilgrims and priests once walked.

In the north, on Mount Carmel, you have the strange feeling that Elijah the Prophet still keeps watch over the site where he once defeated the prophets of Baal. In Jaffa, you think of Jonah who set out on his sea journey from here, hoping to escape the will of God, but found himself unable to flee. At the Dead Sea, your guide points to a rock pillar and tells you this is "Lot's wife," and then recounts the biblical story of how that poor woman looked back and was turned to a column of salt. At Eilat, in the south, you stare out at the blue waters where once Solomon launched ships that traveled to Africa and Asia. You breathe the same air his sailors did, see the same coral reefs below, and enjoy the same exotic fish.

You, too, are a part of Jewish history now. You are one with the Land to which Israel, our people, has given its name: the Land of Israel. Being Jewish binds you to this place.

I: THE COVENANT

Ancient history tells of many journeys. The hero or heroine goes away to find fortune, to do great deeds, to learn great secrets, to wander foreign lands. One after another, these men and women of legend return home, whether vanquished or victorious.

The Jewish journey begins in the biblical saga of Abraham and Sarah (first called Abram and

3

INTRODUCTION

"Lot's Wife," a vertical pillar of crystalline salt, near the Dead Sea.

Sarai). Abraham and Sarah set out from Ur to Canaan to *complete* a promise and, as part of that promise or *Covenant,* to find their home in a faraway place.

וַיֹּאמֶר יְהֹוָה אֶל־אַבְרָם לֶךְ־לְךָ מֵאַרְצְךָ וּמִמּוֹלַדְתְּךָ
וּמִבֵּית אָבִיךָ אֶל־הָאָרֶץ אֲשֶׁר אַרְאֶךָּ: וְאֶעֶשְׂךָ לְגוֹי
גָּדוֹל וַאֲבָרֶכְךָ וַאֲגַדְּלָה שְׁמֶךָ וֶהְיֵה בְּרָכָה: וַאֲבָרֲכָה
מְבָרֲכֶיךָ וּמְקַלֶּלְךָ אָאֹר וְנִבְרְכוּ בְךָ כֹּל מִשְׁפְּחֹת
הָאֲדָמָה: וַיֵּלֶךְ אַבְרָם כַּאֲשֶׁר דִּבֶּר אֵלָיו יְהֹוָה וַיֵּלֶךְ אִתּוֹ
לוֹט וְאַבְרָם בֶּן־חָמֵשׁ שָׁנִים וְשִׁבְעִים שָׁנָה בְּצֵאתוֹ
מֵחָרָן: וַיִּקַּח אַבְרָם אֶת־שָׂרַי אִשְׁתּוֹ וְאֶת־לוֹט בֶּן־אָחִיו
וְאֶת־כָּל־רְכוּשָׁם אֲשֶׁר רָכָשׁוּ וְאֶת־הַנֶּפֶשׁ אֲשֶׁר־עָשׂוּ
בְחָרָן וַיֵּצְאוּ לָלֶכֶת אַרְצָה כְּנַעַן וַיָּבֹאוּ אַרְצָה כְּנָעַן:
וַיַּעֲבֹר אַבְרָם בָּאָרֶץ עַד מְקוֹם שְׁכֶם עַד אֵלוֹן מוֹרֶה
וְהַכְּנַעֲנִי אָז בָּאָרֶץ: וַיֵּרָא יְהֹוָה אֶל־אַבְרָם וַיֹּאמֶר
לְזַרְעֲךָ אֶתֵּן אֶת־הָאָרֶץ הַזֹּאת וַיִּבֶן שָׁם מִזְבֵּחַ לַיהֹוָה
הַנִּרְאֶה אֵלָיו:

The Lord said to Abram, "Go forth from your native land and from your father's house to the land that I will show you.

I will make of you a great nation,
And I will bless you;
I will make your name great,
And you shall be a blessing.
I will bless those who bless you
And curse him that curses you;
And all the families of the earth
Shall bless themselves by you."

Abram went forth as the Lord had commanded him.... Abram took his wife Sarai and his brother's son Lot, and all the wealth that they had amassed, and the persons that they had acquired in Haran; and they set out for the land of Canaan.... The Canaanites were then in the land.

The Lord appeared to Abram and said, "I will give this land to your offspring." And [Abram] built an altar there to the Lord who had appeared to him. (Genesis 12:1–7)

4

INTRODUCTION

Our first Jewish ancestors did not return to Haran. They found a new home in Canaan, in the Land that one day would be called Israel. Much of what follows may already be known to you; in order to understand it fully, however, we review it here briefly.

It may be that the Bible tells the beginning of the story in a kind of shorthand, using Abraham's family to stand for the many families of a tribe called the '*Abiru* or *Habiru* (from which we get the English word, "Hebrews"). This group of people came into Canaan some four thousand years ago. Their tribal name gives us a clue: the word "Hebrews" or *Ivrim* means "those who crossed-over." It was the first name by which our people was known.

The Covenant, God's promise, was passed from parent to child. Abraham entrusted it to Isaac; Isaac gave it to Jacob. The Bible tells us that Jacob cheated his elder brother Esau, usurping the blessing of the birthright from him. One night, Jacob wrestled until dawn with an angel, much as a person might wrestle all night with his or her conscience. Dawn came, but still neither Jacob nor the angel had triumphed. Then the angel gave Jacob a blessing of his own, renaming him Israel, "the one who wrestled God." So the children of Jacob, each of whom came to stand for a tribe, gave rise to the Tribes of Israel. Thereafter, the Children of Israel became the second name by which our people was known.

In Jacob's time there was a famine in Canaan causing him and his sons to move south to Egypt. Historians say that many of the Hebrews stayed in Canaan, but the Children of Israel who journeyed to the land of the pharaohs soon found themselves enslaved.

For many generations they dreamed of returning to their Promised Land, the land of the Covenant.

II: THE JEWS

It was Moses who led the Israelites out of Egypt, brought them into the wilderness of Sinai, taught them and cared for them, and made them into a nation. They stayed forty years in the desert—long enough for the old generation born in slavery to give way to a new generation born in freedom.

History cannot tell us what happened at Mount Sinai. But the Bible story tells how our ancestors thought God appeared to the Children of Israel:

וַיְדַבֵּר יְהוָֹה אֶל־מֹשֶׁה לֵךְ עֲלֵה מִזֶּה אַתָּה וְהָעָם אֲשֶׁר
הֶעֱלִיתָ מֵאֶרֶץ מִצְרָיִם אֶל־הָאָרֶץ אֲשֶׁר נִשְׁבַּעְתִּי
לְאַבְרָהָם לְיִצְחָק וּלְיַעֲקֹב לֵאמֹר לְזַרְעֲךָ אֶתְּנֶנָּה:
וְשָׁלַחְתִּי לְפָנֶיךָ מַלְאָךְ וְגֵרַשְׁתִּי אֶת־הַכְּנַעֲנִי הָאֱמֹרִי
וְהַחִתִּי וְהַפְּרִזִּי הַחִוִּי וְהַיְבוּסִי: אֶל־אֶרֶץ זָבַת חָלָב
וּדְבָשׁ כִּי לֹא אֶעֱלֶה בְּקִרְבְּךָ כִּי עַם־קְשֵׁה־עֹרֶף אַתָּה פֶּן־
אֲכֶלְךָ בַּדָּרֶךְ:

Then the Lord said to Moses, "Set out from here, you and the people that you have brought from the land of Egypt, to the land of which I swore to Abraham, Isaac, and Jacob, saying, 'To your offspring will I give it'—I will send an angel before you, and I will drive out the Canaanites, the Amorites, the Hittites, the Perizzites, the Hivites, and the Jebusites—a land flowing with milk and honey. . . ." (Exodus 33:1–3)

Whatever happened at Sinai, the Israelites were now one people, the Jewish people. Our God was the One God, and our Land was the Promised Land.

III: THE LAND

The Promised Land—Canaan, the Land of Israel—has often been a battleground for the empires of the world. It was conquered by Canaanites, Hittites, Egyptians, Hebrews, Philistines, Assyrians, Babylonians, Persians, Greeks, Syrians, Romans, Arabs, Mamelukes, Crusaders, Turks, French, English, the Jews, and the Arabs.

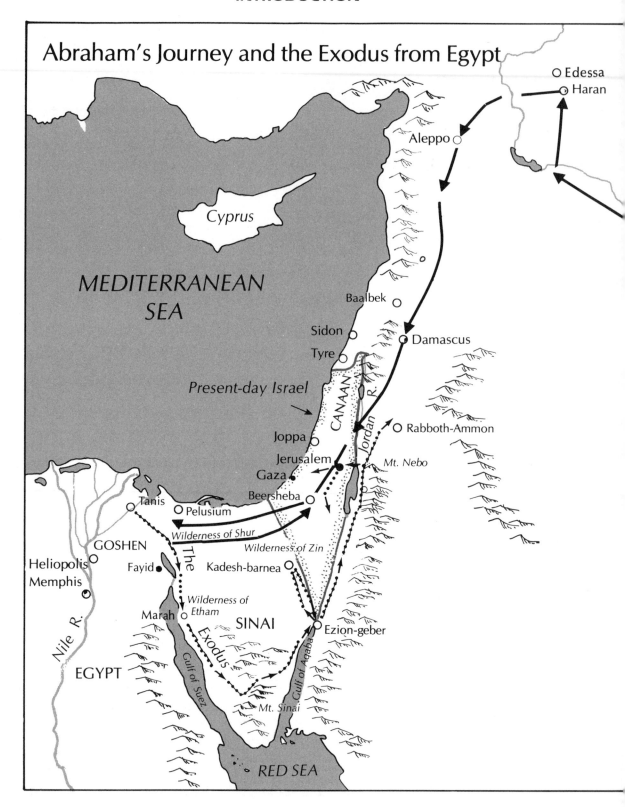

Abraham's Journey and the Exodus from Egypt

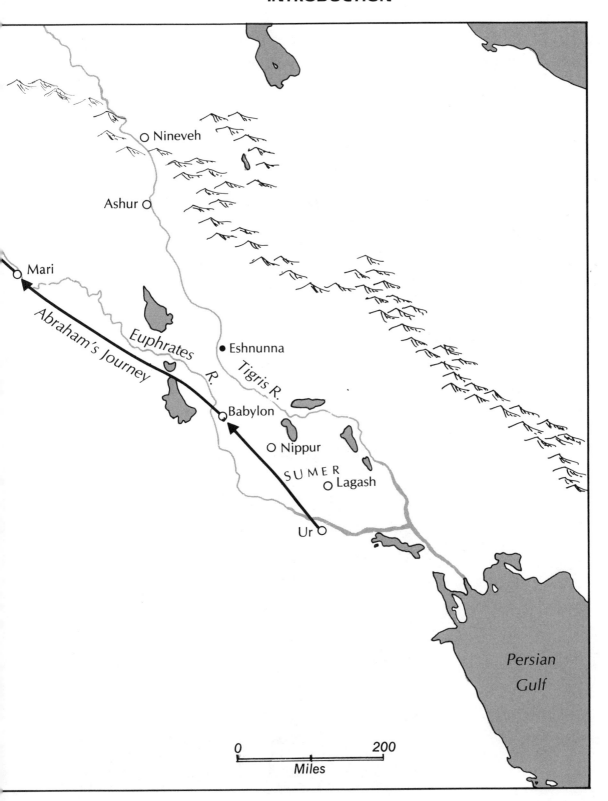

INTRODUCTION

It lies at the meeting place of Africa, Asia, and Europe; and it has always been a center of trading—both of merchandise and of culture and ideas.

It is told that, when God began to create the world, God first built a small model. Into this model, God placed every kind of weather, every kind of land and water formation. Then God filled the model with animals of every kind, and with flowers and fruits that grow in the tropics and those that grow on the mountains. When the world was completed according to the model, God placed the model in its center. This model was the Land of Israel, the Land flowing with milk and honey.

From the burning soil of the Negev where the summer heat may reach 103°F to the Galilee where the winter rains are plentiful, some 2,500 different kinds of plants grow wild. Gazelles, hyenas, lynx, shrews, porcupines, cheetahs, badgers, wolves, wild boar, and jackals roam where the mighty lions of Samaria once ruled the forests. Eagles and gulls, ravens and quail, hoopoe and stork, buzzards and kites, pelicans and swans fill the air. Pilgrims through the ages learned to watch for snakes, scorpions, and spiders; farmers kept an eye out for the black clouds of locusts.

The Bible tells of crops of wheat and barley and vines and fig trees, pomegranates, olives, and honey. Modern Israelis have added many others. The Bible may be forgiven for bragging a little, claiming that the twelve spies sent into the Land of Canaan by Moses returned with a cluster of grapes so heavy that two men had to carry it on a pole between them. In terms of what the Land had to offer the Children of Israel, this was a small exaggeration.

IV: AHAVAT ZION

These are the three elements in our attachment to this ever-changing, never-changing place: the

Covenant, our people, and the Land itself. There has never been a time in history, from the moment the Hebrews first crossed over into Canaan, when some of our people were not living in the Land of Israel. At times, there were few of us, at times there were many. Sometimes, we ruled, and sometimes we were ruled by others. But, we were always there.

Likewise, there has never been a time when our people did not feel something special about this Land, something sacred. Even in the long years that Jews wandered through other lands and other places, we remembered and celebrated the seasons of the Holy Land, prayed for the dew to appear in its appointed time and the rain to fall on schedule "back home."

Throughout the life of the Jewish people, the Land has been central to Jewish tradition, Jewish learning, and Jewish belief. It is a part of us today, whether we live in London or Wyoming, Maine or California, Montreal or Pennsylvania, Moscow or Baltimore, South Pole or North Pole. At the Passover seder Jews everywhere utter the words, לְשָׁנָה הַבָּאָה בִּירוּשָׁלָיִם , *Leshanah habaah birushalayim!* "Next year in Jerusalem!" So we declare our love for the Land of Israel; our hope to see it in our lifetime; our prayer that our people may always inhabit it, even as they always have.

We have given a name to this feeling. We call it אַהֲבַת צִיּוֹן , *Ahavat Zion,* "The Love of Zion [the Land of Israel]." Being Jewish binds us to this place.

PREVIEW

It is Israel, the Land, that this book is about. We will study together the beginnings of our attachment to the Land, our belief that the Land is sacred, and how this attachment and belief shape us and make us into the kind of Jews we are today.

9

INTRODUCTION

And this is a book about the Jewish people, too. Why do Jews feel a special tug when we hear the word "Israel" on an evening news report? What causes so many of us to long to see the Land for ourselves? Why do Jews feel a special pride when hearing of a great Israeli accomplishment? Why is there a special sense of loss when we hear of a tragedy in Israel? What, precisely, makes Israel so precious to so many of us? These are feelings we must define, questions we must answer, all of us, as Jews, as human beings.

Above all—and part of them—is the question of honor. What causes us to honor our ancient Covenant, our exquisite belief that each of us— you and I—stood beneath the mountain of Sinai that day when the Jewish people received the Ten Commandments and entered into the Promised Land "flowing with milk and honey," to test these words, to live by these commandments?

UNIT ONE

From Entry to Exile

1

THE FIRST IN THE LAND

Moses stood on the mountaintop looking over into the Land of Canaan, the Promised Land. He would never enter the Land. For forty years he had led the Israelites as they moved from oasis to oasis, settling for a while, then moving on, knowing only the wilderness. In that time, a generation had passed and a new generation had grown into strong men and women. Moses knew that he was a part of the old generation. The new world—the Promised Land, the land of the Covenant—was for the new generation to conquer.

The old generation thought like slaves. In many ways, they acted like slaves. The new generation had grown up in freedom, thinking and acting like free people. There was a world of difference between them. The old generation still recalled the whips of the Egyptian slavemasters. There were no scars on the backs of the new generation. And in the eyes of the new generation burned the light of freedom.

But there was still another, greater difference: the new generation had sweet and clear memories of the great event at Mount Sinai. Something had happened there—in the midst of fire and clouds and thunder and lightning—that had changed them forever. One part of this was the Ten Commandments. One part of this was the feeling that God had spoken to the people of Israel. One part of this was that a Covenant—an agreement—had been reached between the people and the One God. The promise of God to Abraham, Isaac, and Jacob would come to pass—they would possess the Land of Israel.

There might be questions in the minds of the older folks. Why had God allowed them to suffer in Egypt? Why had God waited so many generations before coming to their rescue? Why had God not just given them the Land? Why had they been made to wander for so many years in the harsh countryside of Sinai?

But the new generation had answers. God had come to their rescue. God had saved them at the Sea of Reeds and destroyed Pharaoh's armies and chariots. God had given them the years in the wilderness to grow up strong and self-assured, ready to do battle against the Canaanites who held the Land. God had prepared them for life on the Land by giving laws for them to live by.

They would need to do their part, now. It was up to them to conquer the Land, to settle in it, to set up a government for themselves, to follow God's laws, to live in freedom. But they were ready. And in Joshua, the son of Nun, they had a new leader—appointed by Moses.

I: JOSHUA

It was Joshua who brought the Israelites into the Promised Land, led their armies against the Canaanites, and began to settle the twelve tribes of Israel on the Land. Those Canaanite cities that were too strong to conquer, Joshua did not attack. All around them, he settled the Israelites, and they became farmers. These cities were finally forced to open their gates and welcome

13

Jebel Musa (in Arabic, "Mount of Moses") on the Sinai Peninsula. Arabs think this is where Moses received the Ten Commandments.

their Hebrew neighbors. In fact, many Canaanites eventually became Hebrews.

Living side by side with the Canaanites, these early Jewish settlers found themselves becoming more like their neighbors, just as we today—living among the mainly Christian populations of America and Europe—find ourselves much like our neighbors. Just as we and Christians today use the word "God" in English (even though we mean different things when we say "God"), so too the God of Israel was called *Elohim* and the Canaanites called their "old god" *El.* Both names came from the same root. Just as the Canaanites brought sacrifices to their gods, the Israelites brought sacrifices to the One God. Just as our services and our synagogues are much like those of our Christian neighbors, so the Israelite religion was much like the religion of the Canaanites.

It was this that worried Joshua most. As he grew older, he saw the Israelites forgetting the differences that separated them from the Canaanites and beginning to accept the ways of the Canaanites more and more. He saw many of the Israelites placing idols in their households and offering prayers to the local gods of the Canaanites. Canaanite farmers taught the Israelite farmers which of their gods "controlled" the rains and the soil and—even though it was more out of superstition than belief—many Israelites offered prayers and sacrifices to the Canaanite gods. It troubled Joshua, just as it would trouble many Jewish leaders after him, even as it troubles us today.

When he was old, Joshua called the leaders of the Israelites to the Tabernacle—the portable sanctuary that had been their place of worship in the wilderness. He reminded them of their his-

The Twelve Tribes of Israel

tory, of the wonders that God had done for them. He told them again the stories of Abraham, Isaac, and Jacob; how Jacob and his sons followed Joseph into Egypt. He told them how the Israelites became slaves in Egypt; how God sent Moses and Aaron to lead them to freedom; how God saved the people at the Sea of Reeds.

> " . . . Thus said the Lord, the God of Israel: . . . Then you crossed the Jordan and you came to Jericho. . . . I sent a plague ahead of you, and it drove them out before you . . . not by your sword or by your bow. I have given you a land for which you did not labor and towns which you did not build, and you have settled in them; you are enjoying vineyards and olive groves which you did not plant.
>
> "Now, therefore, revere the Lord and serve Him with undivided loyalty. . . ." (Joshua 24:2, 11–14)

Joshua's message was clear and sharp: so long as the Israelites lived by the Covenant, they needed no human leader or hero or king. Thus Joshua appointed no one to take his place. Instead, he left behind twelve tribes, settled in the Promised Land, linked by one religion and one idea—that there was a Covenant between God and them.

II: WHAT IS THE COVENANT

The Covenant made at Mount Sinai was similar to the one made between God and Abraham. But it was different, too. In a sense, in the Covenant at Sinai, God agreed to be King over Israel, so long as Israel would follow God's laws. That was the agreement. The laws were given in the form of the commandments, particularly the Ten Commandments, which are, in a way, a summary of all the other commandments to be found in the Torah.

In the Ten Commandments, God first demanded the loyalty of Israel and made it clear that there was a good reason to demand this loyalty; after all, God had just saved the Jewish people from slavery and from Pharaoh's armies. So the commandments begin with the simple statement, "I the Lord am your God who brought you out of the land of Egypt, the house of bondage." (Exodus 20:2)

Next God commands that Israel respect the Oneness, the unity, of God:

> You shall have no other gods beside Me. You shall not make for yourself a sculptured image, or any likeness. . . . You shall not bow down to them [idols] or serve them. . . . (Exodus 20:3–5)

This is followed by a commandment which asks us to honor God in yet another way, by not making false statements while taking an oath in God's name.

Then God commands us to keep the Sabbath, again because of what God has done for us:

> "For in six days the Lord made heaven and earth and sea, and all that is in them, and rested on the seventh day. . . ." (Exodus 20:11)

The Land of Israel is mentioned in the laws of the Covenant only in the fifth commandment, "Honor your father and your mother. . . ." If you do so, "you may long endure on the land which the Lord your God is giving you." (Exodus 20:12) The Bible offers no further explanation of the connection between honoring parents and possessing the Land, but we may guess.

As we have seen, a covenant is passed from one generation to the next, from parent to child, just as Abraham's covenant was passed to Isaac and from Isaac to Jacob. How can one honor the teachings and agreements of one's parents without honoring one's parents? But this is just one possible explanation. You may have one of your own. The commandment itself is simple, merely stating the law: Honor your parents and you will possess the Land of Israel; stop honoring them and the Land will be lost.

THE FIRST IN THE LAND

These, then, are the first five commandments. Five more follow: (6) You shall not murder; (7) You shall not commit adultery; (8) You shall not steal; (9) You shall not bear false witness against your neighbor; (10) You shall not covet your neighbor's house, your neighbor's servants, your neighbor's animals, nor anything that belongs to your neighbor.

The Ten Commandments are the basic terms of the agreement, the *berit* (covenant) between God and the people of Israel. The rest of the *mitzvot* (commandments) spell these ten out in great detail, making them easier for us to understand, easier to follow. Just before giving the commandments to the people at Sinai, God made a promise which is really a part of the Covenant:

" . . . If you will obey Me faithfully and keep My Covenant, you shall be My treasured possession among all the peoples. Indeed, all the earth is Mine, but you shall be to Me a kingdom of priests and a holy nation. . . ." (Exodus 19:5–6)

This is the great secret of being the "chosen people." When we chose to keep the laws of the Covenant, we became God's "treasured possession . . . a kingdom of priests and a holy nation."

Promulgation of the Law on Mount Sinai.

17

All that remained was for the people to agree to the *berit* that God placed before them. The Torah tells us:

Then he [Moses] took the record of the Covenant and read it aloud to the people. And they said, "All that the Lord has spoken we will faithfully do!" (Exodus 24:7)

The people of Israel took an oath. In effect, we swore to behave in ways of righteousness. We swore to live up to the models of Abraham and Isaac and Jacob who had been rewarded by covenants.

From that moment, the Covenant became a way of life for our people, constantly being renewed. Today we renew the Covenant on the High Holy Days, on Sukot, on Passover, and especially on Shavuot—the day on which we commemorate the *berit* made at Sinai. We renew it, too, when we keep Shabbat, as we were commanded in the Covenant. We speak of God's love through which Torah with its commandments was given to us, and we say the *Shema* prayer, promising to teach the Covenant to our children.

We renew the Covenant when a child is born, when a male child is circumcised or a female child named. We renew the Covenant each time there is a consecration, a *Bar* or *Bat Mitzvah,* a confirmation, a wedding ceremony; even as we mourn for those who have died.

And whenever we renew the Covenant we recall the Land of Israel, the Promised Land given to the "chosen people." So long as Jews continue to choose the way of the Covenant, the Promised Land remains part of our agreement with God. So long as Jews choose not to forget, we honor the Covenant and prove ourselves worthy of possessing the Land of Israel.

That is the full meaning of the Covenant which was given at Mount Sinai. It is the agreement between God and the people of Israel; it is the laws which spell out the terms of that agreement. But the Covenant only *began* at Sinai. As we

shall see, it continues to grow through every generation, and every generation leaves its own special mark on the Covenant, changing it slightly, adding to it, renewing it in unique and creative ways.

III: THE JUDGES

For nearly two hundred years, the twelve tribes each had their own government and their own territory, like the thirteen early colonies of North America before the United States was created. Here and there, whenever one was needed, a leader would arise who might unite some of the tribes to do battle against a strong enemy. Such leaders were called judges, and their story is told in the Book of Judges in the Bible.

Deborah the Judge led several of the tribes against the armies of the king of Hazor. Just as the king appointed a general to lead his troops, Deborah also appointed a general. But, in the end, Deborah and her general led the battle together, defeating the enemy.

In another time and place, a judge named Gideon led a few hand-picked men against the fierce camel-riding raiders called the Midianites. His small group fell upon the Midianites at night, taking them by surprise. In the moment of victory, many wished to make Gideon a king, but, wisely, he refused. Perhaps he recalled the lesson that Joshua had taught.

Even Samson, who used his great strength to fight against the Philistines in the plains along the coast, did not seek to become a king. Though he was able to kill many Philistines single-handed before he was captured, though he killed many more when he forced apart the columns of their temple and brought the roof down upon them and upon himself, he was not the kind of king that his people needed. He, too, believed in this great new idea of freedom, that people could live under the rule of God alone.

Whether they led only the people of their own tribe, or united all the tribes in a region, the

The "Lion of Israel" medal, designed by sculptress Elizabeth Weistrop, depicting the basic source of Judaism. The obverse shows the symbolic lion guarding a nine-branched menorah and the Star of David; the reverse represents Moses, after his descent from Mount Sinai, delivering the Ten Commandments to the Israelites.

judges appeared to help the people mainly in times of trouble. For two centuries the Israelites lived in their land, for the most part, without a king, united by their history and Covenant.

IV: THE ARK OF THE COVENANT

It was the Ark of the Covenant that reminded the twelve tribes that they were really one people ruled by the One God. It was this Ark that once stood at the center of the Tabernacle. In it, Moses had placed the Tablets of the Ten Commandments, along with the fragments of the broken tablets that he first brought down from Sinai. The Ark, then, was Israel's most treasured possession.

No wonder the people were shocked when, in 1050 B.C.E., the Philistines captured the Ark of the Covenant and carried it away. The Tabernacle at Shiloh was destroyed. The people had no general to unite them, no king or hero to lead them. And the Philistines were the most powerful enemy they had ever faced.

In fact, many Israelites were afraid that God had deserted them. This was the first of many lessons the Israelites had to learn. In truth, many of them had deserted God by growing too much like the Canaanites. They had turned their backs on their history and forgotten their Covenant.

PREVIEW

In this sad hour a new kind of leader arose. His name was Samuel. He was the last of the judges and the first of a long line of prophets. In his heart and in his mind Samuel carried the message of Joshua—that the Israelites needed but one leader, God.

Things to Consider

Moses dreamed of the Promised Land but was unable to enter it. Like Moses, we often have dreams we cannot complete; like Moses, we often turn to our children—the next generation— to complete some of these dreams for us. Ask your parents or grandparents what dreams they hope *you* will make real.

UNIT ONE: From Entry to Exile

Three great events helped to form the Jewish people: (1) going out of Egyptian slavery, (2) receiving the Covenant and the Law at Mount Sinai, and (3) the years of wandering. In a way, all three were part of one struggle—the struggle to understand and learn to live in freedom. Can you identify some struggles for freedom in the world today?

The Jews lived in separate tribes in the days of the judges; yet they still felt part of one people. In what ways are the Jews today divided? What are some of the things that remind us we are one people?

Throughout the reading, you will be reminded of the Covenant between God and the Jewish people. But the meaning of the word "covenant" will slowly grow and change. Look back over the chapter and make a list of the things that are part of the Covenant in this early period in Jewish history.

2

THE DAYS OF EMPIRE

"In those days there was no king in Israel; every person did what was right in his own eyes." (Judges 17:6; 18:1; 19:1; 21:25)

Four times the Book of Judges tells us that "there was no king in Israel," that each person decided "what was right." For Joshua, this was the ideal. In another way, this was a dangerous situation: no one was in control, no one could call the tribes together to act as one people. And, as the Israelite tribes acted more and more on their own, in pursuit of their own interests, fighting broke out among themselves.

The loss of the Ark of the Covenant underlined the crisis. Even though the superstitious Philistines soon returned the Ark, believing that it was bringing them bad luck, the Israelites felt more strongly than ever that they *should* have a king. So they turned to Samuel, demanding: ". . . Appoint a king for us to govern us like all other nations." (1 Samuel 8:5)

Samuel, though raised as a priest and revered as a judge and prophet, knew that he could not rule over Israel. In his younger years, he sometimes acted as a general, helping the tribes to keep the Philistines at bay. But, as he grew older, and seeing that his own sons were unfit to rule, he knew that he had to help the Israelites in the way they wished—by appointing a king for them. Yet he did this against his better judgment.

The Bible preserves *two* versions of the origin of the monarchy. In one version, Samuel was afraid of what a king might do to the Israelites. He warned them that a king would take their sons for the army, make their daughters into royal servants, and force the people to pay taxes and tributes. In the other version, Samuel knew that a king would bring unity to the tribes, so he chose to appoint the best king he could.

I: KING SAUL

Samuel chose Saul, who was large and strong and who could be "looked up to" by the people. But Saul was soon a disappointment to Samuel.

Saul wished to unite the Israelites—politically, militarily, and religiously. He probably thought he was chosen to do so. But Samuel, who longed for the old days of freedom, was not ready for such a radical change. When Saul offered sacrifices and decided the proper moment for a battle against the Philistines, he assumed the role both of priest and prophet. This caused Samuel great pain and he turned away from Saul and visited him no more.

Without Samuel, Saul was incomplete, falling into periods of depression, rage, indecision—even madness. Saul's own son, Jonathan, found it difficult to be loyal to his father.

Under Saul, both the kingship and the kingdom remained weak. But the groundwork was laid and David, Saul's son-in-law and a soldier in his army, emerged as a second king. David had played his harp to ease Saul's depression, proved himself as a warrior against the Philistine champion Goliath, married Saul's daughter, and be-

"Samuel Anointing Saul," engraving by Matthaeus Merian, 1625.

friended Saul's son Jonathan. Samuel's last act was to announce that he had chosen David as the next king of Israel.

When Saul's army met the Philistines again at Mount Gilboa, his sons were killed in the fighting and he took his own life. Still the people longed for a king, so David rose to rule them.

II: KING DAVID

In his final months, Saul drove David away and sought to kill him. But David learned to live by his wits and even made a pact with the Philistines.

As an outlaw, David gathered a small band of followers who traveled with him and fought by his side. He took money to protect the local herdsmen in the wilderness of Judah and almost agreed to fight *with* the Philistines against Saul at Mount Gilboa, so deep was his argument with Saul. Yet the death of Saul and Jonathan hurt him deeply. "Your glory, O Israel," he lamented, "lies slain on your heights; how have the mighty fallen!" (2 Samuel 1:19)

Following Saul's death, David returned to the city of Hebron and brought together all the tribes under his strong leadership. He turned against the Philistines and defeated them. He drafted the strongest Philistine warriors. By war and treaty he extended the Land of Israel to the north, south, and west.

His most important conquest was the Jebusite city of Jerusalem. This small village stood between the tribes of the north and the southern tribes of Judah and Benjamin, belonging to none

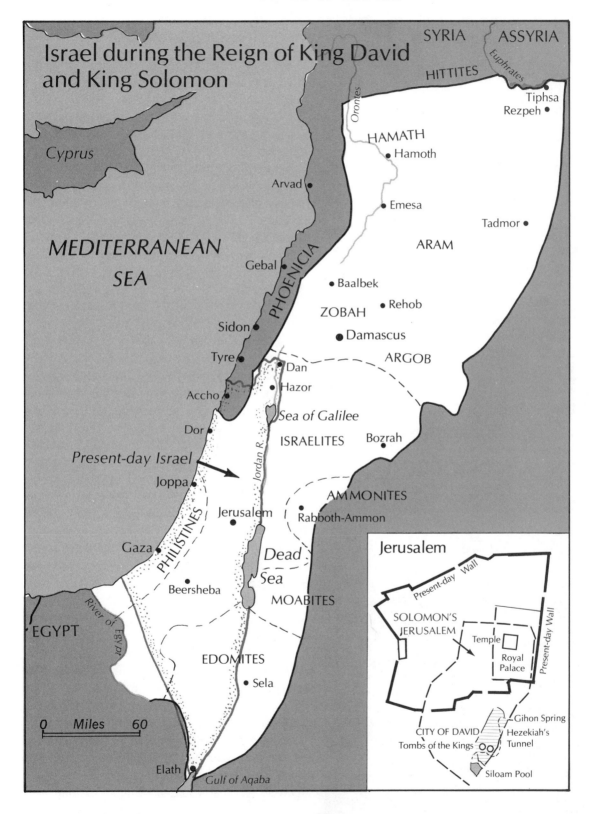

Israel during the Reign of King David and King Solomon

SYRIA
ASSYRIA
HITTITES
Euphrates
Tiphsa
Rezpeh
Oronto
HAMATH
Hamoth
Cyprus
Arvad
Emesa
Tadmor
MEDITERRANEAN
SEA
ARAM
PHOENICIA
Gebal
Baalbek
Rehob
ZOBAH
Sidon
Damascus
Tyre
ARGOB
Dan
Accho
Hazor
Sea of Galilee
Dor
ISRAELITES
Bozrah
Present-day Israel
Jordan R.
Joppa
AMMONITES
Jerusalem
Rabboth-Ammon
Gaza
PHILISTINES
Dead
Sea
Beersheba
MOABITES
River of Egypt
EGYPT
EDOMITES
Sela
0   Miles   60

Elath
Gulf of Aqaba

Jerusalem

Present-day Wall
SOLOMON'S
JERUSALEM
Temple
Royal
Palace
Present-day Wall
Gihon Spring
CITY OF DAVID
Hezekiah's
Tombs of the Kings
Tunnel
Siloam Pool

of them. It soon came to be called "the City of David." Here, David brought the Ark of the Covenant, placing it on Mount Zion and planning for the building of a temple to the Lord. From Jerusalem, David united the empire under his rule, using the strength of his personality to hold it together. The Land was truly a Davidic Empire. Its laws were the laws of the Covenant; David's loyalty to God and the Covenant never faltered.

Yet the man who could rule an entire empire could not rule his own family or his own desires. David came into conflict with the prophet Nathan when he fell in love with Bathsheba, another man's wife, arranged for the man to die in battle, and then claimed Bathsheba as his own bride. He was punished when the first child of his union with Bathsheba died in infancy.

And within his family David was weak and uncertain. His elder sons—even his most beloved son, Absalom—rebelled against him, one by one, until his only choice for the next king was his young son, Solomon.

Pillar of Absalom. This monument in the Valley of Kidron is traditionally regarded as Absalom's burial site.

III: KING SOLOMON

The Bible paints two different pictures of Solomon. One speaks of the wise, goodly king who ruled over his people with love and devotion. The other reveals a king who forced great labor upon the Israelites, built palaces and stables for his pleasure, and did little to improve what his father had left him.

Solomon was wise enough to know that his father's plan to build a temple in Jerusalem was brilliant. He hired architects and craftsmen and brought materials from neighboring Phoenicia, using forced laborers from among the Israelites to do the construction work. And he built the Holy Temple, which became—just as David had envisioned—the center of sacrifice and worship for all Israel.

Solomon went on to build a palace for the many foreign wives he placed in his harem. The palace and the Temple nearly doubled the size of the small city of Jerusalem. But the costs were heavy, and they had to be supported by heavy taxes on the people.

Solomon sent fleets of ships on international trading journeys, sold weapons to other nations, and traded heavily with Egypt and Phoenicia. He rebuilt Gezer, Megiddo, and Hazor—important military centers—and drafted soldiers from among the Israelites and stationed them throughout the country. Yet he made no new conquests. He redivided the land into twelve units and placed the burden of supporting the large royal court on each of these units for one month a year.

Throughout his life, the people of Israel were loyal to him. He was, after all, the son of their beloved David. He was renowned for his wisdom. He was a colorful king, living in Oriental splendor in his palaces, surrounded by many wives. And, like David, he remained true to the Covenant, bringing sacrifices to the Temple.

But the taxes, the forced labor, and the army necessary to maintain all this splendor were too much of a burden for the people to bear. So, upon Solomon's death, the kingdom collapsed.

Solomon's stables at Meggido.

IV: THE KINGS AND THE COVENANT

These were the kings of Israel's First Commonwealth: Saul, David, and Solomon. Together, they ruled nearly one hundred years, from c. 1000 to 922 B.C.E. In that brief period, they changed Israel from a land of farms and villages into a land of walled cities, an empire. It was David and his family that held this empire together, and it is to David that tradition still turns.

David became the model of kingship despite his personal weaknesses. He became for all time a symbol of Israel's unity, and it came to be said that the messiah, the king who would rule Israel in the end of days, would be a descendant of the family of David. The Land of Israel had taken shape under David who expanded it to its furthest borders. The kingdom would never again be so large, rule over so many foreign nations, or attain such glory.

The Temple, built by Solomon, became the center of the Covenant people. Jewish legend claims that it stood at the center of the world itself. Just as the Covenant was the center of Jewish religion, so the Temple became a symbol of the attachment of our people to the city of Jerusalem and the Land of Israel.

No wonder that Jerusalem is the capital city of modern Israel and that Israel's soldiers fought so bravely to regain the Old City of Jerusalem, the site of the ancient Temple, in the Six Day War of 1967. They were fighting for the unity of the City of David, which stands for the unity of the Jewish people!

PREVIEW

In the days that followed there would be much division and confusion. The Land of Israel would be divided into two kingdoms. Yet the people would always recall their former glory.

Models of the Temple in Jerusalem. Top model is at the Holyland Hotel in Jerusalem.

THE DAYS OF EMPIRE

Part of our deep love for Israel today goes back to these days of the kings. Like Samuel, we have come to love and honor the kings, even as we look for a better way to rule ourselves and our people. Like Samuel, we wish that all we really needed was one ruler, God.

Things to Consider

Samuel dreamed of a "kingdom of God," but the people were not yet ready. They wanted "a king to judge us like all the nations." It is human to want things we see around us. What are some of the things you *want,* and why? Could any of them bring you harm?

The text states that, "without Samuel, Saul was incomplete." Even the greatest of leaders needs help and support from others. None of us can do everything alone. Who are the people helping you now, and how are they helping you?

Our tradition tells us that each of us has "an urge to do good" and an "urge to do evil." Just so, King David and King Solomon were real people. Using the information in the chapter, make a list of the good things each of these two kings did and a second list of some of the evil things. Then, consider the following: Is being evil built into the condition of being a king or powerful leader?

3

THE DIVIDED KINGDOMS

Each of the first three kings of Israel was great in his own way. Saul gave the people hope; David gave them Jerusalem and the empire; Solomon gave them the Temple. If another king of equal wisdom had followed Solomon, our history and the history of the Land of Israel might have been different.

Upon Solomon's death, the leaders of the ten northern tribes spoke with Rehoboam, son of Solomon. The tribes of the north had been loyal to Solomon, they said, and they would be loyal to Rehoboam too—*if* Rehoboam would listen to them. They wanted a say in how the country would be run. But Rehoboam refused to listen. Instead, he promised heavier taxes and said he would whip any who would not follow him.

This angered the northern tribes. They refused to make Rehoboam their king. And the Davidic Empire split into two smaller kingdoms: the northern kingdom, Israel; and the southern kingdom, Judah.

I: THE PROPHETS

In both kingdoms, the old spirit of freedom gave rise to new spokesmen and spokeswomen. These strong-minded individuals, the prophets, identified with Moses and Samuel. The Hebrew word נָבִיא , *navi,* can mean "one who is called" or a "messenger."

In the days of King Saul, individuals calling themselves prophets traveled in small bands; they were often known for their strange behavior. Many were "false" prophets, making their living by fortune-telling and locating lost objects. But some spoke out in ways that caused people to see the truth of their message. Even when a prophet was not popular, his words were often heeded. These prophets did not seek to rule the people. They taught the lesson of Moses, Joshua, and Samuel, that the people should be ruled by their Covenant with God. When the prophets did lead, it was usually for brief periods, like the judges before them. In all, they were a bit mysterious, speaking the words of God as if commanded directly from Heaven.

The prophets were fierce lovers of the people and the Land of Israel. They believed that the Land was a sacred trust given by God; that it would expel those who did not live by the Covenant; that the people who lived in the Land of Israel were set apart from other peoples of the world and had a special mission or purpose.

Real religion, the prophets taught, is not measured only by the observance of ritual but even more by the way we deal with one another—with other Jews and with other nations. True faith in God is proved by the way we behave. It is also often stated that "we are God's hands in the world." What we do reflects upon God and our Covenant.

The good we do brings God closer to us and to all peoples; the evil we do makes God seem more distant. In this way, the Land of Israel is a proving ground, a place where the Covenant

King Saul medal. Richard Baldwin sculpture. Franklin Mint photograph. Issued by the Judaic Heritage Society.

Israel, but now they took orders from the Assyrians.

One of the last kings of Israel made a treaty with Egypt, hoping that Egypt would come to Israel's aid in a battle against the Assyrians. But, when the Assyrians attacked, the Egyptians did nothing. In 722 B.C.E., the Kingdom of Israel was destroyed by Assyria and the ten tribes of the north were sent as captives and slaves to Assyria. They disappeared forever from Jewish history. The writers in the south said this was their punishment for not obeying the Covenant and for not following the kings of the line of David.

Yet all was not well in the southern kingdom, either.

could be made to work. It is up to us, up to our people, whether we bring light to the nations of the world or not.

In the time of the prophets, things did not go well for the Israelites. The split in the kingdoms caused a division of the faith, too. But the words of the prophets became important keys to understanding our links to the Land.

II: THE NORTHERN KINGDOM, ISRAEL

The Kingdom of Israel in the north lasted about two hundred years. Its first king, Jeroboam, soon proved unworthy. His son was assassinated and a long series of rebellions and assassinations moved the kingship from one family to another. To keep the people of the north from visiting the Temple of Solomon in Jerusalem, the northern kingdom set up temples at Bethel and Dan. But some of the kings were so weak that they allowed idols to be worshiped.

Prophets like Elijah and Amos warned the people not to forget the Covenant. But the people were stubborn and refused to listen. Israel was attacked from the north by the Assyrians who took many Israelites captive and sold them into slavery. For some time, the kings still ruled over

III: THE SOUTHERN KINGDOM, JUDAH

A prophet named Micah told the southerners that God was displeased not only with the people of the north. The Israelites, he said, were one people. And now the southerners were in danger, too. Like an infected wound, he said, the suffering would spread southward even to Jerusalem. The Assyrians would soon strike at Judah.

About this time, the weak king of Judah, Ahaz, removed the bronze altar of the Lord from the Temple and replaced it with a huge altar dedicated to the worship of the Assyrian deities. This came as good news to the Assyrians, but the prophet Isaiah warned that this angered God. Now all would be lost, Isaiah said. No sacrifice, no prayer would help the people of Judah so long as the altar to Assyrian gods was allowed to remain in the Temple.

Hezekiah, the next king, destroyed the idols that had been brought into the Temple and brought back the worship of the Lord. He led the celebration of Passover—a feast that had been neglected and almost forgotten. But he, too, refused to listen to Isaiah.

Isaiah said that Assyria was too strong, their

Stone found during archeological digging at Tel Dan. The Greek and Aramaic inscription, part of which translates "To the God of Dan Zuilus," proves the existence of the place Dan.

armies too mighty. It was better for Judah to make peace than war.

Nevertheless, Hezekiah made war. Not once, but twice. The first time, he was defeated and forced to give up gold and silver from the Temple to the Assyrians. The second time, the Assyrians were forced to retreat. But Hezekiah's son, the next king, Manasseh, brought back the idols to the Temple. In his time, Isaiah disappeared; it was said that Manasseh had the old prophet put to death, but none could prove it.

Years later, a man named Josiah became king. Josiah removed the idols again and purified the Temple. In his time, the priests discovered a scroll written, they said, by Moses. (Some scholars think it was the core of the Book of Deuteronomy, the fifth book of the Torah, that

the priests found.) Josiah ordered that the book be read—and he listened to its words.

Then he called the people together to hear the book of the Covenant which had been discovered. He made the people vow to keep the Covenant that had been made at Sinai between God and the Israelites. There was a great celebration, and the people of Judah, the Jewish people, felt strengthened and renewed in spirit.

But after Josiah died fighting the Egyptians, his son brought back all the evil his father had tried to undo. The people were told to worship idols, and idols were brought back into the Temple. The new king put to death a prophet who spoke out against him. And he was angered by the words of the prophet Jeremiah who warned that the kingdom would soon be destroyed. In fact, he publicly burned the scroll of Jeremiah's warnings. But Jeremiah's secretary, Baruch, rewrote the scroll, expanding it into the Book of Jeremiah we have today.

A short time later, the Babylonians (who now ruled Assyria) attacked the people of Judah and put an end to the family of Josiah. A new king, Zedekiah, came to the throne of Judah, promising to continue the war.

Jeremiah spoke to Zedekiah, urging him to surrender to Babylonia. But the new king refused. He threw Jeremiah in prison, accusing the prophet of being a traitor. Soon, the Babylonians encircled the city of Jerusalem, keeping it under siege for six long months. Many Jews died of hunger and disease. Finally, in 586 B.C.E., on the ninth day of Av, Nebuchadnezzar, the ruler of Babylon, destroyed the Temple of Solomon and forever put an end to the Kingdom of Judah.

The prophet Jeremiah joined the Judeans who

Hezekiah's water channel in Jerusalem.

fled to Egypt. He was old now but still longed to return to the Land of Israel. He promised that God would one day bring the people back. And this prophecy, too, came to pass. Eventually, the people *did* return.

Meanwhile, thousands of Judeans were carried off to Babylon where, as the Psalmist put it, they sat by the river banks and wept, remembering Zion, the Land of Israel.

The prophets, whose bitter words had warned of the coming destruction, would in the course of time bring comfort and unity to the Jewish people, maintaining the strong ties between Israel, its Land, and its Covenant.

What was the most crucial difference between the prophets and most of the people to whom they preached? The people assumed that the Covenant was unconditional—that God would favor them under all circumstances and at all times. The prophets insisted that God would keep His part of the Covenant only so long as the people kept theirs. The Land would belong to them only so long as they used it to demonstrate how a society could be governed by righteousness and justice. This tension has continued throughout Jewish history, to this very day.

PREVIEW

In Babylonia, a powerful Jewish community would arise. In time, it would be stronger even than the former Kingdom of Judah. The Jews of Babylonia were the first to live in גָּלוּת , *galut* (exile), the first to have possessed the Land of Israel and lost it. What was new for them was the *idea* that they were still a people, that the Promised Land still belonged to them, and that one day they would return to it. Throughout the ages, Jews living outside the Land of Israel would continue to feel they were a part of the Land. Like the Jews of Babylonia, they would sit beside foreign rivers and weep as they remembered the promise that was the Covenant.

UNIT ONE: From Entry to Exile

Things to Consider

Some prophets were rich; others were poor. Some lived in the northern kingdom; some in the southern kingdom. Altogether, they added a new meaning to the Covenant. Look back at their definition of "religion" and add some of these thoughts to your list of the parts of the Covenant.

How does what you do in the world serve to bring God closer or make God seem more distant?

Now that you know something about the prophets, look back at the story of Samuel in chapter two. In what ways was Samuel a true prophet?

THE DESTRUCTION OF THE TEMPLE OF SOLOMON

The Temple had been a sacred landmark. Three times a year, at Pesach, Sukot, and Shavuot, people had come from all over the countryside to bring sacrifices and yearly taxes to the priests there. It was a center for the religion of Israel in the years of Solomon and the later kings; after the Kingdom of Israel was lost, it was the single place of worship for the remaining nation of Judah.

Now, in 586 B.C.E., it was gone. And there were those who thought that all was lost with it—the faith, the Covenant, the people, and the Land. Two thousand years of history and tradition seemed to go up in the flames that consumed the altar of the Lord.

In ancient times, many nations had ruled and then vanished forever. The Sumerians and Akkadians were distant memories, if they were remembered at all. When they lost in battle, their faith in their gods disappeared, their lands were taken over by others, and their identity as a people vanished. New nations, worshiping other gods, took their place. It seemed to the ancients that these other gods must have been more powerful, since their human warriors were more powerful.

What made the people of Israel different? How did they survive, even when their Temple and their Land fell into the hands of foreign powers?

In the end, two things set Israel apart from those nations that disappeared.

The first was the Covenant itself. The Israelites had not made a Covenant with one of many gods. They had made a Covenant with the One God. If the Israelites had been exiled to Babylonia, it was not the work of Babylonian gods, they thought, but the work of the One God—their punishment for the evil they had done. It was not too late for them to change their ways, to follow the Covenant, and be forgiven for their transgressions. What God had taken away, God could return to them.

The second thing making the Israelites different was their precious possessions—the words of the Torah and the words of the prophets. The Torah remained a handbook for the right way to live; the prophets had assured them that Israel would one day return to its Land.

So the Judeans—all that remained of the people of Israel—began to dream of return, to speak of the time when Jerusalem and the Temple would be rebuilt. While many resided in Babylon, some still made their home in the Land of Israel, waiting for their families and friends to return. Belief in the Covenant did not disappear; it grew stronger. Against all odds, the Judeans kept strong their one advantage: hope that they would one day return to the Land of Israel.

Book of Isaiah, part of the Dead Sea Scrolls in the Shrine of the Book.

4

THE TEMPLE REBUILT

The prophet Ezekiel had been among those who warned that Judeans would be defeated and Jerusalem destroyed. When word reached him of the destruction of Jerusalem, he declared that the people would soon be reunited in the Land of Israel, even though at the moment they seemed like a valley of dry bones whitewashed by the sun. Those very bones, Ezekiel prophesied, would rise up and join together. New muscles would cover them, new flesh would grow, and the people would once again live. "For it is not My desire that anyone shall die—declares the Lord God. Repent, therefore, and live!" (Ezekiel 18:32)

Ezekiel promised that the people would once again have a king to guide them—a king from the line of King David. And this king would follow the laws of the Covenant; and, what is more, the prophet even saw a vision of the Temple standing again!

Another prophet arose in Babylonia whose name is lost to us. We call him Second Isaiah, because his words were added to the scroll of the first Isaiah. The Second Isaiah spoke of a new time, a new future for the people of Israel. He spoke in God's name saying, "Do not recall what happened of old, or ponder what happened of yore! I [the Lord] am about to do something new...." (Isaiah 43:18–19) If the people would remember the story of Moses and the Covenant, there would be a new beginning for the Jews.

The Second Isaiah was a prophet of hope. When the Persians, under Cyrus the Great, con-

quered the Babylonians, he called Cyrus, God's "shepherd" who will gather the people from the ends of the earth and return them to Israel, their Land. "For this to Me is like the waters of Noah: . . . For the mountains may move and the hills be shaken, but My loyalty shall never move from you, nor My covenant of friendship be shaken, said the Lord. . . . " (Isaiah 54:9–10)

I: THE FIRST TO RETURN

In 539 B.C.E., Babylonia fell to the armies of Cyrus the Great of Persia. Just as Second Isaiah said, Cyrus was a new kind of ruler. He did not wish to wipe out the peoples he conquered. Instead, he ruled over subject nations. Neither did he require others to worship the Persian gods; he allowed each nation to follow its own religion. In 583 B.C.E., he issued a famous decree saying that the Judean exiles could return to their land and rebuild it. The sacred objects taken from the Temple would be returned to Jerusalem, and Cyrus may even have offered money so that the Judeans could rebuild the Temple.

Within a few years, the first group of Judeans was ready to return to Israel. They were followers of Sheshbazzar whom Cyrus appointed prince of Judah. As soon as they reached the Promised Land, they began to rebuild the Temple. But the work soon halted—perhaps they ran out of money, certainly their spirit was low because they found the land to be barren and

Reconstruction of the Temple.

unplanted. And there was another problem: those who returned from Babylon felt superior to the few Jews who had remained behind in the Promised Land when the Babylonian Exile began.

Those who had stayed in Israel were among "the poorest of the land" (Jeremiah 52:16), but, in time, they had acquired the best farms and orchards. The Judeans who returned from exile demanded the return of the farms and orchards left behind by their families but now owned by other Judeans. Conflicts arose between the two groups.

Many of the Judeans living in Babylonia were comfortable in their new home and had no desire to return to a land they remembered in ruins and flames. They liked living under the rule of Cyrus and saw no reason to leave. Although a few groups of "pioneers" set out for the Land of Israel, most Judeans stayed behind, at home in the new empire of Persia.

It was this way, too, centuries later when the modern State of Israel was formed. The land was barren and rocky, and the pioneers from the Diaspora found life difficult and demanding. Many Jews outside the Land of Israel, in Europe and in America, were comfortable in their new homes and happy with the governments that ruled them. They did not wish to return to Israel to struggle. So it was up to the few who did return to rebuild the land and replant it, to turn a wasteland into a garden.

II: THE RETURN CONTINUES

After the death of Cyrus and his son, it seemed that the Persian Empire would collapse. Two prophets, Haggai and Zechariah, spoke urgently to the Jews, saying, now is the right time to restore Israel.

Haggai called for the Temple to be rebuilt, and by 515 B.C.E. it was completed. The new structure was not as magnificent as the Temple of Solomon, but sacrifices resumed and the priests again led the services as they had in days of old. Then Haggai and Zechariah searched for a new king, hoping Israel could once again become an independent nation.

They settled on Zerubbabel, a man from the family of King David. But soon a new ruler arose in Persia who put an end to the hopes of the Jews for an independent nation. Zerubbabel vanished one day and all that remained of the restoration of Israel was the new Temple. But that was enough. It became the center for the revival of the Land of Israel. Like a small seed, once planted it sprouted into life and grew into a mighty tree.

III: EZRA AND NEHEMIAH

Nehemiah heard of the rough conditions in the Land of Israel in the early years of the fifth century B.C.E. while serving as an adviser to the king of Persia. He told the king of his desire to return to the Land of Israel and help rebuild the nation, and the king sent him there as the governor.

Nehemiah began by rebuilding the walls of Jerusalem. Then he turned his attention to community problems. For many years, the Judeans had been marrying non-Jewish wives and husbands. If this continued, Nehemiah thought, the Jews would soon lose their distinct identity. He tried to break up these marriages with new laws but was only partly successful.

Meanwhile, another leader arrived from Persia, Ezra, a Jewish "deputy of Israeli affairs" for the Persians. He brought with him a scroll. It seems that this was the Torah, in the form we know it today. Like a second Moses, Ezra had this Torah read to all the people, one part each week. As the parts were read, they were explained so that all could understand them. Because of his work, Ezra was called "the Scribe," and the Torah became the basis for the laws of the new settlement in Israel.

Ezra and Nehemiah turned over the govern-

THE TEMPLE REBUILT

Ezra reading the Law to the people.

ment of Israel to the priests, the same ones who held sacrifices in the Temple. The new Temple became a center for the Jews, just as the new and protected city of Jerusalem became the center of Jewish life in the Holy Land.

The return to the Land of Israel by Judean exiles was a new beginning, but in a short period of time—about one hundred years—Alexander of Macedon would conquer the Persians and life in the Holy Land would change again.

PREVIEW

Something had been added now to the Covenant and the Land, the fully formed Torah. It is no exaggeration when we call the Torah our "tree of life." For it was a tree of life both for the people and for the Land, and, with it, all was saved that might otherwise have vanished. Once again, the ancient Covenant had been renewed in the Promised Land. This time it would bloom into a new nation under new leaders. The people who had remained found new hope; those who had been carried off returned. Israel was born anew.

Things to Consider

Not everyone is the pioneer type. Most Jews in Babylonia were comfortable in their new homes and reluctant to return to the Holy Land. Think about yourself. Make a "pioneer" chart by putting a line down the middle of a piece of paper. On one side, list some reasons you would make a good pioneer. On the other, list some reasons you might dislike being a pioneer. Do you think you would have returned to the Holy Land from Babylonia?

Some of the Babylonian Jews called Cyrus a "messiah." Do you think that the rebirth of the Jewish nation in the Promised Land was a miracle? What do you think the word "miracle" means to Jews?

What did Ezra and Nehemiah do to add to the Covenant? Did they add something to Judaism that you should add to your list of the Covenant's parts? And why do you think it was necessary to "explain" the Torah to the people, as it was being read?

5

THE HASMONEANS

The world changed toward the end of the fourth century B.C.E. A young general, Alexander, from the small kingdom of Macedon, near Greece, set out in 333 B.C.E. to conquer the world. When he died ten years later, after defeating the Persian Empire and the ancient land of the pharaohs, the world empire he created was split into three parts. The smallest part—Macedon, Greece, and neighboring lands—stayed in the hands of the kings of Macedon. The eastern lands, including most of the Persian Empire, fell to General Seleucus and was called the Seleucid Empire. The lands of Egypt and Israel fell to General Ptolemy, beginning the Ptolemaic Empire.

The borders between the Ptolemaic Empire and the Seleucid Empire were unclear and the Land of Israel once more became a battleground for the great nations to the north and south. Most Jews lived outside of Israel, in the Diaspora, in what had once been Babylonia, then Persia, and was now the Seleucid Empire. Those in the Land of Israel (the province called Judea by the Alexandrian Greeks) were now practically cut off from Jews in the Diaspora.

Along with the coming of the Greeks, came Greek culture: Hellenism. In the Land of Israel, the Greeks set up trading posts along the coast and built gymnasiums and theaters in the Greek fashion. They did not set out to draw local people like the Jews into their religion, their dress, or their language. But many Jews found Hellenism attractive, especially because it was the culture of the rulers.

In Alexandria, Egypt, a Jewish community arose that experimented with combining Greek and Jewish ideas. The Hebrew Bible was translated into Greek (the translation was called the *Septuagint,* meaning "70," since it was said that seventy-two scholars had translated the Bible independently, but all the translations were the same). As increasing numbers of Jews attended the gymnasiums and the performances in the Greek theaters, Greek ways and ideas became the greatest challenge to the Jewish religion since the days of the Canaanites.

I: THE MACCABEES

You may already know the story of the Maccabees since it is part of the story of Chanukah. Around 200 B.C.E., the Seleucids under Antiochus III seized the Land of Israel from the Ptolemies of Egypt. Many peoples, though, began to dream of breaking away from the overextended Seleucids. Small rebellions continually erupted. Many broke out during the reign of Antiochus IV, called Antiochus Epiphanes (175–163 B.C.E.).

Antiochus Epiphanes was a strict ruler, determined to unite the people of his empire by forcing Hellenism on all his subjects, including the Jews. He made circumcision a crime, banned the study and possession of the Torah, forbade the observance of Shabbat, and forced Jews to eat the forbidden flesh of pigs. He set up a statue

Greek amphitheater, Alexandria, Egypt.

of the Greek god Zeus in the Temple in Jerusalem and ordered sacrifices of pigs on the Temple altar. Then he tried to force Jews to bow down to Greek gods in public. In short, he declared war on the Jewish religion.

Many Jews had adopted Greek ways. They had Greek names in place of, or alongside, their Hebrew names. They studied the Greek language, ate Greek food, and participated in the contests of physical strength in the Greek gymnasiums. Some of the men even underwent painful surgery, hoping to hide the mark of their circumcision as they performed naked in the contests.

Some Jews, faced with deciding whether to worship Greek gods as Antiochus demanded or be put to death, chose life. After all, the One God had commanded this, saying, "I have put before you life and death. . . . Choose life. . . . " For those Jews, it seemed that the only possibility was to do what was commanded by Antiochus.

But others opposed Antiochus with all their might—willing even to be put to death in the defense of their right to practice the Jewish religion. They were called Chasidim, "the faithful ones." They looked down upon those who chose Hellenism, calling them traitors and cowards. And they forced other Jews to take a stand, to choose openly between God and Antiochus.

A rebellion finally broke out in Judea, led by a family of priests. When Antiochus' soldiers reached the small city of Modi'in in the hills near Jerusalem, Mattathias and his sons refused to bow down and worship the symbols of Greek authority. They even killed a Jew who agreed to bow down. Then they fled to the hills.

Around Mattathias and his son Judah (who was called the Maccabee or "Hammerer"), a small army of farmers and Chasidim formed.

(Top) Scene from the Maccabean Revolt, reproduced from a translation of Jewish Antiquities *by Josephus Flavius. (Bottom) Tombs of the Maccabees in Modi'in.*

When Mattathias died, Judah took charge of this army and led them against the Seleucids.

Against great odds, the Maccabees succeeded in capturing Jerusalem. They cleansed the Temple, purified the altar, and celebrated the beginning of sacrifices with a late observance of the most important holiday of the ancient Jewish calendar, Sukot. Later, this fall celebration was repeated each year and was separated from Sukot and given the name Chanukah ("Dedication"), since on this holiday the Temple had been rededicated to God.

Judah and the Maccabees succeeded in creating a new Jewish kingdom in and around Jerusalem—the first independent Jewish kingdom since the fall of Judah in 586 B.C.E., more than four hundred years before.

II: THE HASMONEANS

The Hasmoneans (the family of the Maccabees) ruled for almost one hundred years. In that period, they made two grave errors. One was combining the position of king with that of high priest. The Hasmoneans hoped to gain greater power by doing this, but many Jews objected, insisting that these two roles should be kept separate as a system of checks and balances on one another. Many believed that, since the Hasmoneans came from a minor family of the priests, they had no right to become high priests. In addition, many Judeans regarded the Hasmonean kings as more Greek than Jewish. Though the first Maccabees had been defenders of the Covenant and protectors of the Temple, their descendants seemed to live and rule in the Greek fashion.

The second error was worse. One of the Hasmonean kings made a treaty with the world's first superpower, Rome. But in 63 B.C.E. the Roman General Pompey entered Jerusalem and took over the government. There was no battle. The independent Jewish nation disappeared overnight and the Land of Israel was again ruled by a foreign power.

PREVIEW

In the following 130 years, as the Romans ruled over Judea, a number of different groups of Jews claimed they were the true followers of the Covenant. Each of them believed that theirs was the true path that Judaism ought to follow. The Land of Israel became the center of a struggle between these different kinds of Jewishness, just as before it had been the center of the struggle between the great powers of the ancient world. And at the center of the struggle was the Covenant and the Temple, just as it had always been.

Things to Consider

In most times and places in Jewish history, Chanukah was a minor Jewish holiday, less important even than Purim. Today, Chanukah seems to be almost a major holiday. Why do you think this is so?

What was the "most important holiday of the ancient Jewish calendar"? What made this holiday so important to the Jews in ancient times? What makes it less important to us?

From this chapter, and the others you have read, it seems that becoming like the other nations and forgetting the Covenant go hand in hand. Can you make this idea a part of your growing definition of Covenant? Do you think this is happening in our community today?

6

THE JUDEANS AND THE SUPERPOWER

In many parts of the world, Rome ruled wisely. But in Judea they made many mistakes. Their first was to appoint Herod, a man from Idumea, to rule in Jerusalem. Herod was the child of a Jewish father and a non-Jewish mother. In those times, he was not looked upon as a Jew. He tried to make himself more popular to the Judeans by marrying Mariamne, a princess of the Hasmonean family. But the people's loyalty was still divided. In fact, for the remainder of his life, Herod lived in fear that the Jews would rebel against him. This fear drove him insane; in his madness he destroyed his own family, even sending his beloved Mariamne to death.

The Jews, for their part, were adjusting to living under Roman rule. Before, the Jewish religion had meant loyalty to the Covenant and the laws of the Torah; bringing sacrifices and paying taxes to the Temple in Jerusalem; making pilgrimages to visit Jerusalem especially on the three pilgrimage festivals of Sukot, Pesach, and Shavuot; and living a life of justice and *tsedakah*. Now Judaism itself began to have more than one meaning, even as today we have the Reform, the Orthodox, the Conservative, and the Reconstructionist views. In Roman times, it was even more complex, since the views of Judaism had both a religious and a political aspect.

I: PHARISEES AND SADDUCEES

The wealthiest Jewish families belonged to a religious and political group called the Sadducees. They claimed to be followers and inheritors of a tradition begun by King David's priest Zadok (the word "Sadducee" may be a Greek form of *Zadokite*). In this way, the Sadducees felt an attachment to the Temple and the priesthood and, by way of the priesthood, to the Hasmoneans. They were suspicious of Herod, since he had taken the throne away from a Hasmonean, but they were willing to accept Herod and the Romans because they feared change.

For the Sadducees, being Jewish meant bringing sacrifices to the Temple at the proper times and living according to the laws of the Torah. They did not think that being Jewish meant being holy. They felt that the laws of purity *(kashrut)* found in the Torah were meant for the priests to observe in the Temple. Outside the Temple, Sadducees lived and worked happily side by side with the Romans.

They also thought that the Torah was the complete word of God. It needed no changes or additions; it needed no explanations. It was what Moses had taught and what King David had practiced. They rejected new ideas—such as belief in a life after death, belief in angels and demons, belief in a final day of judgment.

The Pharisees, however, separated themselves

42

Scale model of Jerusalem at the time of Herod on the grounds of the Holyland Hotel. The children are standing next to the Holy of Holies.

from the Sadducees and from the Roman world as well. (The name "Pharisee" probably comes from the Hebrew word פָּרֹשׁ, *parosh,* meaning "cut off" or "separate.") Originally, they may have been the descendants of the Chasidim (see chapter five). But they opposed the Hasmoneans when that family combined the priesthood with the kingship; this began a long struggle for control of Judea.

One of the Hasmoneans had many Pharisees put to death and forced many others to flee Judea. When a Hasmonean who favored the Pharisees came to power, the Pharisees turned on their enemies and put many of them to death, driving others into exile. In time, they controlled many parts of the Jewish government of Judea, particularly the Sanhedrin (the Jewish congress or assembly where 71 scholars met to discuss and debate important issues of the day) and the *bet din* (the Jewish supreme court).

But, in Herod's time, the Pharisees abandoned the Sanhedrin and the *bet din,* which had become corrupted by Herod. In so doing, the Pharisees ended their political struggle and became a religious sect.

This change may have come about through the work of Hillel. This great teacher—and his colleague, another great teacher, Shammai—began a new kind of Pharisaism. To separate his followers from politics, Hillel turned his attention to the Jewish laws of diet and purity, *kashrut.* He, and the other Pharisees, taught that *all* Jews, not just the priests in the Temple, should observe these laws. Using the words of Exodus 19:6, they said God had commanded all of Israel, " . . . You shall be . . . a kingdom of priests and a holy nation." Not only the Temple, but each Jewish home and table could be a sacred place of meeting, a place for teaching Torah.

The Pharisees drew on a long tradition of stories and explanations of the Torah that had been passed down orally through the generations, claiming that these traditions were as sacred as the Torah itself. These oral laws were a part of Jewish tradition, they insisted, and were as binding a part of the Covenant as the laws of the Torah. More than any other, this teaching—that there was an Oral or Spoken Torah equal to the Written Torah—set the Pharisees apart.

Later, these oral traditions were set down in writing—first in the Mishnah, then in the Gemara. New areas of Jewish law, particularly of purity, were explored. The Pharisees remained a small group, but they and their teachings became more popular as time went on. And, as we shall see, it is basically the Judaism of the Pharisees which was passed on from generation to generation until our own time.

II: OTHER JEWISH MOVEMENTS

The majority of the Jews felt they had lost control, not only of their government, but of the Temple. It had fallen into the hands of the wealthy, the Sadducees. Most people continued to pay their taxes to the Temple and to bring sacrifices there, since that was the part of their religion easiest to understand and practice. But some joined the Pharisees and others rejected both.

One small group, the Essenes, moved to the desert. They did not trust the Hasmonean priests and said the Temple was now in the hands of "the sons of darkness." The Sadducees, they said, were traitors to the Torah and the Covenant. Above all, they believed that the end of days—when God would judge the peoples of the earth and send a warrior-messiah to lead the righteous in a holy war—was about to begin and that they would become the army of the righteous, "the children of light."

To prepare themselves as a holy army, they left Jerusalem and settled near the Dead Sea. Here they lived in ritual purity, as if every one of them were a priest. Some swore to have no more children and they obeyed strict laws controlling their lives from dawn to dusk, calling themselves the only true believers in the Covenant, the true "chosen people."

By setting themselves apart from the other Judeans, they removed themselves from history, too. In fact, they nearly vanished without a trace. History recorded little about them until the discovery, in modern times, of the Dead Sea Scrolls—part of their library (see chapter nineteen). As it turned out, unlike the Pharisees who held many of the same beliefs, the Essenic plan led nowhere.

In the north, where Samaria had once been the capital city of the Kingdom of Israel, lived the Samaritans. They built a temple on Mount Gerizim, near the city of Shechem. Here they studied Torah and like the Sadducees refused to accept any additions or explanations to it, rejecting the oral tradition.

The Samaritans may have been a remnant of the ten tribes of the north. Or they may have come later, when most Jews were in exile in Babylonia. But the Judeans refused to accept the Samaritans

Qumran, near the Dead Sea, where the Essenes lived and stored their writings.

as Jews. Once the Judeans even attacked and destroyed the Samaritan temple (in 128 B.C.E., before the Romans came). Later, the Romans destroyed it again.

Yet the Samaritans, like the Judeans, kept their faith alive through Torah study. To this day there are small groups of Samaritans living near Tel Aviv and Nablus (where once Shechem stood), and their temple is again on Mount Gerizim. The Samaritans thought—like the Pharisees, the Sadducees, and the Essenes—that they were the only true followers of the Covenant.

And there was yet another Jewish movement that grew up at this time in Israel, the early Christians. They taught that God had already sent a messiah, a leader who was both king and priest. But their idea of a messiah was unacceptable to most Jews. The majority of the Jews thought the messiah would be a princely warrior who would help the Jewish nation rule over all the nations of the world and would set up a kingdom of peace under God. The Christian idea that the messiah had already appeared, had suffered for his people on the cross and died, and had risen to heaven was not at all what most Jews expected of the messiah. During the first century C.E., the early Christians remained a Jewish sect. Followers of Jesus of Nazareth thought of him as a teacher or rabbi but still called themselves Jews. They, too, believed that theirs was the true path, and they spoke of a "new Covenant."

III: THE ZEALOTS

A kind of "religious fever" infected the Land of Israel in the time of Herod. Because Rome was so powerful, politics were of little use against it. So many turned inward to religion.

Here and there, scattered Jews shared the belief that Roman rule was evil and had to be removed from Judea. Some of these political rebels were a

Two of the pottery jugs in which Dead Sea Scrolls were found at Qumran. The partially rolled "Thanksgiving Scroll," one of the original scrolls, contains 40 psalm-like hymns starting with "I thank Thee, O Lord."

little like the Maccabees and a lot like the Freedom Fighters for Israel that arose in the days when the British controlled Palestine and the state had not yet been born. They had high principles and wanted freedom of religion and independence for the Jews.

Others were more like highwaymen and thieves, using the idea of independence as an excuse for attacking wealthy Sadducees and robbing Romans on the road. Some were even murderers—they were called the *Sicarii* or "dagger men." They slipped into crowds in the cities, especially in Jerusalem, and murdered Romans and Sadducee leaders using the daggers they hid beneath their cloaks. Altogether, these extremists and rebels were called Zealots. There were never many Zealots, but the few succeeded in drawing the Judeans into the wars against Rome that ended in destruction and devastation for the people of the Land of Israel.

IV: HEROD'S LEGACY

Herod ruled from 37 B.C.E. to 4 C.E. He left behind a bleeding nation, a people divided into many political and religious parties. On the other hand, he also left behind a legacy of great works, for Herod was a builder.

He built aqueducts like those in Rome to carry water inland. He built cities like Caesarea, with Roman amphitheaters and heated Roman baths. He built new forts throughout the land. He even built a palace in the desert overlooking the Dead Sea on the mountaintop called Masada. Some of the forts and palaces that he built were meant as places for his escape if the Jews should ever rise in rebellion against him. Some were dedicated to the Roman emperor who had put him on the throne. A few were actually meant to make the lives of the Judeans better.

It seems that Herod really wanted to be liked by

the Jews. He made improvements to the Temple, turning it into a two-story structure, building many outer courts around it, surrounding it with a stone wall. But he spoiled all this by placing a Roman eagle, symbol of the power of Rome, on the gateway to the Temple mount, and by building a temple in Samaria dedicated to the worship of the Roman emperor.

As Herod lay dying, the people of Jerusalem tore the eagle from its perch on the Temple gate. And Herod, from his deathbed, ordered the rioters arrested and their leaders burned to death.

After Herod's death, the Romans placed new kings on the throne, but these kings were given little power. The Romans sent men called procurators to manage the collection of taxes and the work of government. Many of these procurators were cruel. One crucified nearly two thousand Judeans for rioting. He had them hung on wooden crosses and left to die of hunger or thirst. Crucifixion was a common Roman punishment; it was Pontius Pilate, one of the procurators, who ordered the crucifixion of Jesus. Still another, Gessius Florus, ruled so harshly that the Zealots finally convinced many Judeans to rebel against Rome.

Roman aqueduct near Caesarea.

Roman theater excavated at Caesarea. In the background is Kibbutz Sdot Yam.

V: THE GREAT REVOLT

The Great Revolt began in 66 C.E. It was a bloody affair from beginning to end. The Judeans, under the leadership of the Zealots, murdered hundreds of Romans. The Romans were afraid that a successful revolt in Judea might encourage other nations in their empire to revolt. So Rome sent its best general, Vespasian, to lead the war against the Judeans.

Vespasian marched first against the Judeans of the Galilee, forcing the armies of the north to surrender. Then he slowly made his way to Jerusalem. Perhaps he was hoping that the rebels in Jerusalem would surrender. One of the Pharisee leaders, Yohanan ben Zakkai, also hoped for this. He argued that surrender was the only sensible thing to do, for then Jerusalem and the Temple might be spared. But the Zealot leaders refused to speak of surrender and called Yohanan a traitor.

In the end, the Roman armies encircled Jerusalem. Many Jerusalemites died of starvation or disease before the Romans attacked the walls of the city with their battering rams.

In 69 C.E., Vespasian was called back to Rome to become the new emperor. He left his son Titus in charge. It was Titus who led the armies into the city in 70 C.E., in the Hebrew month of Av. It was Titus who put the city to flame and burned the Second Temple to the ground on the ninth of Av—the same day of the year on which the First Temple had been destroyed. It was Titus who ordered that all Jerusalem be destroyed, saving only a small bit of the outer Temple wall and three towers built by Herod so that all could see what Rome had destroyed.

THE JUDEANS AND THE SUPERPOWER

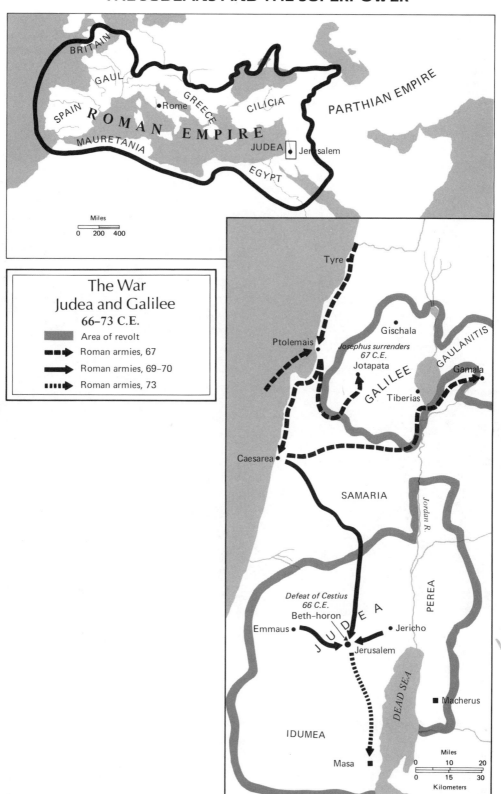

BRITAIN

GAUL

SPAIN

GREECE

ROME

CILICIA

ROMAN EMPIRE

PARTHIAN EMPIRE

MAURETANIA

JUDEA · Jerusalem

EGYPT

Miles
0 200 400

The War
Judea and Galilee
66–73 C.E.
Area of revolt
Roman armies, 67
Roman armies, 69–70
Roman armies, 73

Tyre

Gischala

Ptolemais

Josephus surrenders
67 C.E.
Jotapata

GALILEE

GAULANITIS

Gamala

Tiberias

Caesarea

SAMARIA

Jordan R.

PEREA

Defeat of Cestius
66 C.E.
Beth-horon

Emmaus ·

JUDEA

Jericho

Jerusalem

DEAD SEA

Macherus

IDUMEA

Masa

Miles
0 10 20
0 15 30
Kilometers

The fortress at Masada, where the Zealots held out for three years against the Romans, testimony to the bond between the people and the Land.

VI: MASADA

Some of the Zealots escaped Jerusalem and made their way to the desert fortress of Masada. They lived on top of the mountain for three years while the Romans set up camps encircling the mountain. Then Titus had his soldiers construct a ramp of wood and garbage and sand from the desert floor to the top of Masada.

Nothing—not even the burning oil poured from

the wall upon the soldiers below—stopped the Romans. In the end, as the battering rams rolled up the ramp and crushed the mighty walls, the Zealots made a suicide pact. They killed their families and themselves so that none of them would fall into Roman hands. As the Roman soldiers forced their way into the fortress with their swords drawn and ready, they found only the dead.

The Great Revolt had lasted seven years. In the end the superpower defeated the Judeans and destroyed the Temple. Many captives were sold into slavery, and the Land of Israel was renamed Palestine in honor of the old enemy of the Jews, the Philistines. But Jews still lived in the Land.

PREVIEW

Israel would continue to be a place of Jewish creativity and learning. Even in the terrible days following the destruction, the Jewish religious revolution continued. The Jews were finding a new meaning in their ancient Covenant. The Land of Israel would again be a land of Jewish rebirth.

Things to Consider

Look back at the many choices facing Jews in the years before the Great Revolt. What choice would you have made? Would you have become a Sadducee, Pharisee, Essene, Samaritan, early Christian, or Zealot? What makes you think so?

Is there a kind of "religious fever" in your community? To test the temperature of the Jewish community today, try asking parents, friends, or synagogue leaders to list all the Jewish organizations and institutions in your community.

Hillel said, "If I am not for myself, who will be for me? If I am only for myself, what am I? And, if not now, when?" Having read a little about the Pharisees, can you imagine what he may have been talking about?

YOHANAN AND THE RISE OF YAVNEH

Yohanan ben Zakkai, one of the last students of Hillel, was in Jerusalem when the Romans encircled the city. He was certain that they would soon overpower it and feared, not only for the destruction of Jerusalem and the Temple, but for the destruction of the Jewish religion, too. When the Zealots refused to listen to him, he risked his life to save the form of Judaism that the Pharisees loved.

Pretending to be dead, Yohanan had his students carry his shroud-wrapped body outside the walls of the city for burial. But once outside the "corpse" proved very much alive. Yohanan took off the shrouds and walked into the Roman camp, asking to be taken to see Vespasian, the commanding general. Legend says that Yohanan greeted the general with, "Hail, Emperor Vespasian!"

According to the story, Vespasian was surprised. "I am not the emperor," he replied. "You soon will be," said Yohanan. (It was true. A short time later, Vespasian was called back to Rome to become the new emperor.)

Yohanan asked Vespasian to grant him permission to set up a small school in the village of Yavneh for the purpose of teaching Torah. Vespasian saw no harm in this. In fact, he may have hoped that his generosity would cause the Judeans in Jerusalem to surrender, especially once they saw Yohanan leave in peace. But the Judeans inside the walls of Jerusalem were led by the Zealots, and the Zealots branded Yohanan a traitor.

Just as Yohanan feared, Jerusalem was destroyed and the Temple with it. But the Pharisees under Yohanan created a new Sanhedrin in Yav-

neh. There they ordained students as rabbis and continued the work of Hillel and Shammai. The Pharisees supported the synagogues that were sprinkled through the country; these became centers of study, prayer, and assembly. And the Pharisees spread their teachings to the Judeans of the Galilee, and even to the Jews of the Diaspora.

To many Judeans it seemed that the destruction of the Temple meant the end of Judaism. The only Judaism they had known was based on the Temple and its sacrifices. After all, the Temple was known to be God's dwelling place on earth. Perhaps God had finally grown weary of the Jewish people and deserted them forever.

Yohanan did not think so. He and the other Pharisees had another, more positive message.

One day, the Talmud tells, Yohanan and Rabbi Joshua were walking near Jerusalem and they saw the place where once the Temple had stood. Joshua began to weep. "Woe to us," he said, "for the Temple has been destroyed. How shall we atone for our sins now that we cannot bring sacrifices to the Temple?"

Yohanan did not weep. "Be comforted, my son," he said, "the Temple may be destroyed, but we have another way of atoning for our sins. Instead of sacrifices, we can perform deeds of loving-kindness."

The answer of the Pharisees was that good works and the observance of the laws would keep alive the Jewish people. By following the Covenant they would survive. And the people could still be "a kingdom of priests and a holy nation."

UNIT TWO
Between East and West

7

JUDAISM AND CHRISTIANITY

The memory of defeat burned in the hearts of the Judeans. To many, it seemed that the days of the messiah were near: things were so bad that God would have to send a warrior-leader to save the "chosen people." A new group of Zealots encouraged the people to believe this, and, in 132 C.E., a new revolt against Rome broke out in the south. It was led by a man named Simon bar Coziba. Like Saul, Bar Coziba was tall and broad-shouldered, and it was rumored that he was the warrior-messiah sent by God. So his followers called him Bar Kochba, "son of a star."

The early battles went well for the army of Bar Kochba. Then the Romans assembled a great attack force. This time, they set out, not just to put down the Jewish rebellion, but to punish the Judeans as well. After the Romans defeated Bar Kochba in 135, they put to death some 580,000 of his soldiers, destroyed 900 Judean villages, and allowed thousands to die of starvation. They even uprooted the great olive groves and orchards, turning Judea into a wasteland.

The Roman armies hunted down rabbis one by one, torturing them and executing them. Akiba, the greatest rabbi of his generation, was thrown into prison for teaching Torah, then tortured and burned at the stake. With his last breath, he spoke the words of the *Shema,* dying as he uttered, " . . . One." Ten great sages were murdered. The tenth, Yehudah ben Bava, gathered all Akiba's students and ordained them as rabbis just before he was captured. Then he commanded them to flee and to continue teaching the Torah among the Judeans.

As a final insult, the Romans plowed under the ruins of the ancient Temple and built a new temple over the same site—a temple for the worship of the Roman god Jupiter. Jerusalem was declared a forbidden city—no Judean was allowed to enter it.

I: THE WORK OF THE PHARISEES

A few Jews continued to live in Judea, but the majority lived in the north, in Galilee. Since the people of the Galilee had taken little or no part in the Bar Kochba Revolt, the Romans left their villages and towns standing. It was in the Galilee that the Pharisees continued their teaching.

Before the Bar Kochba Revolt, Yohanan and his students at Yavneh began shaping a new Judaism. They studied the ancient scrolls and decided which of them should be included in the Bible. What they decided to save remains today. What they decided not to include mostly disappeared. In this way, we lost some books mentioned in the Bible and others that might easily have been included, such as the ancient Chronicles of the Kings of Israel and Judah and the

Bar Kochba archive scrolls, showing the separate bundles of documents.

Dr. Yigal Yadin working on the Bar Kochba letters.

Book of Jashar (mentioned in Samuel and in Joshua). But the books they included in the Holy Scriptures—the Torah, the Writings, and the Prophets—came down to us from that day. The work they did was called canonization; like all the work of the Pharisees, the canonization of the Bible was meant to preserve the heritage of the Covenant for all times.

After the Bar Kochba Revolt, the school of Yavneh disappeared. But the rabbis who had escaped the destruction gathered together in the Galilee at Usha. There they continued the work that Yohanan had begun. Rabbi Judah became the *nasi* or patriarch—the head of the Sanhedrin—in the year 170. Under Judah's leadership, the great work called the Mishnah ("Repetition") was completed around the year 200. The Mishnah spells out all the laws of the Jews, discussing them and the decisions of the rabbis concerning them. This was the Oral or Spoken Torah of the Pharisees, recorded in writing. It was the constitution of the Jewish people, compiled after the nation was no longer free to live by its laws.

What a strange idea! To issue laws for governing a nation that no longer could govern itself! What did the rabbis have in mind? Did they believe that one day the Jews would again be free of the terrible might of Rome? Or did they think of the Mishnah as a record book, a memory of what it meant to be an Israelite in the good old days?

We have a clue to what they were thinking in a small book of the Mishnah called *Pirke Avot,* the "Sayings of the Founders." Here we read:

> Moses received the Torah on Sinai and handed it down to Joshua; Joshua to the elders; the elders to the prophets; the prophets to the Men of the Great Assembly. (*Mishnah, Avot* 1:1)

In other words, the Mishnah claimed to be a set of laws and teachings handed on by word of

Ancient ruins at Bet Shearim showing the entrance to the tomb of Judah Ha-Nasi. It now attracts many tourists. It became a spiritual center in 170 C.E.

mouth from one generation of leaders to the next. Each generation added to it. And the rabbis at Yavneh and Usha also expanded it. It was as if the Mishnah were alive, always growing.

Even after the Mishnah was accepted as the constitution of the Jewish people, it continued to grow. It was explained and discussed by rabbis for generations. In Tiberias, about 400 C.E., these discussions were recorded in the Gemara ("Completion"). Together with the Mishnah, the Gemara of the Land of Israel became a legacy for all Jews—one which we study to this day.

Another Gemara was completed much later in the academies of Babylonia. It was far larger than the Gemara of Israel and it became—second only to Torah—the most studied work of Jewish learning in history. Though it was more popular than the Gemara of Israel, the Gemara of Babylonia might never have been completed if the Jews of Israel had not first shown the way.

Together, Gemara and Mishnah are called Talmud, from the word for "teaching." Both Gemaras are based on the Mishnah of Rabbi Judah. And both join legal writings (halachah) with folklore (agadah).

The two Talmuds (Talmud Yerushalmi and Talmud Bavli) were blueprints for the Judaism of the future. In them, the sages taught that the people of Israel were the new Temple; charity and good deeds were equal to sacrifices; and each person could live the priestly life of holiness and purity. The Covenant, which began with the events at Mount Sinai, the Ten Commandments, the Torah, and the conquest of the Promised Land, now grew to include the work of the Pharisees.

Through ensuing centuries Jews never surrendered the hope that they would one day be restored as a viable community in the Land which had originally been a major component of their Covenant with God. Meanwhile, the Talmud, which continued to expand and evolve through additional interpretation and commentary, provided them with a kind of charter for their corporate existence.

II: EARLY CHRISTIANITY

The number of Christians in the Holy Land remained small. Few Jews converted to Christianity, finding its message—that the messiah had come and had sacrificed himself as the perfect sacrifice so that no further sacrifices were needed—strange at best. This Jesus was not the kind of messiah they had waited for. Even stranger was the Christian claim that Jesus was the "son of God." In Jewish eyes, all men were the sons of God and all women were the daughters of God.

In the rest of the Roman Empire, however, Christianity took hold and made many converts. This was possible because the early Christians were willing to make changes to suit the needs of local peoples. To make Christianity more popular to those who worshiped the female gods of Rome, special emphasis was placed on Mary, the mother of Jesus. To make Jesus more popular to those who worshiped the male gods of Rome, he was made to seem more and more like Apollo, the best loved of the Roman gods. None of this appealed to the Jews.

Christianity eventually became the official religion of the Roman Empire. And, since the Romans still ruled over the Holy Land, Christianity became an important factor in the life of the Jews who remained there.

The Christians believed that they were the "new Jews," so they declared that Judaism was no longer a real religion. The Jews were just a group of "impure beings," "creatures without law," the Christians said. Jews were forbidden to keep slaves. Up to that time, many Jews operated farms in the Roman manner—using slaves to work large land holdings. Suddenly, these Jews were forced out of farming. In this and other ways the Christians tried to make it difficult to be a Jew.

The Christians noted that some Jews had slowly moved back into Jerusalem, forming a small community. Once again, the city was closed to Jews. Only on the ninth of Av, the saddest day of the Jewish year, the day on which both Temples had been destroyed, were Jews allowed to visit the Western Wall, the outer wall that encircled the Temple mount—the last standing remnant.

For Christian Rome, Palestine became more than just another province. It was the Holy Land, where Jesus had preached and lived. The Church Fathers tried to convert the Jews of the Holy Land time and again without success. Finally, the empire decided to make the country more Christian in other ways. Churches were built, even where the population was mainly Jewish. Monasteries—housing for monks—were set up in Palestine and maintained by Rome.

None of this kept the Jews in the Holy Land (now called the Yishuv or "settlement [of Jews]") from clinging to their Judaism. All the efforts of the Christian Church, backed by the might of Rome, could not make new converts among the Jews.

III: A NEW UPRISING

There was a small Jewish uprising in Palestine against the Romans in the early years of the fourth century. The Church Fathers tell how it was put down and of the great suffering that was inflicted on the Jews because of it. Nevertheless, by the year 351, the Jews of the Yishuv felt forced to rebel again.

New churches were being built in cities like Sepphoris, Tiberias, Nazareth, and Caper-

Remains of a third-century synagogue at Capernaum (Kfar Nachum), near Tiberias.

59

Bas-relief of the Holy Ark sculpted in rock at the synagogue in Capernaum.

naum—all cities with heavy Jewish populations. The Jews attacked the builders and stoned them. The Romans sent legions with orders to burn to death those who had done the stonings.

Then the Roman legions demanded that bread be baked by the Jews during Passover and that work be done by the Jews on Shabbat and the festivals—even on Yom Kippur. This was too much for the Jews. Hoping that at last the mes-

siah would come to aid them, they rose up in open rebellion.

The Jews of Sepphoris attacked the Roman legions by night, forcing the Romans to retreat. With Sepphoris in Jewish hands, they named a Jew, Patricus, to be king. The revolt spread to Tiberias and Lod. Many Romans, Greeks, and Samaritans were killed.

Once again the Romans attacked in force,

putting an end to the revolt. The city of Sepphoris was burned and its people condemned to die. (Some escaped to caves, living there for years.) Slowly, Sepphoris and other ruined cities were rebuilt. Life went on and the Jews continued to live in Israel.

IV: TO REBUILD THE TEMPLE

When Julian I became emperor of Rome in 361, the situation of the Jews improved. No lover of Christianity, Julian believed that the new religion had weakened the Roman Empire and he tried to bring back the old Roman ways and the old Roman gods.

In addition, Julian wished to allow each province—including Palestine—to return to its own ancient religion and ways. In one decree, Julian called on Jews everywhere to return to the Holy Land and to govern it once again. In synagogues throughout the Roman Empire, the *shofar* was sounded and great sums of money were collected for rebuilding Israel and sending Jews on *aliyah* ("going up"—the term for returning to the Land of Israel). Julian was called the "defender of Israel" by many rabbis. After he put one of his close friends in charge of rebuilding a "Jewish Jerusalem," a synagogue was opened near the site of the ancient Temple and some work was begun on rebuilding the Temple itself. But Christians kept the work from progressing, and, when Julian died in 363, the Jewish dream of restoring the Temple came to an unhappy end.

The emperors who followed Julian killed Jewish hopes. Christian scholars were sent to Palestine to teach the Jews of the Yishuv that Christianity was the only "true Judaism." Jews were forced out of farming entirely. Monks living in the Holy Land rioted against the Jews, looting the synagogues. Jews were not allowed to take part in governing their own land.

The Emperor Justinian (527–565) tried to eradicate the practice of Judaism entirely. The last small outpost of Jewish independence, the island of Yotvata in the Gulf of Eilat, which had always been ruled by Jewish laws, was invaded and Christian rulers were set over it.

As a religion, Christianity never conquered the Holy Land. To the very end of Roman rule in 641, the Jews of Israel remained loyal to the Covenant and continued to study the Torah and the Talmud. They hoped and prayed that Rome would somehow be defeated. They rebelled repeatedly.

But, as the official religion of the Roman Empire, Christianity had a terrible impact on the Jews. Christian rulers kept the Jews poor, stopped new Jewish settlements from growing, discouraged Jews from returning to the Holy Land, and persecuted those Jews who continued to live there.

These were the years of great Jewish triumph—the years of the completion of the Mishnah and the Gemara. And they were the years of Jewish hardship.

But why did the Jews *want* to continue living under these conditions, especially as the Jews outside the Holy Land were becoming wealthier and more respected, finding new opportunities, even enjoying new freedoms?

Any Jew—in Israel or in the Diaspora—could tell you why: because the Land of Israel was precious. Three times each day the Jews turned toward Jerusalem, the city where the Temple had stood, and prayed. Their prayers spoke of the hope that God would rebuild Jerusalem and restore the Temple. At the end of every Yom Kippur and Pesach service—in the synagogue and in the home throughout the Diaspora—they chanted, לְשָׁנָה הַבָּאָה בִּירוּשָׁלָיִם, *Leshanah habaah birushalayim!* "Next year in Jerusalem!" At every Jewish wedding a glass was broken to remind the Jews, even in the midst of celebration, of the destruction of the Temple. The Land of Israel was in their hearts and in their minds. Jerusalem was precious. The Covenant was not complete without the Holy Land. That Covenant had been premised on Abraham's settling in "the land that I will show you.'' The Mishnah and the Gemara were more accessible in the Land of Israel than outside. Judaism made more sense in Israel under the Patriarchs than in the rest of the Roman Empire.

So, even in a time when most Jews lived outside the Holy Land, Israel was still the heart of the Jewish people. And the dream of returning and rebuilding was one that would not die. Not then, not now.

PREVIEW

Judaism gave rise to Christianity. In the next scene of world history, it would give rise to another religion, Islam. The followers of Islam would prove to be both enemies and friends of the Jews. But the war between the Christians and the Moslems threatened the Jews in unexpected ways, as you will see.

Things to Consider

The Pharisees added a great deal to the Covenant. Their beliefs and teachings form the basis of Judaism today. See how many things from this chapter you can add to your ''Covenant'' list.

One of the great lessons taught by the Pharisees was that each new generation should receive (learn) the whole heritage of Judaism and should then add something new to it. What new ideas do you think we should add to the Judaism you know?

The chapter lists some of the ways in which Jews kept the memory of the Land of Israel alive through all the generations, even while most Jews lived outside the Land. What are some ways we keep the Land of Israel in our minds and hearts today?

8

THE CALIPHATE AND THE CRUSADES

Every year at Passover, we retell the story of how our ancestors were once Egyptian slaves. "We were slaves; now we are free." So we keep alive the hope of freedom. And, at the end of the *seder,* as Jews did in the past, we chant the final words of the Haggadah, "Next year in Jerusalem!" So it is today as it always was.

The Jews kept alive the dream of freedom. Whenever Rome seemed weak, the Jews of the Holy Land rebelled. They always hoped other nations would join in the battle. And once the Persians did.

In 614, the Persian armies stormed Jerusalem and some of the coastal cities, trying to defeat the Roman armies there. Jews fought side by side with the Persians and, when the Romans were driven from Jerusalem, the city was turned over to the Jews. Then the old hope returned: the Temple could be rebuilt! Plans were laid and materials were gathered. But, suddenly, the Persians made a treaty with the Christians and sent a bishop to rule Jerusalem. All talk of rebuilding the Temple stopped. Jewish hopes were crushed; the Jews were again driven out of Jerusalem.

Fourteen years later, the Jews helped the Romans to reconquer Jerusalem. This time the Romans promised to let the Jews rule the city. But again the promise was broken. Nonetheless, the Jews continued living by the Covenant and praying for an end to Christian rule.

I: THE CALIPHATE

New hope came to the Jews from the south, from the Arabian peninsula where a new religion had been born—Islam. Like the Christians, the Moslems (followers of the Islamic faith) based their religion on the Holy Scriptures of the Jews. And, just as the Christians had added a second set of writings—which they call the New Testament—to the Bible, the Moslems added their own teachings—the Koran—to the Jewish canon.

In 638, the Moslem Arabs captured Jerusalem with the help of local Jewish armies. It was the end of Roman rule forever. The Moslems would rule the Holy Land for the following 460 years. It became a part of the huge Islamic empire called the Caliphate, ruled by the caliph, the "master of all the faithful."

The Moslems were not eager to convert Christians or Jews to their faith, since the taxes they used to run the empire came from non-Moslems. In fact, the Moslems welcomed Jewish help in governing the Holy Land, counting on the Jews to be loyal. The Jews, for their part, were pleased to be part of an empire that counted them as important.

Many Jews from distant parts of the world made *aliyah* to the Holy Land, willingly paying taxes to the Moslems in return for the good life. Jewish farmers took back their lands. Some Jews

Captives under yokes.

even spoke of the days of the messiah coming soon.

In the beginning, Jews and Arabs were allowed to visit the holy places in Jerusalem, but after a while the Jews were shut out. In the beginning, the Jews were allowed to set up temporary dwellings *(sukot)* on the Temple mount on the holiday of Sukot. Later, they were forced to use the Mount of Olives and were kept away from the Temple site on Mount Moriah.

Slowly, the best farms were taken by the Moslems and the taxes on the Jews grew heavier until some Jews could not afford to pay them. In fact, by the eighth century, Jews in the Holy Land were almost totally separated from any landholdings and forced into poverty. Adding insult to injury, the Temple mount was turned into a burial ground for important Moslems. This, the Jews could not tolerate. The "courtyards of the House of God," they said, were now the "courtyards of the dead."

To pay their taxes, the Jews of Palestine called on Jews throughout the world to send *tsedakah* (the charity that is righteousness). In the course of time, sending *tsedakah* to help Jews living in the Holy Land became a part of the everyday life of Jews everywhere. It was as natural as facing Jerusalem when praying.

The Jews were still the majority in the Holy Land and remained so until the eleventh century. But the Arabs were in control. Under Arab rule, the Jews were allowed to govern themselves in all religious matters. The Sanhedrin continued to exist and the head of the community, the *gaon-nasi* (genius-patriarch), was also head of the Sanhedrin.

Many Jewish towns had *yeshivot* (academies or schools) with rabbis and judges as leaders. In addition, a town might have a *chazan* or cantor. The *chazanim* were often poets, teachers, or scribes.

For nearly 250 years (from the early eighth to

the tenth century), the rabbis of the Land of Israel tried to claim leadership of the Jews of the Diaspora. They often argued against the rulings of the Jewish sages of Babylonia. But the Babylonian Jewish community—far larger and far stronger—made its Talmud more important and its decisions more far reaching, so that most Diaspora communities turned to Babylonia's rabbis for advice and help. Still, as if by miracle, the Yishuv continued to survive.

II: THE KARAITES

A new movement within Judaism, later to be called Karaism (from *Mikra,* the Hebrew word for Scriptures), arose in the last half of the eighth century. Its leader, Anan ben David, brought together a small group of followers. Anan taught that the Oral Torah (the Mishnah and the Gemara and the other writings of the Pharisees) was a great error. Only the Written Torah was the true law. If the Written Torah said that no lights were allowed on the Sabbath, it meant that not even candles or fires lit before Shabbat should continue to burn once Shabbat began. He told his followers to observe a seventy-day fast like the Moslem fast-month of Ramadan each year, and he forbade his people from going to doctors, saying that God alone could heal. The next leader of the Karaites, Benjamin of Nahawend, added to the work of Anan, saying that each person was entitled to interpret the law using only the Holy Scriptures.

This small group set up its headquarters in Jerusalem, calling on all Jews to pray for the forgiveness of Israel's sins and to ask God for the speedy end of the exile. Many of the Karaites became "Mourners of Zion," giving up meat, wine, and luxuries and spending long hours in prayer each day. In the following two centuries, some of Judaism's finest writers and thinkers turned to the beliefs of Karaism.

Mount of Olives, seen from Jericho Road, Jerusalem.

Outside the Holy Land, the fight against Karaism was bitter. Jews like Saadiah Gaon of Babylonia wrote books and sermons and openly condemned the anti-rabbinic ideas of the Karaites. In the end, two things happened: first, the Karaites lost much of their following, remaining strong only in a few places in the Holy Land; second, the fact that the discredited Karaites were *from* the Land of Israel caused the Jews of the Diaspora to turn more and more to the schools of Babylonia where, it seemed, the Talmud was taken more seriously.

In 1012, the Caliph Al-Hakim broke the long tradition of allowing Christians and Jews freedom of religion and ordered that they both be forced to convert to Islam. Anti-Jewish riots followed and Jewish men, women, and children were cruelly tortured and put to death for refusing to convert.

Together, the successes of the Karaites and the cruelties of Al-Hakim brought the Yishuv to a new low point in its history. More Jews now left the Holy Land than came to it. Even later when the Moslem tradition of tolerance was restored and Jews again enjoyed freedom of religion, the Yishuv did not fully recover. But it did not disappear.

The Holy Land was still holy. Nothing could change that. The Covenant—that ancient promise—was still in the minds and hearts of the Jews of the Yishuv and the Jews of the Diaspora. The Jews of the Yishuv held on. They wrote poetry. They wrote folktales. They even used Hebrew as a spoken language.

In fact, it was in this bleak period that the Yishuv made one of its greatest contributions to Judaism: the invention of vowels. The scholars of the Yishuv created the system of dots and lines and vowel letters which we still use today and by which we recognize the meaning of the Hebrew words of the Bible. It was the beginning of the true story of the grammar of the Hebrew language, and it made Hebrew a more popular language among Jews everywhere.

III: THE CRUSADES

The Yishuv prayed for relief. Instead, tragedy struck. In 1095, Pope Urban II called for a holy war of the Christians against the Moslems. The men who answered this call wore crosses on their clothing, which gave rise to their name, "Crusaders."

The Crusades were a kind of world war in which Germans, French, Italians, Norwegians, Englishmen, Spaniards, Danes, Scots, and Armenians journeyed to the Holy Land to battle Arabs, Turks, Mongols, and Tartars. For nearly two hundred years, this terrible war raged in and around the Holy Land. But, always, some of the fiercest fighting took place in and near Jerusalem.

The Crusaders conquered Jerusalem in 1099. The battle was hard won. Losses on both sides were heavy. And, on the third day after the battle, the Crusaders took revenge by putting to death all those who still survived within the city. It was said that not even infants escaped the sword that day. Corpses lay in the streets of the City of David—women and children, along with the men who had fought.

The massacres spread to other cities—Jaffa, Ono, Lod, Hebron. Haifa was then the meeting place of the Sanhedrin, and the Crusaders hated it more than any other city in the Holy Land. When they conquered it in 1101, they put to death all those trapped within its fortress-like walls.

The few Jews who remained in the Land of Israel lived primarily in ten settlements in the Galilee, where many were in the shipping business. The Jews and their ships were needed to bring supplies from Europe to the Crusaders. Some Jews were physicians, money-lenders, glass-blowers, peddlers, and dyers of cloth; some worked as travel agents and guides, showing the Christians the places they wished to visit—especially those places in the Galilee mentioned in the Christian New Testament.

The Crusades left a deep scar on the Jews of the Holy Land, just as they did on the Jews of Europe where they began. Many Jews turned inward. They had always prayed for the coming of the messiah, but now their prayers became more urgent. Jews in the Holy Land turned increasingly to mysticism, the attempt to draw nearer to God through prayer, fasting, and meditation.

Far away, in the many lands in which Jews had been scattered, longings for Zion, for the Holy Land, were stirring many Jewish hearts. Judah Halevi, the Spanish Jewish poet, wrote loving poems about the Holy Land. His spirit was elevated by thoughts of returning to Jerusalem. At last, he and a few friends set out to reach the Land, but it seems they got no farther than Egypt (though one legend tells of Judah dying at the hands of an Arab as he reached a hill overlooking Jerusalem). The spirit he felt was felt by many.

In 1187, Sultan Saladin fought against the Christians and defeated them. He recaptured Jerusalem and opened it to the Jews once again, inviting them to settle in it. A new Jewish community grew up there, and some of the greatest rabbis and scholars of the age led groups of Jews to this community, following in the spirit of Judah Halevi. Three hundred rabbis came from France and England. Others came from Spain and later others came from Germany.

One generation later, Rabbi Yehiel of France moved his entire *yeshivah* of nearly three hundred students to the Holy Land. Spanish Jews came seeking refuge from the wars between the Moslems and the Christians there. Even Nachmanides—one of the great scholars and teachers of the Middle Ages—made his way to Palestine when he was forced to leave his home in Spain. He founded a school in Jerusalem, attracting many new students to the Holy City.

The Jews of the Diaspora once more discovered that life in Palestine was possible. The Covenant and the Promised Land were still deeply imbedded in them; they longed for the complete life of Judaism—the full life of the Jewish people in the Jewish Land. The valleys and the hills, the deserts and the orchards, the olive groves and the palm trees called to them. They wanted to walk where King David walked, to stand where Solomon stood, to breathe the air and see the sky just as Elijah and Isaiah and Amos had. No matter that life in the Holy Land would be harsh and difficult. They were willing to make that sacrifice just to be in the Promised Land.

Jerusalem, city of David.

Landscape in the Holy Land.

THE CALIPHATE AND THE CRUSADES

PREVIEW

The Crusades and the long years of warfare left both the Christians and the Moslems weakened in the Holy Land. Into their midst rode the Mamelukes, a warrior nation that would conquer Palestine in 1291 and rule over it for the next 225 years.

The Mamelukes were heartless rulers. They ruthlessly stole everything of value from the people of the Holy Land. Many Jews fled. Only fifteen Jewish communities remained. The Jews in them worked mainly as craftsmen or peddlers. A few more great scholars would soon arrive from the Diaspora. And the new rulers would later be defeated by the Ottoman Turks.

Who could have imagined that a new Jewish age was about to dawn? That the Covenant—based on the Torah and the work of the Pharisees—would grow again to include still another new strain of thought?

Yet this is the strength of our people: to find light where others see only darkness, to draw strength from our past to shape a better future.

Things to Consider

Jewish leaders in the Land of Israel felt they should be the leaders of all world Jewry. Perhaps they had the words of the prophet in mind: "... For instruction shall come forth from Zion, the word of the Lord from Jerusalem." (Micah 4:2) Today in Israel there are two chief rabbis and a *bet din*. Do you think these religious leaders should make decisions that are binding on Jews everywhere? Why, or why not?

Why do some students of Jewish history call the great years of the Caliphate (638–1012), "The Golden Age of Judaism"? To find out, look up at least two of the following people in a Jewish encyclopedia: Saadiah Gaon, Moses Ibn Ezra, Solomon Ibn Gabirol, Maimonides, Judah Halevi, Hisdai Ibn Shaprut, Samuel Ibn Nagrela. ("Ibn" is the Arabic for "ben," meaning "the son of.")

Judah Halevi longed to return to Zion. At age 55, he set out to make this dangerous journey. On board a ship, he wrote:

> I cry to God with a melting heart ...
> On a day when the oarsmen are astounded
>   at the deep ....
> How shall I be otherwise, since I, on the
>   ship's deck ...
> Am dancing and tossed about? Yet this is
>   but a light thing,
> If I may but hold the festival dances in
>   your midst, O Jerusalem! (From "On
>   the Sea")

If you are an artist, illustrate the poem. If you are a musician, try writing music for it. If you are a dancer, create a dance to it. Or, you might try writing your own poem about how Jerusalem makes you feel.

9

THE OTTOMANS

The well known Jewish traveler, Benjamin of Tudela, journeyed through the Land of Israel shortly after the Crusaders conquered it. In his diary, he tells of meeting Jewish shipowners in the city of Tyre. And of Jerusalem he wrote:

> The dyeing house is rented by the year, and the exclusive right to dye cloth is purchased from the king by the Jews of Jerusalem, two hundred of whom dwell in one corner of the city, under the tower of David. . . .

In 1334, when the Mamelukes ruled Jerusalem, another Jewish traveler, Isaac ben Joseph ibn Chelo, visited Jerusalem. Ibn Chelo reported that the Jewish community in Jerusalem was quite numerous, adding:

> Among the different members of the holy congregation . . . are many who are craftsmen such as dyers, tailors, shoemakers, etc. Others carry on rich businesses in all sorts of things and have fine shops. Some are devoted to sciences [such] as medicine, astronomy, and mathematics. But the majority . . . study the Holy Law [Torah and Talmud] day and night and study the true wisdom which is the Kabbalah [Jewish mysticism]. . . . There are also at Jerusalem excellent scribes, and the copies [they write, of the holy books] are sought for by travelers, who carry them away to their own countries. I have seen a Torah written with so much art that several persons at once wanted to purchase it. . . . (Quoted in *The Jews in Their Land,* edited by David Ben-Gurion)

As the Mamelukes grew poorer, they forced new and heavier taxes on the Jews of Israel. Slowly, the fine shops were closed; the students of Talmud grew poorer. Again, there was need for *tsedakah* from the Jews of the Diaspora. And, as before, the Jews of the Diaspora were willing to share what they had with the Jews of the Holy Land.

In 1481, Meshullam of Volterra visited Jerusalem. He told of finding perhaps 250 Jewish families in the city which was much "in ruin." Most of these Jews were scholars, living on charity sent to Jerusalem by Jews outside the Holy Land.

Over the following few years, conditions grew still worse. In 1489, Obadiah of Bertinoro, a famous rabbi from Italy, visited Jerusalem and found only a few Jews living there: "about seventy families of the poorest class . . . scarcely a family does not need the most common things. . . ."

> The Jews of Jerusalem have to pay [taxes] of thirty-two pieces of silver per person. The poor man, as well as the rich. . . . Everyone is made to pay fifty ducats a year . . . for permission to make wine [for Shabbat and the festivals]. . . . *(The Jews in Their Land)*

Obadiah decided to stay, despite the heavy taxes. He soon became the leader of the Yishuv and

Mameluke tombs, Old Cairo, Egypt.

founded an academy. Many students from Spain and Italy followed him to Jerusalem in the following few years. By 1455, there may have been as many as 1,600 Jews in the City of David. And, in the Galilee—especially in the city of Tsfat—there were more.

Better times were coming. The Ottoman Turks attacked from the north in 1517, conquering Palestine and making it part of the Ottoman Empire for the next four hundred years. The Jews and the Turks struck up a friendship. The Turkish sultans never called for Jews to come to the Holy Land, but they also never tried to stop Jews from coming.

New Jewish immigrants came southward from Turkey and northward from Africa to settle in Jerusalem. Most were Spanish Jews, forced out of Spain by the Inquisition. Some were *conversos*—Jews who had been practicing their Judaism secretly since the terrible days of the Inquisition in Spain. With them came Jews from Italy and some from northern Europe.

They built new workshops and new factories. New *yeshivot* sprung up around the countryside, where the study of Bible and Talmud went on constantly. Orchards were planted; some Jews went into farming in the rich soil of the Galilee. On Lake Kinneret, a few Jews became fishermen. The Jews set up courts and schools and collected money for *tsedakah*. Once again, the eyes of all the Jewish world turned toward the Land of Israel where the Covenant was being renewed.

I: FALSE MESSIAHS

For Jews, these were the best of times and the worst of times. The Jews of the Holy Land lived in peace, while those in the Diaspora were caught in a tumult. Constantinople, the last outpost of the holy Roman Empire, fell to the Turks in 1453. But, just as the Church in the east was weakened, the Church in the west turned against the Jews, particularly in Spain where the Inquisition grew so powerful that, in 1492, the Jews were expelled and forced to seek refuge in places like the New World, Northern Europe, North Africa, and Turkey. As we have seen, some of them made their way to Palestine.

Jordan River flowing into Lake Kinneret, as seen from Almagor.

The terror of the Inquisition haunted the Jews. Many expected the world to come to an end. Once again, Jews looked for help from Heaven, hoping a messiah would lead them to freedom in the Holy Land.

In Jerusalem, students at the academies fasted for days, sat up studying all night, read mystical works of the Kabbalah, and prepared for the coming of the messiah. There were rumors of strange "miracles." It was said that pillars inside the Dome of the Rock (the Moslem mosque built over the site of the ancient Temples) had fallen; that the crescent (the symbol of Islam) on the dome's roof had somehow twisted. These were sure signs that Islam was about to crumble.

In 1523, a Jew from Arabia, David Reubeni, came to the Land of Israel and claimed that he knew where the ten lost tribes (see chapter three) were waiting, hoping to return to the Holy Land. Reubeni planned to set up a Jewish kingdom with the help of Palestinian Jews and the kings of Europe. Many Jews thought Reubeni might be the messiah.

Two years later, a student of Reubeni, Solomon Molcho of Portugal, came to Tsfat and Jerusalem to predict that the end of the world would come in 1540. A short time later, Molcho was put to death by the Inquisition in Italy. Reubeni was killed in Spain, another victim of the Inquisition. The year 1540 came and went. No messiah appeared.

THE OTTOMANS

Damascus Gate, Jerusalem, a major attraction of the Old City since its sixteenth-century reconstruction by Suleiman the Magnificent.

The best times were reached under Sultan Suleiman the Magnificent. He set laborers to work for six years from 1536 to 1542 to build the huge wall that still encircles the Old City of Jerusalem. He ordered that the cisterns (underground water tanks) be repaired, the city's water system fixed, and the reservoir called the Pool of Solomon restored. With enough water for all, with the protection against raiders and night riders given by the wall, the Jewish population in Jerusalem increased.

The worst times in Jerusalem came toward the end of the century when a new sultan took away the Jews' most beloved possession—the Nachmanides synagogue, where Jewish services had been held every day for the last 320 years. He gave this building to the Arabs and told them to turn it into a warehouse.

II: TSFAT

When times were hard in Jerusalem, they were usually better in Tsfat. Tsfat, on the side of a mountain, was surrounded by farms. From these fields came the wheat, grapes, sheep, wool, and honey that brought the Galilee fame throughout the Ottoman Empire. The merchants of Tsfat, in turn, brought goods from Syria and Constantinople to sell inside the Holy Land.

Suleiman built a wall around Tsfat in 1549, just as he had done in Jerusalem. Within that wall, the Jews built another wall around the Jewish section of town. For a hundred years, this Jewish section, called the *khan,* gave protection to the community. They slept better at night, knowing the gates were locked and guarded.

In 1538, the leading rabbi of Tsfat, Jacob Birav, called together twenty-five other rabbis and asked them to restore ordination—the official power to appoint Jews as rabbis and judges. The assembly made Birav the first to be ordained and gave him the right to ordain others.

The rabbis of Jerusalem were outraged. They claimed that, to retore ordination officially, *all* rabbis in the Land of Israel would have to agree. The argument smouldered into a flame. Birav was forced to flee for his life to Damascus. But,

View of Tsfat.

before he left Tsfat, he ordained four rabbis, including the great sage, Joseph Karo.

In 1545, Karo became the head of the Jewish community in Tsfat. Through his writings, his fame spread. He collected all the laws of the Talmud, adding many decisions of the rabbis through the ages and a few decisions of his own regarding how a true Jewish life should be led. He brought all this together in a code of Jewish law called the *Shulchan Aruch* ("The Set Table"). This code book was soon accepted by Jews everywhere. By 1577, two years after Karo's death, the first Jewish printing press in the Land of Israel had been set up in Tsfat, and the works of the Tsfat scholars began to circulate widely wherever Jewish books were read.

Maybe it was the majesty of the mountains, or the magic of the evenings and mornings of the Galilee—something gave Tsfat a special spirit. Living on the hillside, breathing the misty air, the rabbis and leaders there turned to mysticism and Kabbalah. Karo himself was a mystic.

It was in Tsfat that the Jewish poet Solomon Alkabetz wrote the mystic prayer *Lechah Dodi,* which we still sing on Friday night to greet the Sabbath Queen. In Tsfat, Rabbi Moses Cordovero completed his mystic masterpiece, *Pardes Rimonim* ("The Grove of Pomegranates"); and Eliezer Azikri wrote the *Sefer Chasidim* ("Book of the Faithful")—both great works of Kabbalah.

And, in Tsfat, in 1570, lived perhaps the greatest of all mystic teachers, the young Rabbi Isaac Luria, known to all as Ha-Ari, "The Lion." Luria taught his secret beliefs for only two years before he died, yet it took his students nearly ten years to set down all they had learned from him.

What did these mystics hope to achieve? Nothing less than hurrying the coming of the messiah. They truly thought that, by settling in the Land of Israel, following the Covenant, ordaining rabbis, setting up a *bet din,* and governing the Jews of the Holy Land, they could draw closer to God and draw God closer to the Jewish people.

set out to show that he, too, was a great lover of his people.

First, he had a wall built around Tiberias. New buildings were erected; old ones were repaired. A palace was built near the hot springs of Tiberias for Dona Gracia (though she probably never lived in it). Next, Joseph brought mulberry trees and silkworms from the Far East, hoping to set up a silk industry. He sent out invitations to the Jews of Italy, calling on them to settle the new city. But he was disappointed. Only a few Jews came, and those who did were not interested in spinning the fine fibers of the silkworm's cocoon into silk. They were students of Torah, wanting only to study. No industry blossomed. The city remained poor. But many scholars came to settle there.

Many fell in love with scenic Tiberias, as Joseph Nasi had done. Centuries before, the greatest Jew of the Middle Ages, Moses Maimonides, left his home in Egypt to visit

(Above) "Ari" Synagogue, Tsfat. (Below) Statue of Maimonides in Cordoba, Spain, his birthplace.

When they found, in the course of years, that these things were not working as they planned, they turned to studying and waiting.

III: JEWISH SETTLEMENTS

Not all Jews lived in Tsfat or Jerusalem. In 1563, a brave group of pioneers returned to the ancient city of Tiberias on the edge of Lake Kinneret. Suleiman gave one of the most famous Jews of that time—a man who was his personal adviser— the task of governing this ancient city.

The man was Don Joseph Nasi, nephew and son-in-law of Dona Gracia Mendes. Dona Gracia Mendes was one of the most outstanding women in Jewish history. She was called "The Angel" by Sephardic Jewry because she used her personal fortune to rescue many Spanish Jews from the Inquisition and to resettle them in Italy, Turkey, and the Holy Land. Now Joseph Nasi

The grave of Maimonides in Tiberias, Israel.

Israel. He was so taken with the beauty of the lake and of the Galilean setting that he decided to be buried there. Just as he asked, his grave was placed in Tiberias, and it became a magnet for scholars as well as a place to visit for all other Jews. In modern times, it was on the shores of this lake, only a few miles from the city of Tiberias, that another Jewish birth took place—the birth of the *kevutsah,* the first Jewish collective settlement (see in Unit Three "Kibbutz and Moshav"). Did these modern pioneers remember the days of Don Joseph Nasi? Did they know that they were finally bringing his dream to life, so many centuries later?

IV: THE END OF GLORY

In Tsfat, Arab raiders finally broke into the *khan,* stealing everything of value from the merchants' warehouses. Then a plague broke out, forcing most Jews to abandon their hilltop paradise. Years of hunger followed in the mystic city and, a short while later, Jerusalem too was clothed in suffering. Cruel rulers placed impossible taxes on the Jews living there, and, when years of drought came, they blamed the drought on the Jews of Jerusalem. Synagogues were looted and burned, and, by 1663, most Jews had fled from Jerusalem to Ramleh, leaving behind everything they treasured. Arab riots then spread through Tiberias and the other settlements in the Galilee.

Slowly the Jews returned to Jerusalem and the Galilee. But for the next hundred years little changed. In 1703, when the sultan sent collectors to gather taxes in Jerusalem, the Jews rebelled. It took three years before the Turks could again enter Jerusalem and collect taxes.

In those times, Jewish leaders were often kidnaped and held for ransom by the Turks—this was another way of getting the tax monies demanded by the sultan. The Jews were forced to turn to Arab money-lenders in order to pay these heavy ransoms. The community fell apart.

Help came from the Diaspora, from the Jews of Constantinople. They sent funds to rebuild the *yeshivot* and Jewish homes. Turkish Jews continued to travel to Jerusalem on pilgrimages. And Jews from other parts of the world began to arrive in numbers, too. In the late 1700s the Chasidim (followers of Rabbi Israel, the Baal

Distinctive dress of Turkish Jews.

Shem Tov) made *aliyah,* as did followers of the Baal Shem Tov's opponent, Rabbi Elijah Gaon of Vilna. But these new immigrants were not farmers, merchants, or craftsmen. They were students and scholars. So the Jews of the Land of Israel relied heavily on *tsedakah* collected among Jews in Turkey and Eastern Europe.

The sheik who controlled Tiberias and the Galilee wrote to the famous Palestinian rabbi, Haim Abulafia, saying, "Arise, come up and inherit the land of Tiberias which your forefathers possessed." Abulafia did. In fact, he and the sheik together rebuilt many of the Jewish settlements of the Galilee, even while Jerusalem and Tsfat were filled with Jews living on *tsedakah.*

PREVIEW

Something strange had happened to the Jews of the Land of Israel under the rule of the Ottoman Turks. The people and the Land had been separated. Only in a few places did Jews still farm or raise sheep. Most Jews now lived on charity from the Diaspora and studied in the *yeshivot.*

The new immigrants lived in the Land because it was holy, but they had no real attachment to the land itself. Yet it was the *Land* that was promised in the ancient Covenant; it was the Land and its treasure that called out to be reclaimed.

Into this new kind of community came news that a new kind of conqueror had appeared. His name was Napoleon Bonaparte, and the next chapter of Jewish history bore his mark, responding to the slogan of his revolution, "Liberty, Equality, and Brotherhood."

Things to Consider

Ashkenazic Jews (from northern Europe) and Sephardic Jews (from countries around the Mediterranean Sea) lived very differently throughout our history. Ashkenazim lived in mainly Christian lands; Sephardim lived mainly among Moslems. They had different versions of the prayer book and made different decisions regarding Jewish law and religious practice. Check at home. Is your family Ashkenazic, Sephardic, or mixed? As far back as anyone in your family remembers, where did your family come from? Bring your notes to class and compare them with your classmates'. What does this tell you about your Jewish community?

Different communities have placed importance on different parts of the Jewish tradition. The Jews of Tsfat placed emphasis on mysticism. What Jewish traditions or values do you think your community considers the most important today? (Another way to ask this question would be: What do most Jews in your community do that makes them think they are acting Jewishly?)

In what negative way did the Covenant suffer during the rule of the Ottoman Turks? Should you remove something from your definition of Covenant? Why, or why not?

SHABBETAI ZEVI

are afbeeldinge van Sabetha Sebi den genaemden hersteller des Joodschen Rijcks.
ry pourtrait de Sabbathai Sevi qui se dict Restaura-teur du Royaume de Juda & Israel.

In Europe, word spread that the messiah had truly arrived. The man called "messiah" was Shabbetai Zevi. He appeared in 1654, shortly after the Cossacks massacred Jews in Russia. His teachings were much like those of Isaac Luria, the beloved sage of Tsfat, and many Jews studied his words as eagerly as they studied the Torah and the Talmud. In 1662, Shabbetai Zevi entered Jerusalem. Here, too, he appeared just after a period of suffering—when Tiberias lay in ruins, Tsfat had been emptied by plague and looting and most Jews lived in Hebron, Gaza, or Ramleh.

Behaving like a saint, Shabbetai fasted and visited the tombs of holy men. Scholars and common people alike fell under his spell. In Gaza, he met Nathan who spent long hours in talk with him. Because Nathan of Gaza was himself thought to be especially holy, the community of Israel was rocked by the news in 1665 that Nathan had called Shabbetai the messiah.

A wealthy scholar in Gaza gave Shabbetai money for the poor of Jerusalem. Instead, Shabbetai spent the money on his own travels and needs. When he reached Jerusalem, the rabbis there excommunicated (banned) him, forbidding Jews to have anything to do with him. Shabbetai was forced to flee, first to Gaza, then to Smyrna.

Meanwhile, the Jews of the Diaspora were

caught up by the dream of the messiah. Thousands sold their businesses, packed their belongings, and began the long walk to Turkey, hoping that Shabbetai would lead them from Turkey to the Holy Land. Shabbetai set out in 1666 to meet them. He led a parade of loyal followers toward the city of Constantinople where the sultan, fearing that this madman would cause trouble, offered Shabbetai a simple choice: convert to Islam or be put to death. Shabbetai converted, saying he was not the messiah after all.

The Jews waiting at the Turkish border soon heard of his conversion. Many refused to believe it was true. Some claimed that Shabbetai was only pretending to convert, waiting for a better time to openly declare himself the messiah. But, a short while later, Shabbetai died, shattering the faith of his "followers."

The idea of the messiah had stayed alive through the ages. It was the same idea that had come alive in the days of Jesus, in the time of Bar Kochba, in the seventh century, in the twelfth century, in the days of Reubeni and Molcho during the tortures of the Inquisition, and now in Shabbetai Zevi. Later, some would call Theodor Herzl the messiah. And, even now, somewhere in the Jewish heart, this idea still dwells—the hope that God will send a leader to the Jewish people, a leader who will bring an end to suffering and herald a time of peace.

10

NAPOLEON AND THE JEWS

Jews have always believed that freedom and the Covenant are intertwined. To live by the Covenant means to be free to live by the word of God. Anything less is slavery. Living in the Holy Land meant living closer to the memory of freedom, but it did not yet mean real freedom for the Jews.

Life under the Ottoman Turks hardly changed for hundreds of years. While Europe entered into a new age of freedom, the Age of Emancipation, the Jews in the Land of Israel still lived as they had in the Middle Ages, hardly dreaming of equality or citizenship, much less of freedom.

Yet in France and, even more, in the new United States of America, an age of freedom dawned that would send sparks flying even as far as the walls of Jerusalem. The message came with the armies of Napoleon Bonaparte.

Napoleon's armies conquered Egypt then entered Palestine in 1799. Napoleon hoped to lead them to Constantinople, to conquer the Ottoman Empire. He was not interested in Jerusalem, since it was inland, away from the coast and the coastal highway by which he hoped to travel northward. But he surrounded Jaffa and took the city by force.

Was he surprised when a group of Jewish leaders told him that he was as welcome as the messiah? They had prayed for his victory, the Jews said. And they wanted to join him to free the rest of the Jews of Palestine.

Napoleon next moved his armies north to the city of Acre, home of the ruler of Palestine. Here, he encountered resistance. Hoping that the Jews of Acre would welcome and help him, as the Jews of Jaffa had done, he sent messages to the city's rabbi. But the rabbi and the Jews of Acre were loyal to the Turks. They stood against Napoleon, and the Turks (with the help of the British navy) held Napoleon off.

So Napoleon tried another stratagem. He called on the Jews of Palestine to help him in "the restoration of ancient Jerusalem." Still the Jews of Acre refused to listen. Acre would not fall. Finally, Napoleon gave up all hope of conquering the city and he and his troops returned to Egypt.

Wherever Napoleon's armies were successful in Europe, Napoleon set the Jews free—opening the gates of one ghetto after another. What might have been the outcome if the Jews of Acre had helped him? Would freedom have come sooner to the Land of Israel? Would Napoleon have kept his promise to rebuild Jerusalem, to give Palestine to the Jews?

One thing is clear: the name of Napoleon became beloved to many Jews, even in the Holy Land. In story and legend, they celebrated the conqueror who had not conquered. They spoke of his wisdom and recalled his might. They prayed for his return while he lived and they prayed for his spirit once he was dead. The rabbi of Jerusalem called Napoleon, "the man after God's heart."

View of Acre and (below) the Citadel with its Turkish tower that was built to guard the city of Acre.

I: IBRAHIM PASHA

Napoleon failed to conquer the Ottoman Empire, but it was crumbling from within, its army weak and old-fashioned, its rulers only local tribe leaders. The empire was poor.

In 1832, Ibrahim Pasha, the Egyptian general, did what Napoleon had failed to do. Coming by land and sea from Egypt, he conquered Palestine—taking even the stubborn city of Acre. He placed good governors in the offices of the old tribal leaders, collected taxes not only from Christians and Jews but from Moslems as well, and drafted Moslems to serve in his army. He allowed the Jews of Jerusalem to rebuild four synagogues and made sure that the Jews and Christians were safe from their Arab enemies.

Port in the Ottoman Empire.

The draft and the new taxes angered the local Arabs who rose up against Ibrahim. Fresh troops from Egypt crushed the revolt, taking revenge on all who stood in their way. They killed the innocent along with the guilty, Jews along with the Arabs who had rebelled. In Tsfat and Hebron, Jews were slaughtered without mercy. However, in Tiberias, the Jewish community gave all their possessions to the soldiers and were allowed to live, and, in Jerusalem, few Jews were murdered.

Britain once again came to the aid of the Turks, helping them to drive Ibrahim Pasha back to Egypt. And, by 1840, the Turks once again controlled the Land of Israel.

II: JEWISH LIFE

The Turks still did not trust the Jews. They added a new "government" tax and forced the Jews to pay "festival taxes" and a monthly tax. Once again, the Jews of the Holy Land called for *tsedakah* from the Diaspora communities.

Rabbi Menachem Mendel, a student of the Gaon of Vilna, came to Jerusalem in 1816. With his help, the Ashkenazic (European) Jewish community there began to grow. The Ashkenazic Jews sent a leader to Constantinople to plead with the sultan to lift some of the heavy taxes, and, surprisingly, they were successful. But now the Ashkenazic Jews were forced to pay a huge sum of money for protection against the local Arabs.

They sent to Europe *tsedakah* collectors known as *meshulahim* or "messengers." But the monies collected hardly paid the debts of the Jerusalem community, and there were still the poor to support.

Four different aid societies were set up to help the Jews: a Poor Fund, a Sick Fund, a Fund for Orphan Girls, and a Fund for Scholars. Every Friday before Shabbat, the collectors for the Poor Fund went from door to door in Jerusalem asking for bread. Most of the money from Europe was spent paying government taxes, so these four funds were supported mainly by the local Jews, out of the small amounts they received from Europe. *Tsedakah* became more than a part of life in Jerusalem; it very nearly became the center of life. The poor gave to the poor.

Moses Montefiore.

III: MOSES MONTEFIORE

Help came from one of the most important Jews of the day, Moses Montefiore. He visited the Holy Land and fell in love with it. In the coming years, despite the great hardships of travel, he visited it six more times, trying to help the Jews living there build a better way of life. Though Montefiore was a lover of the study of Torah, he understood the special connection between the Jews and the Land that many had forgotten.

On his first visit, with his wife Judith, he gave money for education and charity. After his second visit, in 1840, he gave money for a population count and discovered that there were about 3,000 Jews in Jerusalem—five hundred were from Europe, the rest were Sephardim from North Africa, Asia, and Spain. There were perhaps 3,500 Jews in the rest of the Holy Land. Nearly four hundred were students or scholars living entirely on charity. The rest were peddlers, storekeepers, money changers, weavers, tailors, barbers, millers, cobblers, and carpen-

ters. And, in addition, there were a few doctors.

Montefiore did the unthinkable: he built houses for the Jews *outside* the protective walls of Jerusalem! This was the beginning of what we now call the New City of Jerusalem. He set up schools to train young people in trades and farming. To provide for the first Jews brave enough to move outside the Old City walls, Montefiore built a windmill to grind grain.

The windmill, which still stands, never worked, but the settlement around it soon filled up. When Montefiore heard that a printing press owned by a Jew in Tsfat had been burned by Arab *fellahin* (peasants), he helped to set up a new printing press in Jerusalem in 1842. Soon there were others. Newspapers began to appear, along with many books, maps, and pamphlets.

It was Montefiore's plan to build two hundred Jewish settlements in the Galilee, but he could not gain permission from the Turks who were fearful that the Jewish population might grow.

Around 1839, a rabbi named Yehudah Bibas of

UNIT TWO: Between East and West

Montefiore Windmill and Museum, Jerusalem.

Corfu traveled through the Holy Land telling Jews that they would have to learn to help themselves, advising them to study science and learn to fight, just as their forefathers fought against the Greeks. One of his students, Rabbi Alkali, traveled through Europe asking Jews to help revive the Land of Israel, telling them the time had come for Jews to rebuild their ancient homeland.

PREVIEW

The seeds were planted. A new generation—made up of men like Montefiore, Bibas, and Alkali—was not afraid to think that Jews could be farmers again, own land, and control their own lives. They were the first Zionists, active even before the birth of modern Zionism—the idea of creating a Jewish nation in Palestine.

They were religious men, two rabbis and one learned Jew, hoping that the Covenant could again bear fruit where it was first practiced, in the Land that was promised by God to the people of Israel. Unlike previous generations, they were not happy to wait for the coming of the messiah. They wanted a new kind of Jew to live in Israel, a Jew who would work the land and love it. None of them lived to see the dream come true, but they were the first to dream it.

Things to Consider

The Jews of Palestine needed *tsedakah* from the Jews of the Diaspora in order to pay their taxes and live and study in the Holy Land. Yet they set aside a little of the charity money they received to set up four charity funds to help others. In what way is *tsedakah* a part of the Jewish Covenant? Is it something you need to add to your list of the Covenant's parts?

Montefiore's population count showed the Jews of the Holy Land were occupied in many different jobs or professions. Check with your family: What jobs or professions do people in your family hold? Ask what jobs or professions were held by people in your family in past generations. Bring in your list and share it in the classroom. Have "Jewish" jobs changed much over the years?

Moses and Judith Montefiore did what they felt was the right thing to help the Jews of Israel in their time. If you were trying to help the Jews of Israel today, what would you do?

UNIT THREE

The Golden Age of Zionism

11

THE BIRTH OF ZIONISM

From the moment the Hebrews first crossed over into Canaan, there has never been a time when our people has not been living in the Land of Israel. Even though through much of history the Jews in the Holy Land were small in number, the majority of Jews scattered around the world continually turned toward Israel, seeing its small Jewish community as the beating heart that sent blood rushing through the body of world Jewry.

Through the ages, whenever travel was possible, Jews visited the Holy Land, seeking out the City of David, bending down to kiss the ground, standing in prayer before the huge stones of the Western Wall—the last vestige of the glory of the ancient Temples. Sages and rabbis, poets and travelers left homes far away to come and settle in the Promised Land. Some, who never visited while they lived, left instructions that they be buried in the holy soil of Palestine.

They all believed, with perfect faith, in the coming of the messiah. A Davidic prince would arise among the Jews to lead them home, to Zion, to the Land of Israel. Then, they said, the Jews would be one people again in their Land. The dead would rise up to join the living. Those buried outside of Zion would have to make the long journey home. But those buried in the Land of Israel, they said, would be ready to answer the messiah's call—able to see the beginnings of the messianic era, when all nations would learn to serve the One God, the God who had made a Covenant with Abraham, Isaac, and Jacob.

By the middle of the nineteenth century, then, most Jews in the Land of Israel lived in one of the four "holy cities"—Jerusalem, Tsfat, Hebron, Tiberias. They lived the dream of the messiah, believing that the days of the messiah were near, praying and studying. They hoped that God would look with favor upon the holiness and faith of their community, would have pity on them because of their poverty and their suffering, and would send the messiah to save them.

I: JEWISH NATIONALISM

Another path was opening, another way of thinking about the messiah that was different from waiting in perfect faith. It was also Jewish, but it borrowed an idea just beginning to shape the world we live in today. This was the idea of nationalism.

New voices argued that a people had the right to live in its own land, speak its own language, study its own history, and create its own destiny. Each nation would be unique, just as each instrument in the orchestra is unique. Each nation would give its special tone and note and all together would create a music greater than that of any single instrument.

Surely, Jews whose families had lived in France, Britain, or Germany for many years could be part of the French, British, or German nations. And these nations began to reach out to their Jewish citizens, slowly offering them freedom and equality.

The Western Wall.

But the Jews soon came to realize that they were a nation, too. They had a unique history of their own, a language—Hebrew—which was theirs alone, and a special destiny, spelled out long before—to be a kingdom of priests and a holy people. They had much to offer to this great symphony of nations. They lacked only one thing: possession of their own land. Nationalism affirmed their *right* to a homeland, and Jewish nationalism—what we call Zionism—set out to assert that right, to gain a free and independent Jewish state in the Land of Israel.

This was, indeed, another path to the days of the messiah. Jewish teachers and sages had often said that the messiah would come only when the Jews no longer needed the messiah—that is, when the Jews were already in their Land, already a light to the nations of the world, already bringing peace and plenty to the Land of Israel.

As anti-Semitism mounted in late nineteenth-century Europe, a minority of Jews began to believe that the only alternative was to take things into their own hands. They dreamed of building, repairing, restoring, replanting, and redeeming their Promised Land, Zion, the Land of Israel. Zionism became the name for this special combination of beliefs, and, by the last half of the nineteenth century, Zionism was already taking shape in some very real ways.

II: EARLY ZIONISM IN PALESTINE

It was Moses Montefiore who took the first step in this new direction, even as he was trying to help the Jews who still believed in waiting for redemption. In 1856, Montefiore bought an orange orchard near Jaffa, hoping that some of the Palestinian Jews would settle there and learn to work the land. A few years later, the Alliance Israelite Universelle, an international Jewish self-help organization, set up a school called Mikveh Yisrael near Jaffa to teach farming to the Jews. These were small, but important, beginnings.

More important was the work done by the Jews of the Holy Land. Three Jews from Jerusalem bought 844 acres of land near the Yarkon River, naming it *Petach Tikvah* ("Gate of Hope"), and set up a Jewish village there. A couple of years later, more land was purchased,

Publication founded by Hermann Ahlwardt, a notorious nineteenth-century German anti-Semite who arrived in America in 1895 for purposes of agitation against Jewry.

more settlers came from Jerusalem and other cities of Palestine. The area, it turned out, was infested with malaria. Those who did not die of the fever were finally forced to leave. Some Jews of Tsfat bought land about the same time (this was the beginning of Rosh Pina), but there too the first settlers were unable to hold on.

Zionism suffered hard beginnings.

Post office, Pinsker St., Petach Tikva, 1920.

III: HEBREW REBORN

Another part of Jewish nationalism—the language of the Jews—was also of concern to the Jews of Palestine. Up to this time, the Jews of Jerusalem, for example, communicated in many languages. The Sephardic Jews spoke a mixture of Spanish and Hebrew called Ladino and the North African Sephardic Jews spoke Arabic. Ashkenazic Jews spoke Yiddish and Jews from the mountain country of Russia mainly spoke Georgian. Of course, when the leaders of the different Jewish communities came together, they spoke Hebrew. Other than that, Hebrew was used only as a language of prayer and study—it was the "Holy Tongue."

There came a dreamer—really, a family of dreamers. Eliezer and Hemdah Ben Yehudah spoke only Hebrew. Whether they were sitting in their apartment in Jerusalem or shopping in the Jewish marketplace, they spoke Hebrew. They spoke Hebrew to rabbis and to neighbors. And they tried to convince other Jews to speak Hebrew, too.

Offered a job as a teacher in an Alliance school in Jerusalem, Eliezer agreed to teach only if he could teach in Hebrew. Before long, he had talked other teachers there into using Hebrew, too.

Later, when the new Technion college was opened in Haifa, Eliezer heard that the teaching was being done in German, the language of modern science. Eliezer demanded that Hebrew be the only teaching language at the Technion. The scientists argued that Hebrew did not even have words for new scientific inventions. How could it be used to teach modern science?

Eliezer replied that words could be created, formed out of old Hebrew roots, to meet modern needs. The real goal, he said, was to make Hebrew the language of the Jews. The argument spread. Teachers throughout Palestine went on strike, refusing to teach until the Technion would agree to use Hebrew. They understood what Eliezer had in mind. Thus Hebrew became the language of instruction at the Technion.

There was more to be done. Eliezer devoted his life to the study of Hebrew. He formed new words out of Hebrew roots. He compiled a Hebrew dictionary of seventeen volumes. Hemdah wrote novels in Hebrew. Their children were raised—the first in modern times—to speak only Hebrew.

Together with others in Jerusalem, Ben Yehudah formed a group called *Techiat Yisrael* ("Rebirth of Israel"). The members agreed to work toward making Hebrew the spoken language of the Jews. They went even further. They wanted to "revive the nation of Israel on the soil on which it has grown . . . [and to increase the Jewish community] in the Land until we are a majority. . . ."

They found help from the many Jews in the Diaspora already writing and publishing in

Eliezer Ben Yehudah (opposite page); Chaim Nachman Bialik (top left); Achad Ha-Am.

Hebrew—Jews like the great Hebrew poet, Chaim Nachman Bialik, and the famous thinker, Asher Ginsberg, who chose to call himself Achad Ha-Am ("One of the People"). These writers were the heirs of the *Maskilim* ("Jewish Enlighteners") and the *Haskalah* ("Enlightenment") movement. The great difference between the members of *Techiat Yisrael* and the *Maskilim* was that the *Maskilim* did not *speak* Hebrew day by day.

It was in Palestine that Hebrew became the spoken language of the Jews. And it was something of a miracle. For Hebrew is the language of the Covenant. In speaking, writing, reading, and thinking in Hebrew, a door opened for the Jews—a door that led to all the great works of the Jewish tradition. Knowing Hebrew brought the past alive, as much for the Jews of Palestine in the nineteenth century as it does for us today.

IV: BILU

The traditional Jews of Jerusalem and the Land of Israel—those waiting patiently for the messiah—were strongly opposed to the rebirth of spoken Hebrew. They felt that speaking the "Holy Tongue" degraded it. They wanted no more of the new Jewish settlers to come. They objected to those who seemed to want to "force the hand of God" and with their own strength bring on the days of the messiah. Traditional Judaism forbade this. But history chose its own path: Zionism.

In Russia, where most of the world's Jews lived, anti-Jewish riots called "pogroms" broke out. Many Jews were killed. Businesses were ruined. Homes were looted and burned. Many began to seek new homes, safer homes. A great many of these went to America. Some turned to Palestine.

UNIT THREE: The Golden Age of Zionism

At first, small numbers of Russian Jews met together secretly, discussing the return to Zion. They knew their idea was shocking to most Jews, just as it was against the laws of Russia to meet to discuss it. Yet they soon found a leader to unite them and an idea to call them to action.

A physician named Leon Pinsker witnessed the pogroms of 1881, when 160 Jewish communities in Russia were cruelly attacked, and he wrote a small book called *Self-Emancipation.* In it, Pinsker said it was time for Jews to free themselves. Using the words of Hillel, he asked, "If not now, when?"

The small secret groups called Pinsker a prophet. They read his book and agreed with his ideas. In 1882, fourteen members of the "Lovers of Zion" made the long journey from Russia to Palestine. They called themselves the BILU, using the first letters of the Hebrew *Bet Yaakov Lechu Venelchah,* "O House of Jacob, come, let us go up." They made *aliyah,* the "going up" to the Land of Israel.

Leon Pinsker.

Baron Edmond de Rothschild.

They studied and worked at an Alliance farm school then settled on a small piece of land, naming it Rishon le-Tzion ("First to Zion"). Their first crop failed and they suffered from malaria, from the burning heat, and from Arab raids. Six returned to Russia. Life in Palestine was too difficult for them. The rest hung on; soon hundreds more began to come.

From the outset it was clear that they needed help, especially money, to survive until they could make the fields support them. They sent one member to Europe to seek out help. He traveled to Austria and Germany without success; but in Paris he met Baron Edmond de Rothschild. The meeting went well. Rothschild saw a great future for the Jewish people in Palestine. He was willing to give money and send experts to help them, but on one condition. He did not want it known that it was he, Baron Rothschild, who was helping.

THE BIRTH OF ZIONISM

The Russian Jews kept arriving in larger numbers. From 1882 to 1903, some 25,000 Jews came to settle in Israel. These were the years of the First Aliyah, the first wave of immigration to the Holy Land in modern times. These settlers did not head for the holy cities of Jerusalem, Tsfat, Hebron, and Tiberias. They were ready to work on the land. And, with Rothschild's help, they did.

Though Rothschild wanted his gifts to be anonymous, he made so many grants and did so much to help the people of the First Aliyah that it was not long before everyone knew who the "secret" helper was. He created new villages, set up the vineyards and wine industry of Palestine, and purchased land for the Jews on both sides of the Jordan River. He loved most to see that the Jews were helping themselves, working on their own soil. He asked them to speak Hebrew and made sure that Hebrew was taught in all the schools he supported. He never thought he was giving his money away. He was making an investment in the Covenant, using his wealth to bring his people back to life on their Promised Land. The settlers knew that Rothschild did not wish his name known, so they called him *Hanadiv ha-yadua,* "The well-known man of generosity." Later, they simply called him the "Father of the Yishuv."

PREVIEW

The Jews who came to Israel later—the Second Aliyah, Third Aliyah, Fourth Aliyah—saw the wisdom of Rothschild's ways. They, too, turned to the land, purchasing as much of it as possible; living on it and working it. What had been lost in the long years of the Ottoman Turkish rule was the special attachment between the Jews and the soil of the Promised Land. Now, while the Turks still ruled, the Jews remembered their heritage and returned, not just to the Land of Israel, but to the soil of Israel, as well.

Things to Consider

The chapter speaks of "bringing the messiah" and the different paths Jews chose to do this. Another way in which we understand the messiah is as a symbol of the *time* of peace and freedom. We sometimes speak of "the messianic age." Is there a special connection between the Jewish idea of the messiah or the messianic age and the Land of Israel? To check, look up the word "messiah" in a Jewish encyclopedia.

So far, you have met many different kinds of Jewish leaders. Make a "leadership" chart by dividing a piece of paper into four columns. Above the columns place the following: (1) Montefiore, (2) the Ben Yehudah family, (3) Pinsker, (4) Rothschild. Below each name make a list of words that describe each leader and the ways of leading that each of these four chose.

The text says that Rothschild believed he was making an "investment in the Covenant." If you were going to make an investment in the Covenant today, what are some of the ways you might use your talents and your money?

12

HERZL AND THE ZIONIST CONGRESS

Two years after the French Revolution of 1789, the French officially made Jews "citizens." France thus became the first country in Europe to grant equal rights to its Jewish residents. This fact alone gave the French a special place in the hearts of modern Jews. But one hundred and three years later, in 1894, France startled the world—Jewish and non-Jewish—by its anti-Jewish fervor.

Alfred Dreyfus was a Jew by birth. Much more important to him, he was a captain in the French army. He knew little of the Jewish people or Jewish history. But ask him about French army drill, or full dress army uniforms, or military strategy—about these he was an expert. He was devoted to his government. His one ambition was to rise in the ranks at Staff Headquarters in Paris, where he was stationed.

Without warning he was arrested, accused of stealing French military secrets and selling them to the Germans. He knew he was innocent. He trusted the French court system, the fairness of the French. Surely, he would be tried, found innocent, and set free. Or, perhaps even sooner, the true spy would be found and Dreyfus would receive a full apology.

Imagine the shock of Captain Dreyfus when he was put on trial and unfairly convicted; the decision had been reached in advance. He was sentenced to life imprisonment on Devil's Island, a punishment reserved for only the worst

criminals and traitors of France. As it was said, there was no return from Devil's Island.

In 1906, Dreyfus was finally declared innocent and his name was cleared. He was brought back from Devil's Island. But by then he was little more than a skeleton of the man who had been Captain Alfred Dreyfus. Prejudice and politics had ruined his career, shamed his family, and spoiled his health forever. True, the scandal of his so-called trial had shaken the French government to its roots, even toppling the government that had sent Dreyfus into exile. True, his case—the Dreyfus Affair, as it was known—became so important in French politics that two parties were formed, the Dreyfusards and the anti-Dreyfusards. But Dreyfus had no part in any of this. He was just the axle that stood still as the wheel of French politics spun around him.

The *New Free Press,* an Austrian newspaper, sent one of its star reporters, Theodor Herzl, to cover the Dreyfus trial. Herzl, like Dreyfus, had put his Jewishness in the background of his life, preferring to think of himself as a modern citizen of Europe, free and equal to all others. He was offended by the trial. Like others, he was aware that it was unfair. He stood in the crowd, watching the French army assemble in the center of Paris to shame Captain Dreyfus.

Dreyfus was called forward. An officer removed the sword that hung at Dreyfus's side and broke it in two. Then the epaulets were torn from

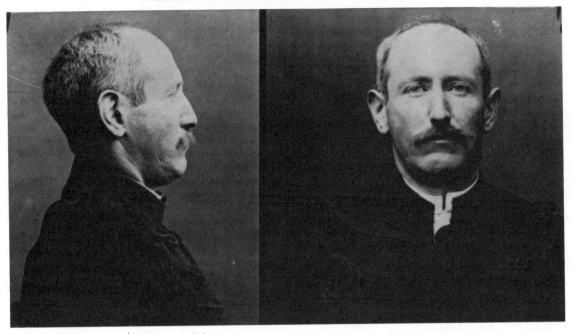

Alfred Dreyfus, January 4, 1895, after being stripped of all insignia of military rank. The Dreyfus trial before the military court, Rennes, August 7, 1899.

The Dreyfus home on Devil's Island, 1899, with guard's barracks, tower, and canteen.

the shoulders of Dreyfus's dress uniform. Dreyfus was disgraced. But the worst was yet to come.

The crowd began to scream, not "Down with the traitor!" but "Down with Jews!" Dreyfus must have been bewildered. The last thing on his mind was being Jewish. Herzl was enraged. How could the French people, the nation of liberty, equality, and brotherhood still be filled with the age-old prejudices against Jews?

Dreyfus went to Devil's Island. Herzl returned home to Vienna. His anger forced him to think again about his Jewishness and about the problem Jews faced. After all the years of freedom, the Jews of Europe remained strangers in strange lands. What they called their homes were not their homes.

In 1896, Herzl published a small book entitled *The Jewish State*. His ideas were much the same as Leon Pinsker's, though he had never read Pinsker's *Self-Emancipation*. Jews, Herzl said, had to take their lives in their own hands, had to create a Jewish nation like the nations of other peoples. Without this, they would always be homeless and helpless.

Unlike Pinsker, Herzl was a man of action. What he said in print, he now set out to accomplish in fact. He sent a call far and wide for Jews to gather together to begin the creation of a Jewish state.

Word of the meeting called by Herzl spread rapidly. About two hundred Jewish leaders came to Basle, Switzerland, in 1897 for a Zionist Congress. Herzl knew the world was watching; he was a wise politician. He wanted the world to see a Jewish summit meeting, so he made sure that all the delegates (even the poorer ones from eastern Europe) were equipped with tuxedos and top hats for the occasion.

Under Herzl's leadership, the Zionist Congress gave birth to the Zionist movement. A formal statement was issued, reported in newspapers throughout the world, stating that the congress had one purpose: "to secure for the Jewish people [a] home in Palestine." Herzl was elected first president of the World Zionist Organization. In his *Diary,* he wrote:

> If I were to sum up the congress in a word . . . it would be this: At Basle I founded the Jewish state. If I said this aloud today I would be greeted by universal laughter. In five years, perhaps, and certainly in fifty years, everyone will see it.

Herzl was not far from wrong. Fifty-one years later, the State of Israel was declared! Herzl, unfortunately, did not live to see it come to pass. Yet, for the rest of his life, he pursued his one great goal: to find a home for the Jewish people.

I: POLITICAL ZIONISM

Herzl believed that "infiltration," the slow buildup by immigration and resettlement of the Jews in Palestine was the wrong path. A better road, he thought, was to negotiate an agreement that would allow Jews the right to govern themselves and call a part of Palestine their own. He started knocking on the doors of world figures, speaking to princes and politicians. Several times he met with the sultan of the Ottoman Empire. He offered to raise the money to pay all debts the Turks owed to the governments of Europe. In exchange, he asked for a charter

Herzl acknowledges his acclaim, First Zionist Congress, 1897.

giving Palestine to the Jews. For a brief moment, it seemed that Herzl might actually triumph. Then the sultan changed his mind. No charter would be given.

Herzl became desperate. In Russia, new pogroms broke out. Jews were being attacked, their businesses and homes were being looted, many were losing their lives. He could not bear to see his people dying needlessly. He turned to Great Britain.

The British were sympathetic. They could not offer him Palestine, they said, but they would offer the country of Uganda, in Africa, which was under their control. He could settle the Jews there and create a Jewish state. It was not exactly what he wanted, but Herzl was a realist. Jews were dying. They needed some place that would be safe, even if it was not in Palestine.

At the following Zionist Congress, Herzl pre-

sented the Uganda plan to the Jewish people. But the majority of Zionists—especially the ones from Russia, where Jews were suffering the most—wanted no part of Uganda. They understood what Herzl only dimly felt: only the Holy Land would satisfy them, only Jerusalem could be their capital city. Zionism, after all, was more than just nationalism—it was tied up with the bringing of the messiah. Nothing less than Palestine would do.

Herzl felt crushed by this defeat. He only wanted to save Jewish lives, and now the very Jews he was trying to save turned against him. Or so he thought. If he could have visited Russia just then, he might have been surprised at what he would have found: he had become the most famous and beloved Jew of his time; his photograph was framed and hung on the walls of Jewish homes all over eastern Europe; he was

99

Herzl and members of the delegation on board ship during their journey to Palestine.

even spoken of as a "modern messiah."

In 1904, at the age of 43, he died. He had literally worn himself out in frantic efforts to establish a Jewish state. The entire Jewish world mourned. Herzl had become the Father of modern Zionism.

II: THE ZIONIST MOVEMENT

Herzl's Zionism was political. After his death, the movement divided itself into many kinds of Zionism. In truth, it had always been many kinds, but Herzl's personal force had kept them united.

Achad Ha-Am spoke of "cultural" Zionism, the belief that Israel should become the center of Jewish life, sending Torah and Jewish learning out to the Jewish communities of the Diaspora. Achad Ha-Am was not so interested in a political Jewish state, so long as a strong and wise Jewish community could exist in the Holy Land.

Religious Zionists wanted to be sure that the new Jewish community of Palestine would be ruled by the laws of the Torah.

Labor Zionists spoke of the need for Jews to be part of every economic group in the new Jewish nation— to be ditchdiggers and farmers, as well as office workers and politicians.

There were other kinds of Zionism, too. Each group came to the Zionist congresses with its own set of ideas and its own program. Later, many of these groups became political parties, forerunners to the many political parties in Israel today.

Still, Herzl's one dream united them. The

Jews needed a safe and secure homeland. The time had come, they all agreed, for "the ingathering of the exiles." The time had come for Jews to help themselves by building their own nation. They could still trust in God, but they could not afford to wait any longer for God to send them help. They had come to believe the old adage that "God helps those who help themselves." Even if the return to Zion was not going to be the exact way it was promised in the Bible and the Talmud, it was still the right time for it to be. Above all, Zionism united Jewish people around the globe, reminding us that we are one people, *Am Echad.*

III: THE SECOND ALIYAH

Herzl had been right about another thing, too. The Jews of Russia were in terrible danger. The outbreak of the pogroms in the last years of the 1800s and the first years of the 1900s was a clear

sign that the time to leave had arrived. Now the young people of Russia, Jews raised in the light of the Zionist dream, chose to act.

Many fled to America, the country their parents called the Golden Land. Some remained in Russia and became socialists and later Communists, hoping that by bringing a revolution to Russia they could change the old patterns of Russian prejudice and become equals in the new order. But many took up the Zionist dream fully.

The old *Choveve Zion* ("Lovers of Zion") gave way to the new *Poale Zion* ("Workers of Zion"). Their chief thinker was Ber Borochov, a Russian Jew who never made *aliyah* to Palestine. The members of his movement pleaded with him to stay in Russia, to keep writing and speaking, and to keep sending more Jews to the Holy Land. And this he did.

Borochov told the Jews that they were in danger *because* they did not own or work the land. The really important people in any nation, he said, were the ones who provided food, cloth

Herzl's grave; lower left is a commemorative stamp in his honor.

Gordon arrived in Palestine in 1904. He was forty-eight years old. Most of the Russian Jews coming to settle were in their teens or twenties. Many of them had read his writings and watched closely to see what he would do.

He immediately went to work in the fields, laboring day after day beside the younger men and women. At the end of a hard working day, he was always ready to sing and dance around the campfire, or to read from his writings. He was tireless. When all others were in bed, he wrote by the light of a candle. The next morning, he was fresh again, ready for another day of field work.

Gordon was putting a challenge before these young people. He *dared* them to work as hard as

for clothing, and materials for building. The Jews could never be really necessary so long as they were in the middle class—buying and selling what others created.

The new settlements in Israel, he said, were a chance for the Jewish people to prove they could create everything a nation needed; the new settlements in Israel were an opportunity for the Jewish people to prove that they could control their own fate and govern themselves. Most importantly, he said, the people who did the actual work should be the people in charge. A Jewish nation in the hands of its workers could become a real light to the rest of the nations of the world. Workers everywhere would turn to the Jewish people as an example of what workers could do if only they would unite.

Borochov's ideas inspired many young Russian Jews. But the ideas of Aaron David Gordon, a Russian Jew who made *aliyah*, set them afire. Gordon preached a "religion of labor." He said that work would "save" the Jewish people, bringing them "close to the Land."

he did, to enjoy the work as much as he did, to love the Land and conquer it. Those who worked closely with him said later that they felt a special force in him, a "holiness" some called it, a "fever" some said. Whatever it was, this force grew in power. Work itself almost became a religion. Attachment to the Land became a Jewish value again. In fact, in the eyes of the people of the Second Aliyah (1904–1914), one of the great sins was laziness.

In 1909, another major figure of the Second Aliyah arrived in Palestine, Berl Katzenelson. He also came from Russia; he, too, went to work in the fields. Like Gordon, Katzenelson spent every spare moment speaking and writing. He spoke, especially, about teaching children the importance of labor. Later, he set up the first labor newspaper, *Davar.* He helped to organize a Labor party to unite the workers of the Second Aliyah. Through his newspaper and the political party, he became the voice of his generation.

PREVIEW

The young people of the Second Aliyah studied hard to learn self-reliance—how to do whatever they needed for themselves. They were fortunate to have good teachers like Borochov, Gordon, and Katzenelson—strong and able, like the generation of Israelites who came out of the Sinai wilderness to settle the Land so many centuries before. They were willing to do whatever needed doing because they believed in the future. Work was setting them free in a new way, so they placed their Jewish faith in a "religion of labor."

In the years to come, they would create settlements, political parties, health and welfare services, trade unions, schools, and a defense force to protect what they built. They always trusted that more Jews would come to join them. They were deeply Jewish, though they hardly paid any attention to the majority of the laws of the Torah and the Talmud. Their Jewishness came from a special sense of what the Promised Land and the Covenant could mean: a people on its own land,

(Opposite page) Ber Borochov (far left); Aaron David Gordon; (above) Berl Katzenelson.

speaking its own language, cherishing and extending its own unique values, united by its history.

Things to Consider

Organize a classroom debate, using the following statement. *Resolved:* Zionism is a part of the Covenant. Prepare yourself to argue both sides of this statement, pro and con.

List the kinds of Zionism mentioned in the chapter. Which of these movements interests you most? Which of them might you have joined, if you had the chance? Why?

Zionists had a definite idea of the meaning of the Covenant. Make sure that all the things they believed are added to your list of the Covenant's parts.

KIBBUTZ AND MOSHAV

The World Zionist Congress voted in 1901 to set up Keren Kayemet Leyisrael, *the Jewish National Fund or JNF. It was a unique idea in world history. JNF was given the task of raising money from Jews around the world to buy land in Palestine—land that would forever belong to the Jewish people. Whatever land the Arabs were willing to sell, the Jews bought. They bought the worst pieces of land—swamps infested with malaria—and the best they could find. All of it became the property of the Jewish people, never again to be sold. So successful was the idea of JNF that today the State of Israel owns 90 percent of its land.*

Next, JNF began to settle Jews on the land, leasing it to groups of Jews for forty-nine years at a time. This idea of a forty-nine-year lease grew out of the Torah where every fiftieth year any land that had been sold returned to its original tribe and owner. In this way, the land was always to be divided equally among the people, as it had been in the days of Joshua.

In 1909, seven farmers leased from the JNF some land on the southern shore of Lake Kin-neret. In one year, they proved that workers could oversee their own work, plant a crop and harvest it, and even realize a profit. The seven went on to other tasks, but a new group came to replace them, and the first kevutsah *("community settlement") was born. The workers named it Deganyah ("God's corn").*

It was to Deganyah that A. D. Gordon came. Here, he helped build a new model for settling the land. The workers were in charge. They worked together, ate together the food prepared in one kitchen, sent their children to a central schoolroom, met together to decide what the kevutsah *should do and how the* kevutsah *should be run. At harvest time, women and men and their children—the entire* kevutsah*—went out to the fields to bring in the crops. The rest of the year, women and men worked together in nearly every task—in the kitchen, the fields, the laundry, the school. In some other lands, people dream of socialism—a system in which there are no bosses, where those who work share the fruits of their labors equally, where all give according to their abilities and receive according to their*

needs. In Israel, in the kevutsah, *the dream had become a reality.*

After a while, children were placed in special houses where they could grow up together in the spirit of the community. Parents visited with their children after work, in the evening hours before bedtime. And the kevutsah *decided to remain a small group so that members would always feel a part of a single family of workers, each as important as the other.*

A second experiment was soon set up to see whether a large group of people could live in the same way. This group, living at En Harod, created the first kibbutz (large kevutsah). *As in Deganyah no wages were paid and no money changed hands on the kibbutz. Members took what they needed from a central storeroom and asked for other things at the regular meetings. Life became sharing. Both kibbutz and* kevutsah *were socialistic in their way of living, but they* were also democratic since they were ruled by the democratic ideal of "one person, one vote." For women, especially, this was a revolutionary idea. For all peoples, it was a new way of life.

Some newcomers to Israel did not wish to share so completely. For them, a new kind of settlement called the moshav ovedim *or "workers' town" was created. Here, each family leased a parcel of land. Together, the families of a moshav bought seeds and goods, owned large farm machinery, dairy cattle, goats, and sheep. But each family lived in its own house, earned the profits from its own fields, and decided for itself what to do with its money.*

Later, another kind of moshav, the moshav shitufi *or "collective town" was set up. This was midway between the kibbutz and the* moshav ovedim. *Here, the land was not divided; it was worked as one farm. All livestock was shared; all farm machinery belonged to everyone. Yet each*

family had its own home and made its own decisions. At the end of each harvest, the profits of the farm were shared equally by all families.

The kibbutzim and the moshavim tried to grow their own vegetables and fruits and whatever else they needed, so that they would be as independent as possible. Some settlements chose to devote their energies to light and heavy industry, setting up factories and workshops. A few moshavim were set up in cities, where small groups shared houses and divided their salaries equally.

The kibbutz and the moshav faced special problems—after all, they were experimental; people had never before lived in such ways. Some settlers found it impossible to share completely. Others did not like farm or factory life. Some left. Others came. By 1948, there were 149 kibbutzim in Israel. By 1964, there were 244. The word "kibbutz" entered into the daily language of Jews and non-Jews throughout the world. The pioneers had truly created a new way of life.

13

WORLD POWERS AND SELF-DEFENSE

In 1904, as the Second Aliyah began, the Yishuv (the Jewish community of Palestine) was split into two parts at odds with one another. Neither group liked or understood the other. Yet both groups thought they held the key to the Jewish future in the Land of Israel.

The first group was made up of the religious Jews living in and around the four holy cities—Jerusalem, Tsfat, Hebron, and Tiberias. They refused to use Hebrew as a spoken language because they were afraid that common, everyday words would lead the Jews away from prayer and religion. They welcomed scholars and students from the Diaspora but opposed Jews who came to settle and farm. They feared that such newcomers would upset the local Arab population (the *fellahin*) and cause anti-Jewish riots.

These religious Jews lived on *chalukah,* the *tsedakah* money collected from Jews in the Diaspora. This was an old and honorable tradition. They were being paid to study by Jews who felt too busy to study, or by those who felt that study was all-important. If the religious Jews earned money in business or trade, it was only in order to pay for *tsedakah* and to support synagogues and *yeshivot.* Few of them earned enough to live on.

The second group was made up of the Jews who came in the First Aliyah (1882–1903). They became managers of vineyards, orchards, and farms and hired the *fellahin* at low wages to do the hard work. They had little contact with the religious Jews living on *chalukah,* feeling superior to them.

When the people of the Second Aliyah (1904–1914) arrived, the First Aliyah farmers offered them jobs at the same low wages they were paying Arab workers. The early settlers were surprised when the newcomers refused to work for them. They were shocked to see the newcomers struggling on their own farms, without hired help. Why did the new arrivals refuse to become "hired hands"?

For their part, the people of the Second Aliyah felt superior to both the religious Jews living on *chalukah* and the "gentleman" farmers. Those early colonists, they argued, had not changed Palestine; they had merely used other peoples' money—Montefiore's, Rothschild's, *chalukah*—to control bits and pieces of the land. They seemed to have no pioneering spirit. The newcomers charged the First Aliyah colonists with behaving like the middle class Jews in Russia—

buying and selling the labor of others. No wonder the Jews of the Second Aliyah did not get along with the Jews already in Palestine. They simply did not share the same ideals.

I: HA-SHOMER

The religious Jews were right about one thing: as the new waves of immigrants poured into the country, the Arabs did grow increasingly hostile. This was nothing new. Troubled by the success of the First Aliyah colonists, the Arabs fell back on their old tribal ways, taking what they could, when they could, by force if necessary. The Arabs formed gangs of mounted raiders. They rode usually by night into the towns and villages, stealing food and cattle, attacking the Jewish settlers.

To protect themselves, the colonists hired Arabs to serve as guards, just as they hired Arabs to do their field work. The guards, however, were only a little better than the raiders. No Arab guard would stand up for long against the horseback warriors; in addition, the guards sometimes would steal what they could, or even open the village gates to allow the raiders to enter.

The newcomers of the Second Aliyah refused to accept this situation. Fresh in their memories were the pogroms in Russia, where Jews had seldom defended themselves. Even in Russia, these young people had felt shame at this lack of self-defense. In fact, in 1904, when the Black Hundreds rioted against the Jews of Gomel, Russia, they were surprised to find the Jews *did* fight back. In that town, the members of the Zionist *Poale Zion* organized a defense force that actually drove the Black Hundreds away. If they could do this in Russia, why not in Palestine?

So a few of the newcomers founded a group called Ha-Shomer ("The Watchman"). They bought and learned to use guns; they bought horses and learned to ride and handle them; they trained and drilled, adopted a flag, and coined a motto: "In blood and fire Judea went down; in blood and fire Judea shall rise again." They kept their force small and their discipline strict.

Ha-Shomer hired themselves out as guards to the new settlements and later to the towns and villages of the First Aliyah. (At first, the early colonists did not believe that Jews could handle weapons. They soon learned otherwise.) Now, when Arab raiders appeared, they found Ha-Shomer waiting for them.

These Jewish guards did not give up when the first shot was fired. They fought back when attacked. They stood their ground and drove the Arabs off. Yet they did not seek revenge. They only used weapons when there was no other choice. If they could turn away the raiders with friendly warnings, they did.

Knowing well the Arab mind, they were patient and cautious. They recognized that, once an Arab was killed, the man's family would demand revenge; a blood feud once begun was like a vicious landslide: a single pebble might topple an entire hillside. It was not blood Ha-Shomer wanted, it was safety.

When the Jews of the First Aliyah finally turned to Ha-Shomer for help, the Jewish guards drove a hard bargain. To hire Ha-Shomer, the colonists had to agree to hire Jewish workers at fair wages. And the colonists had to agree to make Ha-Shomer their *only* official defense force.

It was not long before both the early colonists and the Arabs learned to respect Ha-Shomer. Though the guards were few in number—there were only twenty-six members between 1907 and 1909—they moved in small groups, wherever and whenever they were needed. Like the "conquest of labor," the right to self-defense became a hallmark of the Second Aliyah.

II: WEIZMANN AND BALFOUR

At the Zionist Congress of 1907, a young Zionist leader, Chaim Weizmann, brought new unity to the Zionists with his proposal. What we need, he stated, is a combination of practical Zionism and political Zionism. They could not give up

Ha-Shomer ("The Watchman") members, including Ben-Gurion and Ben-Zvi, about 1910.

Herzl's dream of a charter giving the Jews the right to Palestine; but they should also not wait quietly until the charter was gained. In the meanwhile, practical Zionism—Jewish people moving to Palestine, JNF buying and leasing land in Palestine, setting up new settlements in Palestine —had to be continued. In fact, said Weizmann, the best reason for any great power to grant a charter to the Zionists was the work being done by the Zionists in Palestine.

Herzl had been against what he called "infiltration"—the settlement of large numbers of Jews in Palestine *before* a charter was granted. And his opinion had been so powerful that it had split the Zionist movement into those who were political and those who were practical. Now, with one proposal of common sense, Weizmann reunited the forces of Zionism and became one of its chief speakers.

Chaim Weizmann was born in Russia and moved to England in 1905. He was a scientist of that rare breed, as comfortable attending a formal dinner in high society as he was in his laboratory with his chemicals. In Manchester, England, he struck up with Lord Arthur Balfour a friendship that would remain strong for the rest of their lives. Through their talks and his enthusiasm, he made Lord Balfour a supporter of Zionism. It was Lord Balfour who introduced Weizmann to many important Britishers of the time, giving him the opportunity to speak to them about the need for a Jewish state.

While Weizmann was working in England, another leading Jew of the day, Justice Louis D. Brandeis of the Supreme Court of the United States, was doing much the same thing in America. Brandeis spoke often with U.S. President Woodrow Wilson, who also became a Zionist supporter.

In 1914, World War I began. Britain and

Chaim Weizmann (right) and Lord Arthur Balfour.

France took the side of Russia against the military might of the Austro-German Alliance. The armies of Russia and Austro-Germany fought back and forth across the lands where the majority of European Jews lived. Because of what happened during World War II, we tend to forget how terrible a price was paid by Jews in World War I, a price that prompted the great Jewish writer Sholom Aleichem to say, "Yes, this is a Jewish war—a war for the extermination of the Jews."

In the midst of World War I, the Zionist movement seemed trapped. The elected leaders of the movement were in Germany, prevented from traveling or speaking with the Zionists in Palestine, England, Russia, and the United States. Immigration to Palestine was cut off when the Ottoman Turks took up the side of the Austro-German Alliance. And, in 1915, the Turks exiled several important Zionist leaders from Palestine. David Ben-Gurion and Yitzhak Ben-Zevi—both founding members of Ha-Shomer and important speakers and Zionist leaders—were sent out of Palestine with orders never to return. They went to America, where they continued to write and speak, to raise funds for the Zionists of Palestine, and to try to convince more young people to join the Zionist movement and make *aliyah.*

England very much wanted the United States to join the war effort on its side. And, even before the U.S. did join, important decisions were made by the British in consultation with Woodrow Wilson. At the same time, the British wanted to make sure that, after the war, they would be able to control the Middle East, especially Palestine.

In 1917 the Russian people revolted against the czar and removed him from the throne. It did not escape the attention of the British that many of the revolutionary leaders in Russia were Jews. It seemed the moment had come to enlist the support of Jews in Russia, the United States, and even the small number in Palestine who might help when the British invaded the Ottoman Empire there. The pressure from Brandeis and Weizmann grew. Why not give the Jews what they wanted most? Grant them a charter for a Jewish state. In return, the Jews of the world would give their loyalty to the British and help them in the war effort. Weizmann had already proven just how much help could be gained—through his work on acetones he helped the British army to achieve the edge in modern explosives.

In 1917, the British took action. Lord Balfour was then the foreign secretary of the government, and it must have pleased him to send the following letter to one of England's most notable Jewish citizens.

November 2nd, 1917

Dear Lord Rothschild:

I have much pleasure in conveying to you, on behalf of His Majesty's Government, the following declaration of sympathy with Jewish Zionist aspirations which has been submitted to, and approved by, the Cabinet:

"His Majesty's Government view with favour the establishment in Palestine of a national home for the Jewish people and will use their best endeavours to facilitate the achievement of this object, it being clearly understood that nothing shall be done which may prejudice the civil and religious rights of existing non-Jewish communities in Palestine, or the rights and political status enjoyed by Jews in any other country."

I should be grateful if you would bring this declaration to the knowledge of the Zionist Federation.

Yours,
Arthur James Balfour

The only real opposition to the Balfour Declaration came from a few leading Jews of England. They fought against it bitterly, worried that it might cause other countries to accuse the Jews of being "foreigners" since there was now a Jewish home to which they could go and that the Jews would lose the rights they had won at so great an expense through the years. The British government and Lord Balfour wanted to use stronger language, to say "a Jewish state in Palestine" rather than "a national home." But the opposition of these leading Jews forced Balfour to issue the declaration in softer words.

Even so, the Balfour Declaration was a great triumph. Wherever Jews lived—in Russia, America, South Africa, Canada, England—there were large demonstrations and celebrations. Many Jews who had not been Zionists before now joined the Zionist movement. There was a new hopefulness in the dream of the Jewish state.

III: THE WAR IN PALESTINE

For the moment, however, the Turks still ruled Palestine. The Turks felt no fear from the local Arabs, even though a British officer, T.E. Lawrence (nicknamed Lawrence of Arabia), had led tribes of Arabs in a "Revolt in the Desert." That revolt never reached Palestine.

But the Turks did fear the Jews of Palestine—especially the members of Ha-Shomer, the armed Jewish fighting force. They expelled many of the leaders of the Second Aliyah, arrested others, seized guns and ammunition, tortured, and even put some to death by hanging.

Food became scarce when a plague of locusts struck the crops in 1916. There were plenty of good reasons for Jews to leave Palestine, and many did.

One more reason to leave Palestine was to join Yosef Trumpeldor's Zion Mule Corps. Trumpeldor was an outstanding leader, one of the few Russian Zionists who had true military training and experience. He had served in the Russian army during the Russo-Japanese War and was

decorated for bravery. In one of the battles against the Japanese, he lost an arm. Yet he was the only Jew in the czar's army with officer rank. He was among those expelled from Palestine in 1914, and like many others he went to Alexandria, Egypt.

In Egypt, with the help of Vladimir Jabotinsky, also a Russian Jew, Trumpeldor organized a fighting unit to join the British army. He called it the Zion Mule Corps, and many Palestinian Jews sneaked past the Turkish border guards to enlist and fight with the corps. The Zion Mule Corps saw action during the campaign against Gallipoli; then it was officially disbanded.

Many of the soldiers of the corps stayed on in the Cairo area; when the word came that the British were ready to enter Palestine from the south, Jabotinsky grouped these soldiers and new recruits into another Jewish fighting force, the Jewish Legion.

In America, with the help of Justice Brandeis, Ben-Gurion and Ben-Zevi organized a Jewish battalion that later joined the British army in its campaign in Palestine.

As the British army marched northward into the Holy Land, fighting units of Jews from England, Russia, the United States, and Palestine marched with it. Were they thinking of another small army that once marched from Egypt into the Holy Land to conquer it?

The British army pulled into the south of Palestine and went no further. For an entire year, the Jews of Galilee remained under Turkish rule, cut off from their people in the south. Their situation was very serious. They suffered from hunger and poverty. It was the Zionists of the United States who saved them by raising huge sums of money and calling on the help of the American ambassador to Turkey, Hans Morgenthau, to place pressure on the Turkish government to make certain that no harm would come to the trapped Jews of Galilee.

(Opposite) Yosef Trumpeldor; (below) Vladimir Jabotinsky.

PREVIEW

The British would soon learn what kind of future the Jewish settlers had in mind for the Holy Land. On July 24, 1918, General Allenby received a strange invitation. He was requested to come to the top of Mount Scopus in Jerusalem to witness the laying of the foundation stone for the new Hebrew University. Even as Dr. Weizmann and the other speakers offered prayers and words of dedication, the sounds of artillery fire could be heard coming from the north.

Like many who had conquered the Holy Land before him, Allenby must have been bemused by

The Jewish Legion. (Right) Sarah Aaronsohn, a member of NILI. NILI, an underground intelligence network, collected information about the Turkish forces for British Intelligence, World War I. The NILI group also brought gold into Palestine to help the Jewish community fight starvation.

this ceremony. What an odd people, these Jews, he may have thought. In the midst of hunger and chaos, they begin to build a place of study for the future.

Did these modern Jews know how like their ancestors they were? Did they realize that the Jewish rabbis and leaders of the Middle Ages had done just this—built academies in the midst of suffering and want—to renew the ancient Covenant? Of course they did.

Things to Consider

One of the modern myths about Jews is that we were not warriors or soldiers from ancient times until the modern period. In your reading, you have seen that this is not true of the Jews who lived in the Land of Israel. (There were also great Jewish generals and soldiers among the Sephardim in the "Golden Age.") Why were the Jews in Israel called on to fight so much more often than the Jews in the Diaspora?

What were the reasons that the British decided to give the Balfour Declaration to the Jewish people? What caused some Jews to fear this declaration? If you had been in England then, would you have supported or opposed the Balfour Declaration?

In what sense was the dedication of the Hebrew University on Mount Scopus very much like the rededication of the Temple that took place when the Maccabees freed Jerusalem from the armies of Antiochus? In what ways was this new event different? Does this add any new meaning to the word "Covenant"?

UNIT FOUR

From Yishuv to Nation

14

THE BRITISH MANDATE

In 1908, a few families from Jaffa decided that the city was overcrowded. They bought some sand dunes across the harbor. Then the sixty families met on the dunes to draw lots for pieces of the land. They planned one street—Herzl Street—leaving room at one end for a high school to be called the Gymnasium Herzliyah. They named their new "garden suburb," Tel Aviv ("Hill of Spring"). This was the Hebrew name of Theodor Herzl's novel about the Jewish state. Tel Aviv became the first all-Jewish city in Palestine.

By 1914, fifteen hundred people lived in Tel Aviv. By 1924, there were 25,000. And today there are nearly 400,000. This was only one of the wonders of the new spirit of Jews in the Holy Land.

Each year, from about 1882 onward, Jews kept arriving from the undeveloped Arab country of Yemen. Mostly they came in small numbers, settled in the cities, and worked at the crafts they had learned in Yemen. But, in 1907, the number of Yemenite Jews coming to Israel increased, and some went to work in the fields in Rehovot, Rishon le-Tzion, and Petach Tikvah.

In 1910, the settlers sent a young Russian Jew to Yemen to tell the Jews there about the new labor movement in Palestine. From that point on, the number of Jews coming from Yemen grew even more rapidly. They joined the labor unions, worked in moshavim, and became an important part of the Yishuv.

What could possibly stop a people who could turn a sand dune beach into a city, a people who sent missionaries to lands where Jews still lived as they did in the Middle Ages? In 1918, when World War I ended with the British in control of Palestine and the Balfour Declaration on the record, it seemed that the Jewish state would soon become a reality.

I: BRITISH AND ARABS

In 1918, at the end of the war, Dr. Weizmann was sent to Palestine at the head of the new Zionist Commission to plan the future of the country. One of his first acts was to meet with Emir Feisal of Mecca. The British had promised Feisal an Arab state in 1916, one year before the Balfour Declaration. Palestine was not part of the British promise, but Weizmann wanted to meet with Feisal to set up friendly relations between the two peoples, both of whom soon expected to be free and independent.

Just as the British had issued the Balfour Declaration in the face of Jewish nationalism or Zionism, so, too, they responded to the Arabs—especially the Arab leaders—who were learning about nationalism, too. They also wanted freedom and independence, and this the British had promised to them.

The meetings between Feisal and Weizmann went well. At a historic conference in 1919, the two leaders signed an agreement saying that the Arabs and the Jews would live side by side in the Middle East in friendship.

But the British had other plans. Now that the

View of Tel Aviv-Jaffa from the air.

Middle East was in their hands at last, they were not eager to give it up. In Palestine, they refused to allow new Jewish settlers to enter the country or any more land to be bought or sold. Nor were they friendly toward the Jews of the Yishuv. The Arabs of Palestine soon began to feel that the British were opposed to a Jewish state. Some Jews also began to feel that way.

The British and French agreed in 1919 that the French military government would control the Upper Galilee. In September, before the French were ready to move in, the British troops left the northern part of Palestine. The local Arabs saw an opportunity. In April 1920, they attacked four Jewish settlements, including Tel Hai. The Jews of Tel Hai were at first able to drive the Arabs

back, but the Arabs soon gathered in larger numbers and attacked again.

In the south, no one knew how dangerous the situation really was. Yosef Trumpeldor led a small group of defenders to Tel Hai only to find that food was running low and the settlers were growing desperate. The Arabs pretended that they wished to talk, but when Trumpeldor came out to meet them he was shot and badly wounded. As he lay dying, he spoke the words that became a slogan for the defense of the Holy Land: "No matter, it's good to die for our land."

By the end of March, the settlers fled south from the four villages. The first round was won by the Arabs. But on April 24, 1920 the British were given a mandate by the League of Nations.

They would rule all of Palestine and be responsible for the implementation of the Balfour Declaration. The British army returned to the Upper Galilee and the settlers returned with them. The last stand at Tel Hai became a symbol for the defense of the whole Yishuv.

Only a year before, another kind of battle had been fought and won without any shots being fired. The Yishuv called a meeting to set up a Provisional Committee to rule all the Jews of Palestine. At the meeting, the religious Mizrachi party demanded that only men should be allowed to vote. There had never been a question about the equality of women in Palestine and all the other organizations objected violently. The vote against the Mizrachi proposal was overwhelming. Women would always be considered equal in the Jewish state. A Provisional Committee

was then elected, but the British never allowed it to meet.

Also in 1920, an Arab sheik, stirred by Arab nationalism, spoke to hundreds of Moslems who had come to Jerusalem on pilgrimage. His speech ended with the cry, "Kill the Jews!" The Arabs obeyed. They ran into the Jewish Quarter of the Old City, breaking into Jewish shops and stoning the Jews in the streets. Arab police joined the mob, yelling, "Don't be afraid. The government is on our side!" The rioting lasted three days. The whole time, the British were busy in the New City, arresting all Jews who were armed. On the last day, Jabotinsky and nineteen other Jewish defenders were thrown in jail. They were brought to trial for owning weapons and "causing" the riots. Jabotinsky was given fifteen years at hard labor. The others were

Dr. Chaim Weizmann (left) and Emir Feisal of Mecca.

Haganah boy and girl arrested by British soldiers for bearing arms to ward off Arab attacks.

given three years apiece. Later, all were pardoned.

II: HAGANAH

The riots in Jerusalem were followed by riots in Tel Aviv. This was the year that Sir Herbert Samuel, an outstanding English Jew, was sent to become the high commissioner of Palestine. Many among the Yishuv believed that he was a modern Nehemiah (see chapter four), sent by the ruling power to help the Jews rebuild their land. But the rioting did not stop, and even Sir Herbert Samuel could not bring peace between the Arab nationalists and the Zionists.

Now the Jews of the Yishuv met to take matters into their own hands. The members of Ha-Shomer agreed to join a new, national defense force. A secret and—so far as the British were concerned—illegal army was set up in 1920. Command was given to the Histadrut—the union of Palestinian workers founded two years earlier. The new force was called Haganah ("Defense").

Looking back, the miracle of the modern State of Israel seems almost natural. The people of the Second Aliyah (1904–1914) came to a country of marshes and sand dunes, built new settlements, and took up arms to defend themselves. They united in labor unions and self-help groups. They raised money abroad and traveled in search of new immigrants to join them. They lived through the difficult and dangerous years of World War I and held the Yishuv together even when it was ruled by two separate foreign powers.

THE BRITISH MANDATE

PREVIEW

The next wave of immigration, the Third Aliyah (1919–1923), will bring new pioneers. Yet, as we shall see, the members of the Second Aliyah became the first leaders of the new State of Israel. They—not Sir Herbert Samuel—were the true Ezras and Nehemiahs of the modern return to Zion.

Things to Consider

In earlier chapters, you read about the many times that Jews thought the Temple was about to be rebuilt. Their hopes were raised then dashed. In this chapter, you read that the Zionists believed the Jewish state was about to be founded any day. Once again, their hopes were high, but they were disappointed. It was the same way with dreams of the messiah. What kinds of things do you hope for? In what way is hope an important part of religion? Does hope deserve a place on your list of the parts of the Covenant?

What event in the chapter makes you think that the Jewish settlers in Palestine sincerely wanted to live in peace with the Arabs of the Middle East? What happened that made this impossible? Do you think it is possible today?

The text calls the people of the Second Aliyah "the true Ezras and Nehemiahs of the modern return to Zion." What did Ezra and Nehemiah do for the Jewish people in the Land of Israel in their time? What were the people of the Second Aliyah doing that was similar?

15

THE THIRD ALIYAH

The popular Jewish writer and teacher, Maurice Samuel, visited Palestine in 1924, at the end of the Third Aliyah. He had heard from others about the work of these *chalutzim* ("pioneers"), as the people of the Third Aliyah called themselves. Seeing the changes for himself, he was amazed. In Deganyah, where once a small ferry had been the only way of crossing the Jordan River, there was now a bridge built by the *chalutzim*. He asked one of the members of Deganyah, "Who built this bridge?"

> "The *chalutzim*."
> "Who built these houses?"
> *"Chalutzim."*
> "Who laid that road [from Deganyah to Tiberias]?"
> *"Chalutzim."*
> "Who taught them?"
> "I don't know."

Nobody knew who taught them. The *chalutzim* taught themselves, by experimenting, by trial and error. The *chalutzim* of the Third Aliyah were Israel's great builders.

I: THE NEW YISHUV

At the end of World War I, the Jewish population of Palestine was half what it was at the start of the war. Only 55,000 Jews remained in the Yishuv. But the Jews who arrived from Russia between 1919 and 1923—the Third Aliyah—brought the population of the Yishuv back to nearly 100,000. In Russia, they heard of the Balfour Declaration and they came in the hope that the Jewish nation would soon be born in Palestine. Many also came because they were disappointed in the 1917 revolution.

The Russian Revolution began as a workers' revolt, but it later fell into the hands of the Communist party, which claimed it was acting only until the workers were ready to be in charge. But it was soon obvious that the party

Instructing Russian immigrants in agriculture.

The Valley of Jezreel after the swamps were drained.

did not intend to give up its control. Many young Jews—Zionists and non-Zionists—had helped in the fight against the czar. Now, in their disappointment, they looked to Palestine, hoping things would be better there.

In Palestine they joined the Histadrut, the workers' union, making it the most powerful organization in Palestine. The Histadrut assigned them work. The land they worked on was leased from the JNF. The money to pay them came from the new *Keren Ha-Yesod* ("Palestine Foundation Fund") set up by the Zionist Congress.

The work was hard and they loved it. In 1921, the JNF bought land in the Valley of Jezreel. Most of the land was swamp, infested by malaria spread by mosquitos. It was dangerous, often deadly. The *chalutzim* were given the task of planting eucalyptus trees (which need a great deal of water to grow, thereby helping to dry the land) and of draining the swamps. The first season, more than a third of the *chalutzim* caught malaria. The second season, nearly 22 percent more were stricken. But eventually the swamps were drained, malaria disappeared, and five kibbutzim and one moshav were established on the land for farming.

Help came from the Jews of the Diaspora, especially from America. Hadassah, the American Women's Zionist Organization, sent medical teams to the Holy Land in 1920. Medical care was hard to find at the time, and the Hadassah teams performed wonders against diseases such as malaria and trachoma (an eye disease that was common in Palestine).

Even with help, the *chalutzim* had to struggle. They sometimes would go hungry so their cattle could eat. They found themselves building barns before they could build homes. A huge tent or a single-room shed would house all the members of a work group. Even a newly-wed couple was given only a small corner with a drape to separate them from the rest of the group. There was no privacy. But this was their *kevutsah*. They were willing to struggle as long as they were free to live in *Eretz Yisrael*.

On Friday evenings, after a week of work,

they dressed in fresh clothing and celebrated Shabbat. They sang. They sat beside campfires. They danced the *horah*, a circle-dance in which all could join in equally. They were trying to find a home for themselves on the Land, to build a place their children would love. And they wanted it to be a Jewish home—not in the way of the Old Yishuv city-dwellers who lived on *chalukah*, but in their own way. They were the New Yishuv.

Sometimes they visited Tel Aviv, a city of 25,000. They walked beside the seashore or along Allenby Street. They tasted the faster life of the city then returned to their own, harder life.

On Sunday morning—*Yom Rishon*, the "first day" in Hebrew—they returned to work.

II: THE LEGION OF LABOR

The *chalutzim* began to organize as workers. In the summer of 1920, they formed the *Gedud Ha-Avodah Al Shem Yosef Trumpeldor*, "The Joseph Trumpeldor Legion of Labor." The idea was to create one huge *kevutsah* of all road-makers, stone-quarryers, and builders in Palestine. Most of the Legion members believed that workers

First delegation to Palestine of the Hadassah medical organization, 1920.

should have the right to control themselves—the basic idea of communism. The Histadrut had grown powerful, however, and wished to direct and control the laborers. This led to arguments.

Belief in communist ideas also led to the political party called *Ha-Shomer Ha-Zair* ("The Young Watchman"). *Ha-Shomer Ha-Zair* first organized in Russia then came into Palestine with the *chalutzim*. Socialism—such as the system in use on the kibbutzim and the moshavim— could be democratic. But communism taught that the freedom guaranteed by democracy was false, that everyone should be *forced* to live as workers. The great majority of the Jewish workers did not believe in communism. They formed political parties built on socialist ideas—the sharing of labor and the sharing of profits. Histadrut was itself a socialist organization.

These new parties were more than just political. In eastern Europe (and in the United States), parties like *Ha-Shomer Ha-Zair* set up work farms called *hachsharot* to train young people and prepare them for *aliyah*. The later immigrants of the Third Aliyah studied farming and kibbutz life *before* they came to Palestine.

But it was building more than farming that was important to the *chalutzim*. A Russian Jew who had been living in the United States, Pinchas Rutenberg, came to Israel and directed the *chalutzim* in the construction of huge electrical plants along the Jordan and Yarmuk rivers. Power stations were built in Tel Aviv, Haifa, and Tiberias.

With electricity, it was possible to build factories—to make salt and oil and to grind flour. And, in 1925, the Nesher cement factory was completed, along with several factories for manufacturing cloth.

Nesher cement works.

The *chalutzim* also built schools, laying the foundation for national education. And the roads they paved tied the country together, making travel safe and inexpensive.

They drained the swamps of the valley of Jezreel and the swamps of Nahalal. They settled on these lands and learned to farm them. They built bridges and apartments. They made the kibbutz experiment work.

All this was done in a time when arguments over how to raise money had split American Zionists into two camps—those who thought money should be sent only as investments in the Land and those who wished to continue sending money as charity to the Land. All this was done when even the money raised was smaller than what was needed. All this was done while the British remained on the sidelines, giving little or no help at all.

III: UNDER THE BRITISH FLAG

Sir Herbert Samuel was the first to admit that little had been done by the British to keep the promises made in the Balfour Declaration and by the League of Nations, which had given Britain the Mandate over Palestine. The British had given practically no new land to the Jews. They had let the Jews carry the whole burden of educating Jewish children and had even taken money raised by taxing the Jews to help support the Arab school system.

In his report to the Mandate Commission in 1924, Herbert Samuel said that he had tried, in every way, to treat the Arabs as if there were no Balfour Declaration. In fact, leaders like Ben-Gurion pointed out that he had also treated the Jews as if there were no Balfour Declaration. After the riots in 1921, Samuel stopped Jews from coming into Palestine for a while. Lands were set aside and given to the Bedouin Arabs, who already owned more land than they could use. When British money supported building projects, only Arab workers were hired. And

Sir Herbert Samuel.

Samuel had helped to write the first British "White Paper" in which the Transjordan (the land of Palestine east of the Jordan River) was said to be outside the new "Jewish national home."

The Jews had good reason to be disappointed in Sir Herbert Samuel. They had counted on him to help establish the Jewish state. Instead, he bent over backwards to keep things as they were before the war. The Yishuv breathed a sigh of relief when Samuel was removed from his office as high commissioner and replaced by Lord Plumer. Plumer immediately showed that he could be fair to both Arabs and Jews. But, a short two years later, Plumer was also replaced, this time by Sir John Chancellor. And Chancellor proved nobody's friend.

THE THIRD ALIYAH

In terms of practical Zionism, things were going well. The Jewish people of Palestine held elections and voted for their first "government," the National Assembly. Buildings went up everywhere, settlements proved successful, and new crops were tried.

But political Zionism—the dream of an independent Jewish state—was making no headway. In fact, the Jews of the Yishuv began to wonder whether Britain ever meant to give them "a national homeland."

PREVIEW

Four challenges faced the Yishuv in 1925, at the beginning of the Fourth Aliyah (1924–1928). The first was something quite unexpected— unemployment. There were not enough jobs to go around, not enough money to pay for new building projects.

The second challenge came from the Arabs of Palestine. Anti-Jewish riots broke out again, as the Arabs tested the British to see whether they would try to stop them from driving the Jews out.

The third was a worldwide challenge. The entire Western World was headed toward the Great Depression. It struck first in countries like Poland, where the Jews were already poor and barely able to make a living.

The fourth challenge was the British Mandate government. Britain ruled Palestine, but not fairly. Britain was asked by the League of Nations to help create a Jewish state, but it did not. Britain made the rules. The Yishuv—Old and New—had to live by them.

Yet each week, on Friday evening, as Shabbat approached, the Jews of the New Yishuv took off their work clothes and donned their Sabbath best. They danced and sang and told stories. They spoke of the days of the BILU, spun tales of Ha-Shomer and self-defense, recounted stories of the Zion Mule Corps and the Jewish Legion, and spoke in almost mystical ways about the building done by the Labor Legion. A new kind of Jewish life came into being, a new kind of Jew—a true lover of the Land, a child of the Covenant.

Things to Consider

Like Solomon and Herod, the Jews of the Third Aliyah were builders in the Land of Israel. The difference was that the people of the Third Aliyah taught themselves to build by trial and error. In what ways did their faith in the Jewish people help them?

Imagine that you are one of the *chalutzim*. Write a letter to your mother and father in Russia telling them what life is really like in the Land of Israel. Be sure to include both the hardships and the brighter moments, too.

In the past, many of the Jews who cared deeply about the Covenant were scholars and rabbis and their students. Now, the text speaks of the Jews of the first three *aliyot* as "children" of the Covenant. Yet they were farmers, soldiers, and builders. Does your definition of Covenant agree with the text? If not, what needs to be added now?

16

THE FOURTH AND FIFTH ALIYOT

The Jews who came to Palestine in the first three waves of immigration chose Palestine because of hopes, dreams, and ideals. The First Aliyah was made up of members of the Lovers of Zion. The Second Aliyah came seeking a "religion of labor." The *chalutzim* of the Third Aliyah arrived after the Balfour Declaration, hoping to see the birth of the Jewish homeland.

If it had not been for these dreams, these young people would have gone elsewhere—to America, as many others did. They were, first and foremost, a part of a great transfer of Jewish population out of Russia. It was more than their dreams that made them move.

The Jews of the First Aliyah left Russia after the pogroms of 1881. The Kishinev pogrom in 1903 led to the Second Aliyah. The shattered hopes of the Russian Revolution led to the Third Aliyah.

In 1919, the Yevsektsia, the Jewish section of the Communist party in Russia, declared Zionism to be "counterrevolutionary." They banned Zionist writings and closed down Zionist immigration offices. They arrested, tried, and imprisoned many Russian Zionist leaders. By 1923, the Yevsektsia had very nearly wiped out all traces of the Zionist movement in Russia.

Now, all immigration from Russia had dried up. The Yishuv was forced to face the fact that Great Britain was in no hurry to carry out the promises made in Lord Balfour's letter. And the Arabs of Palestine showed clearly that the Jews would not win their homeland without a fierce struggle.

I: THE FOURTH ALIYAH

The next wave of immigrants—the Fourth Aliyah (1924–1928)—also came to escape persecution. They were mostly Polish Jews. Like the immigrants before them, they came mainly from the cities. Unlike the earlier immigrants, the people of the Fourth Aliyah liked city life.

After 1926, they left Poland because of the depression spreading through eastern Europe. They were middle class, and they hoped their money would buy them a better life in Palestine where food was cheaper and property less expensive. Few of them had dreams of living on the kibbutzim, or of working to build roads and drain swamps. But most wanted to open small businesses, buy and sell, live in villages and cities, and work as tailors, cobblers, greengrocers, lawyers, merchants, or tradesmen. A few bought farms with their money, slowly turning their farm villages into towns like Herzliyah, Kfar Ata, and Bnai Brak. But the vast majority flocked to the major cities of Tel Aviv, Hebron, Tsfat, Jerusalem, and Haifa.

Their dream was different from the others. In the 1920s, there were few jobs open to workers;

there was even unemployment. For the first time, the Histadrut had very few new building projects. The Yishuv was in need of a middle class, of people who were interested in making the cities grow and in buying and selling what the workers produced.

So the Jews of the Fourth Aliyah found a new way of helping the Zionist idea to grow. The Land was home for them, even though they did not share the "religion of labor" that had united all the immigrants before them.

II: THE WHITE PAPER OF 1930

The mufti of Jerusalem, head of the Supreme Moslem Council of Palestine, preached a holy war against the Jews. On August 23, 1929, the Jewish Quarter in Jerusalem was attacked. The next day, Jews in Hebron suffered heavy losses as Arabs murdered sixty men, women, and children. Tsfat, too, was the scene of Arab rioting and Jewish killing. Villages all across the country were raided. At Mishmar Ha-Emek, the British police ordered the Jews to leave. Then the British watched as the Arabs raided the town, taking everything of value. Almost everywhere, the Jews tried to defend themselves. But they had few weapons and the attacks took them by surprise.

In one week of rioting, the Arabs left 187 Jews wounded and 105 murdered. The Jews of Hebron left their homes, never to return.

The British ordered an investigation. After looking into the problem, they issued a report blaming the Jews! The Arabs were upset by the number of Jews coming into Palestine, the report stated, and by the amount of land being bought by the Jews. A White Paper was issued in 1930, mapping out the official British policy, limiting the number of Jews allowed into Palestine each year and the number of new settlements to be built. The Jews of the Yishuv were bitter.

Back in England, Chaim Weizmann was shocked. In protest, he resigned from the presi-

Haj Amin el Husseini, mufti of Jerusalem.

dency of the Zionist Organization. The White Paper was never put into effect. Instead, a new high commissioner was appointed over Palestine with instructions to give fair treatment to the Jews there.

The workers of Israel now united in a single political party, *Mifleget Paole Eretz Yisrael* ("The Workers' Party of Israel"), called by its abbreviation, Mapai. The Mapai party joined together nearly all the smaller labor parties except the communist *Ha-Shomer Ha-Zair*. Since

Arab disturbances in Jerusalem, 1929.

almost all Mapai's members were also members of the Histadrut, Mapai gave the New Yishuv a unified voice. Yitzhak Ben-Zevi was made the first head of Mapai.

As a political force, the power of Mapai was first felt in the Zionist Congress of 1933. Leadership of the Congress was in the hands of the Diaspora Jews before this. For the first time, with Mapai in control, the world Zionist executive leadership came into the hands of the Jews of Palestine. Mapai leaders like David Ben-Gurion and Moshe Sharett brought the Zionist executive home to the Holy Land.

III: THE FIFTH ALIYAH

In the meanwhile, the Great Depression struck in America and Europe. The rich found themselves suddenly poor. The poor lost what little money they had. Banks closed. Food was expensive to buy and difficult to find. Jobs were scarce and work was nearly impossible to get.

Palestine looked a little like the Garden of Eden in those hard times. Thousands of acres of new orange groves were planted. New settlements were set up, and those destroyed in the 1929 riots were rebuilt. The new town of Netanyah came to life twenty miles north of Tel Aviv.

The Great Depression did not strike at the Jews of Palestine, but it was to hurt the Jewish people in other parts of the world. And, as Adolf Hitler was rising to power, the German Jews who were already Zionists began to leave their homes and flee to Palestine. From 1933–1935, more than 150,000 Jews left Germany and other western European countries and arrived in the Holy Land. But, because most of Germany's

THE FOURTH AND FIFTH ALIYOT

Jews still felt safe in their adopted land, they did not take seriously the anti-Semitic propaganda of Hitler's Nazi party that was blaming the Jews of the world for causing the Great Depression. They thought this was just a thunderstorm. Surely, it would soon pass and more sensible Germans would be elected to government.

The German newcomers of the Fifth Aliyah (1933–1939) brought skills and know-how, more than any other group which had come before. They were scholars and scientists, engineers and industrialists. They invested in orange groves and farms, in water companies and land drainage. Some joined the kibbutzim. Some went to work as teachers and professors.

New Arab riots broke out in 1936 when sixteen Jews were killed by a mob in Jaffa. The Arabs then closed the port of Jaffa by going on strike. They demanded three things: to stop Jewish immigration, to stop Jews from buying any more land, and to elect a new government for Palestine.

The Yishuv offered to build a new port at Tel Aviv, and the British Mandate government, wanting to put the Arab strike to an end, agreed. The port was built. There were more Arab riots. But, in October, the strike came to an end.

The 1936 strike had two results: For the Jews, it was an unexpected blessing. When the Arabs refused to work, more Jews were hired in their place. New settlements were set up and a new Jewish port put in operation. For the British, the strike raised new questions and a committee was sent to investigate the riots.

The Peel Report (as the committee's final document was known) said that the Mandate was

Arab riots, Jaffa, 1936.

not working. It suggested that the land west of the Jordan be divided into two parts. The larger, southern part—what was once Judea—was to be set aside for the Arabs; the smaller, northern part—most of Galilee—was to become the Jewish homeland. Between the two a small section of the land, including Jerusalem, would remain in British control. The British sent this plan to the League of Nations, suggesting that it be adopted.

The Zionist Congress of 1937 strongly opposed the Peel Report. How could the Jewish state be born without Jerusalem, without Judea? So the British sent another committee to Palestine, and a new plan was suggested which neither the Arabs nor the Jews liked. In the end, the British invited Arab and Jewish leaders to London to discuss the future of Palestine.

PREVIEW

The world was headed toward war again. The Jews who stayed in Germany would soon find themselves trapped. The thunderstorms they hoped would soon pass turned into a typhoon that destroyed six million of our people. Hopes for a Jewish state were set aside in the struggle to save the Jews of Europe.

The Jews of Palestine would play an important part in the rescue efforts. Yet, no amount of help would be enough. Nothing before or since the Holocaust showed so clearly the need for a Jewish state. And not just the Jews, but all the peoples of the earth learned a lesson from the Holocaust that could not be denied or ever forgotten.

Things to Consider

Abraham was told to "go forth from your native land and from your father's house to the land that I will show you. I will make of you a great nation. . . ." (Genesis 12:1–2) The people who made *aliyah* in the first five *aliyot* were doing just that. They were leaving the homes of their parents and grandparents and trying to create a great nation in the Land of Israel. But they all had different dreams. Make a chart showing the five *aliyot,* and below each one tell what the people hoped for when they arrived in the Land.

The British helped establish the custom in Israel of having a chief rabbi (there is one for the Ashkenazic community and one for the Sephardic community). One of the early chief rabbis was Rav Abraham Isaac Kook. Kook wrote that "Jewish original creativity . . . is impossible except in the Land of Israel. . . . A Jew cannot be true to his own ideas, sentiments, and imagination in the Diaspora." Do you agree or disagree with Rav Kook's statement? Why?

The Jews of the early *aliyot* believed that all Israeli Jews should be involved in labor. In this chapter, you read how the Jews of the fourth and fifth *aliyot* went to the cities or invested in business. Was this good or bad for the Land of Israel?

17

THE HOLOCAUST YEARS

Haj Amin, the leader of Palestine's Arabs, the man known as the mufti of Jerusalem, visited the German consul-general in July, 1937. As a result, Arab rebels were soon carrying German weapons and reading Arabic translations of German propaganda. When the Arabs paraded on the birthday of Mohammed, founder of Islam, they waved German and Italian flags, carried photographs of Mussolini and Hitler, and shouted support for fascism and nazism.

The Arab attacks in 1937 were worse than those of 1936. Two British officials were assassinated by Arab rebels, and the British ordered the arrest of the Supreme Moslem Council. The mufti escaped by hiding in the Mosque of Omar in Jerusalem, then slipping out of Palestine to Damascus, which was in French territory. From Damascus, he continued to direct the rebels.

Arab rebels cut the railway lines between Jaffa and Jerusalem. They attacked busses and cars, planted mines and explosives on highways. Within a month, they were in control of the Old City of Jerusalem. The British needed help, from outside and from within.

The British were forced to bring more troops into Palestine, to set up police stations along the major roads, and to add new Jewish volunteers to help them keep order. These new Jewish troops were placed under the command of Captain Orde Wingate, a British officer sent to Palestine because the British government thought he was pro-Arab.

Wingate surprised everyone by his love for Zionism. This love grew out of his belief in the importance of the Bible. It grew into a crash training program for Jewish soliders. Wingate, along with the British government, was well aware that the new soldiers were also members of the secret Haganah force. He also knew that the Jews would have to fight the Arabs if there was ever to be a Jewish state. So he turned his knowledge of Arab warfare and tactics into a plan for Jewish defense.

Wingate trained the new soldiers as "Special Night Squads." He taught them to use the darkness as a friend, to walk along the hills in absolute silence, and to strike the Arabs at night, taking them by surprise in their hideouts. He led the night squads on their attacks, taking them even into Lebanon and Syria. In 1938, the Arabs felt this new force and suffered heavily from what the Haganah was calling "active defense."

The British sent Wingate home in 1939. By that time, the Scotsman had become close friends with Weizmann and many of the other Jewish leaders. What he taught the members of the Haganah, they later used in fighting the War of Independence. They might have learned it all on their own, but Wingate gave them a headstart that proved precious. And, with Wingate's help, the Haganah was able to protect Jewish villages and towns throughout the Land through the years of the Arab revolt.

All the same, the Arab attacks went on. While the killing and looting continued, the British sent a committee which recommended a new partition plan that would separate the Jews and the Arabs in Palestine into two states, leaving both

Captain Orde Wingate; (right) David Raziel.

equally clear in their opposition. Ben-Gurion warned the British that the Jews would rebel against any Arab rule and that stopping "a Jewish rebellion against British policy will be as unpleasant a task as the repression of the Arab rebellion had been."

A group of Jewish extremists, the *Irgun Tzevai Leumi* ("National United Army"), commanded by David Raziel, began bombing British government buildings in Tel Aviv and Jerusalem and used explosives to cut off rail lines. The official Zionist executive was opposed to this Jewish "terrorism," even though it was aimed at British property, not at British lives. But the Irgun continued its attacks for many years.

For the Jews, the worst thing about the White Paper of 1939 was the limit on immigration. It under British control. In defiance, the Arabs renewed their attacks on both the British and the Jews.

The London conference rejected all plans for partition. Instead, giving in to Arab demands, the British issued a new White Paper in 1939, stating that Jewish immigration would be limited to just 75,000 in the next five years. After that, immigration would be limited to a number to be agreed upon by the British and the Arabs. Land sales were also kept to a small number. This capitulation, this giving in to Arab violence came just as Arab attacks were declining. The end of the rioting came in August of 1939, after three years of fighting. By then, nearly 2,500 Jews had been murdered.

I: THE WHITE PAPER OF 1939

Arab leaders were pleased by the White Paper of 1939, saying that it would put an end to Jewish hopes for a state in Palestine. The Jews were

came at a moment when the Jews of Europe were trapped by the start of World War II. With Palestine closed to those needing rescue, the Jews of the Holy Land found themselves in a terrible dilemma.

On the one hand, they supported the Allies against Hitler. The idea of Hitler's winning the war and controlling Palestine would mean the absolute end of all Jewish hopes. On the other hand, they could not agree to the White Paper which called for Jewish immigration to stop.

David Ben-Gurion defined the only solution possible for the Yishuv: "To fight the war as if there were no White Paper and to fight the White Paper as if there were no war."

To help the British, they planted more fields than ever before. They set up new factories to make weapon parts, antitank mines, uniforms, tank engines, tank treads, and small boats. The Haganah set up an advance strike force called the Palmach, made up of those who had been members of Wingate's Special Night Squads. The new force was led by Yitzchak Sadeh, who had been the leader of the Haganah in the days of Wingate.

The Palmach leader sent two companies, led by Moshe Dayan and Yigal Allon, as advance scouts in Syria for the British invasion. The companies were divided into twelve squads. Moving ahead of the British troops in 1941, they cut telegraph wires, ambushed guards at bridges and river crossings, and placed explosives in the roads in front of the enemy troops. In one battle, Dayan lost an eye to gunfire. The work of the Palmach made the British advance into Syria successful, protecting Palestine against invasion from the north.

II: THE BOAT PEOPLE

The Germans, in the early years of the war, wanted to send Jews out of Germany and the conquered territories. For about a year after the White Paper was published, these Jewish refugees poured into Palestine. Then the British

Yigal Allon.

decided that this immigration was planned by the Germans to cause the Arabs of Palestine to revolt again. So they tried to put a stop to all illegal immigration of Jews into the Holy Land.

In November 1940, the British loaded an old ship named the *Patria* with 1,900 Jews who had entered Palestine illegally. They planned to send these Jews to Mauritius Island in the Indian Ocean where they would be held at least until the end of the war. The Jews of the Yishuv, hoping to force the unloading of the vessel, planned to blow a small hole in the vessel's side, making it unseaworthy and unable to leave Haifa Harbor. The explosion went off, but the ship was so weak it sank almost at once; 240 Jews and a number of British police lost their lives in the tragedy.

A month later, the SS *Atlantic,* another aged ship reached Haifa with 1,600 European Jewish refugees aboard. This ship was sent to Mauritius Island. A few weeks after this, the SS *Salvador,* with 350 Jewish refugees on board, was turned away from Haifa Harbor by the British patrols. The *Salvador* sailed north and sank in the Turkish Straits, leaving only 70 survivors.

The SS *Struma* left Rumania bound for Palestine. It carried 769 Jews. But it was leaking and its engines were not working well. It came to port in Istanbul Harbor, in need of repairs. The Turks, however, refused to allow the ship to dock and refused any repairs. For two months, the ship sat in the harbor, as people aboard began to die of starvation. The Jewish Agency begged the British to allow the *Struma* to land in Palestine, even if it meant sending the refugees to Mauritius. If the British would agree, then surely the Turks would allow the boat to be repaired and send it on its way. But the British refused and the Turks had the *Struma* towed out of the harbor. Five miles out, the *Struma* sank and all 769 Jews on board drowned. Even the British public was horrified when the tragedy was reported. But several more ships tried to land in Palestine, and the British continued to stop them when they could.

III: THE HOLOCAUST

By 1941, it was not just anti-Semitism that the Jews of Europe were fleeing, it was death. The truth—that the Germans were placing Jews in concentration camps and murdering them in death camps—was already becoming known to the Allies and to the Jews of the Diaspora and Palestine.

The Jewish Agency asked the British and American governments for money to pay for the rescue of European Jews, but the Allies refused. The money would just fall into German hands, they said.

In 1943, a plan to rescue 10,000 Jewish refugees from Nazi Europe was turned down by one of President Roosevelt's staff. When Bulgaria offered to allow its Jews to leave if only Allies would pay for transportation costs, the British refused. "If we do that," the British Foreign Secretary Anthony Eden said, "then the Jews of the world will be wanting us to make a similar offer in Poland and Germany. . . . Hitler might well take us up on such an offer and there simply are not enough ships . . . in the world to handle them."

The United States, in 1943, agreed to a plan to rescue Jews from France and Rumania, if the British would allow them to enter Palestine. Again the British refused, saying there were "difficulties in disposing of a considerable number of Jews."

Perhaps the strangest loss came when the Hungarians offered to trade Jewish lives for trucks and goods. The offer was made to Joel Brand of the Hungarian Rescue Committee. Brand was arrested by British police and sent to Cairo where he was kept under guard. The British called this deal Nazi "blackmail." Their refusal to even talk with the Hungarians resulted in some 434,000 Hungarian Jews being sent to Auschwitz, where they were murdered in the gas chambers.

Members of the Haganah took part in heroic rescues of Jews from Europe. Yet the number saved was very small. More successful was the "underground railroad" set up along ancient caravan routes in the Middle East. Here, the Haganah managed to rescue a few thousand Jews from Persia and Iraq.

Late in the war, the British turned to the Haganah for another reason. They needed native speakers of the Balkan languages to send as spies to Rumania, Hungary, Bulgaria, Yugoslavia, and Slovakia. The British knew that many of the Palestinian Jews had come from these countries originally and could speak the languages fluently. Thirty-two Jewish volunteers were chosen for this mission, including three women. They were trained by the British in Cairo then sent in by parachute to the various countries.

When volunteering, the thirty-two had more than one mission in mind. They would spy for the British, but they would also set up rescue routes for Jews to escape to Palestine. Unfortunately, only a few Jews were saved by the parachutists. Some information was gathered and radioed back to the British. But, for the most part, the mission was a failure. Seven of the Haganah volunteers were captured and put to death by the Nazis.

Among those who died, the most famous was Hannah Senesh. She had escaped Hungary in 1934 to settle in Palestine. Ten years later, she fell into the hands of the Gestapo, was tortured, and murdered. The poetry she left behind be-

Hannah Senesh.

came a part of Zionist legend. One poem began, "Blessed is the match consumed in lighting flame."

Another quite different rescue effort was much more successful. It was headed by a woman, Henrietta Szold. She was born in Baltimore and studied in New York at the Jewish Theological Seminary. She was one of the founders of Hadassah (see chapter fifteen) and came to Palestine to help set up hospitals and medical clinics. Beginning in 1934, she was put in charge of the new organization called Youth Aliyah. Through their work, this organization brought out of Nazi Europe nearly 30,000 Jewish young people, helped them reach Palestine, placed them on kibbutzim and in villages around the country, and began training them for a new life on the Land.

None of the rescue efforts had been very successful. Six million Jews were murdered by the Nazi Germans and their collaborators in Europe before World War II ended in 1945. The destruction was nearly total. Thousands more died of disease and starvation after the war ended. The survivors had no homes to which they could return. They shared the only dream left—Palestine. But Palestine was still sealed off from Jewish immigration by the British Mandate government.

PREVIEW

Jews throughout the world were enraged by this needless loss of lives. They wondered if they had done everything possible to save the Jews of Europe. They blamed the Allies for not saving more Jewish lives.

The Jews of the Yishuv were more determined than ever to have an independent Jewish state. More than ever, they saw the need for a place where Jews could go in times of crisis, a place where Jews could defend themselves, a place free of anti-Semitism. Their fight for independence was now a life-or-death struggle. If the nations of the world would not give them their

(Above) Henrietta Szold greeting the first Youth Aliyah group, 1934. (Below) A Youth Aliyah group.

independence, they would seize it for themselves. There was no turning back. In the Torah, God had commanded, "Choose life!" Now the Jews forged a new part for their ancient Covenant: a promise never to let Jews be murdered again.

Things to Consider

Zionists played an important part in the Jewish resistance against the Germans during the years of the Holocaust. To find out more about this, look up the story of Mordecai Anielewicz in a Jewish encyclopedia, or look up the story of the Warsaw Ghetto Revolt. You'll find even more information in articles about the Holocaust, in the sections on Jewish resistance.

The chapter speaks of many missed opportunities when Jews might have been rescued—by the British, by the Allies. Reading it, you may feel that the British, especially, were almost as evil as the Nazis. Yet, Ben-Gurion once observed that it was fortunate for the Jews that it was the British who ruled over them in those early years, for any other nation would have crushed the Jews in the Land of Israel, instead of putting up with their constant rebelliousness. Why did the Jews of Israel like the British yet hate British rule?

What new idea has to be added to your list of Covenant beliefs?

18

THE STRUGGLE FOR STATEHOOD

In World War II, just as in the earlier world war, the Jews of Palestine helped the British by enlisting to fight against the Axis powers. More than 130,000 Jews signed up for the Jewish Brigade formed in 1944. They fought in Italy and in the last battles of the war. In the meanwhile, the Zionists felt that the United States, having entered the war, would have much to say about the world after the war was over. Ben-Gurion was sent to the U.S. in 1942 to speak to American Jews about the need for a Jewish state.

In May 1942, a meeting of all American Zionist groups was held at the Biltmore Hotel in New York City. A declaration was made demanding that after the war the gates of Palestine be opened to all Jewish immigrants, the Jewish Agency be allowed to develop the land and control immigration, and Palestine be established as a Jewish state. This declaration, the Biltmore Program, later became the official policy of the Zionist movement throughout the world.

After the German surrender in 1945, Ben-Gurion was certain that the British would soon be forced to leave Palestine. In that case, the Arabs would revolt against the Jews again. The Jews needed weapons. Ben-Gurion met with seventeen American Zionists who gave him money. Two members of the Haganah were sent to New York to buy machinery which was then smuggled past the British into Palestine. And this machinery became the foundation for a small arms industry in Palestine.

Not everyone in the Zionist executive agreed with Ben-Gurion. There were many who felt that the Jews of the Yishuv were not yet ready to rule themselves. After all, most Jews in Palestine then were newcomers and a minority despite the fact that they lived in villages and cities throughout the country. Also, there were great advantages to being a part of the British Empire—the British nations were a ready marketplace for the produce and industries of Palestine, and the British did give the Jews military protection, even if it was not always evenhanded.

The largest issue was not statehood but immigration. If the new British government, elected after the war, had opened the doors to Palestine (as it promised in its campaign speeches), then the Jews—even Ben-Gurion—would have waited far longer before demanding statehood. But the new government adopted the 1939 White Paper. And keeping out the survivors of the Nazi terror was something that no Jew could accept.

I: ALIYAH BET

At the end of the war, the Haganah went back into action in Europe. The plan was to smuggle into Palestine as many Holocaust survivors as possible. The idea was to show that the White Paper could not put an end to the growth of the Jewish population of the Yishuv. The members of the Haganah met with the survivors in their

Displaced Persons (DP) camps in Europe, telling them of the plan and the idea behind it. The DPs were eager to reach Palestine and willing to take great risks to do so.

The Haganah set up headquarters in Paris, taking the name *Mosad le-Aliyah Bet* (The Institute for the "Other" [or "Illegal"] Aliyah). More offices were set up in port cities to buy, rent, or lease old ships—everything from small fishing boats to dilapidated ocean-going vessels—and to load them with the Jewish DPs and send them out on secret sailings to Palestine.

Thousands of DPs left each month, walking or riding trains from the middle of Europe to small ports along the coast of the Mediterranean Sea. Sometimes the harbor police were willing to ignore the loading of the ships; sometimes the ships were loaded under cover of darkness. One Mosad agent even dressed in the uniform of a British sergeant and ordered British troops to help in the loading of ships in Italy. Papers were forged to "requisition" food and clothing for the refugees and to get fuel for the ships. At times, even British army trucks were used to take the refugees down to the ports. Palmach troops from Palestine ringed the inlets, keeping watch over the refugees as they were put on board. All was done with military precision.

It was the same when the ships reached Palestine. But first the ships had to make their way through the Mediterranean past the British naval blockade of Palestine. And, arriving in Palestine was more dangerous than leaving Europe. After all, in Palestine there were 100,000 British troops guarding against illegal immigration.

The Mosad was cautious. The ships were brought close to land only after the Haganah knew where the British troops were going to be and radioed messages to the ships directing them how to avoid the British. If a ship managed to get past the British, smaller ships were sent out to meet it, or the lifeboats were lowered and the illegal immigrants were brought ashore. Almost at once, they were given false identity papers and taken inland to the kibbutzim and villages. In this manner, illegal DPs entered Palestine under the noses of the British army and navy.

Even so, most did not make it. Sixty-three ships sailed for Palestine between April 1945 and January 1948. They were packed tightly with some twenty-five thousand refugees. Fifty-eight ships were caught by the British, and only five thousand immigrants managed to land safely. Yet the rescue effort was a success.

It was a success because people around the world heard about it and sympathized with it—they sympathized with the Jews of Palestine and against the British. Newspapers in England and America carried front-page pictures of the DPs aboard the *Beauharnais*, defying British destroyers. The DPs hung out banners that read, "We survived Hitler. Death is no stranger to us. Nothing can keep us from our Jewish homeland. The blood will be on your head if you fire on this unarmed ship."

Another ship, the *Exodus 1947,* an old American riverboat, was loaded with 4,500 refugees when the British navy stopped it off the coast of Palestine. Six British destroyers and one cruiser closed in on it, and the British began to board the *Exodus*. But the DPs on board fought back, and the British used machine guns and gas bombs, killing three Jews and wounding a hundred. The crew of the *Exodus* agreed to surrender only when the British said they would sink the boat. All the while, the crew had sent radio messages to the Haganah headquarters in Tel Aviv, and these messages were later broadcast by radio throughout the world.

When a ship was captured, the British usually sent the refugees to camps on the island of Cyprus. But, this time, the British wanting to make an example of the refugees aboard the *Exodus* placed them in cages and sent them back by prison ships to France, where their journey had begun.

But the Jews on board these ships decided to make an example, too. They refused to leave the prison ships. They demanded to be taken to Palestine. The whole world watched and waited

to see what the British would do. The British sent the refugees back to DP camps in Germany. Around the world, people everywhere were enraged at this cruelty.

They were enraged, too, by pictures appearing in their newspapers showing the terrible conditions in the DP camps set up by the British on Cyprus. Increasingly, public opinion sided with the Jews of Palestine and turned against the British policy of excluding Jews from Palestine.

II: OIL AND THE MIDDLE EAST

The British hoped that the United States would support their tough policy on keeping the Jews of Palestine under control. The British were well aware of the fact that the United States had much to lose if there were a serious conflict in the Middle East. For one thing, the U.S. and the British were both interested in keeping Russia out of Palestine and Transjordan. For another, there was the matter of oil.

World War II proved that fuel was crucial to both military and non-military progress. Vast oil fields had been discovered in Saudi Arabia, Kuwait, and other countries of the Arab world. The United States had been quick to invest millions of dollars in developing these fields and placing air bases and military installations in Arab lands to protect the oil companies. In fact, the United States was planning a huge pipeline that would lead from the Arabian peninsula right to the Mediterranean Sea—and that meant through Palestine.

The British had every reason to believe, therefore, that the United States government would stand by them in preventing Jewish immigration and in keeping the Middle East tightly under Great Britain's control. But Americans were deeply moved by the suffering of the DPs and the terrible treatment the British were giving them. And, American Jews, in ever-increasing numbers, were becoming Zionists.

While only 100,000 Jewish families belonged to the Zionist Organization of America in 1939, by 1945 there were more than 400,000 members. The Conservative movement of American Judaism began teaching spoken Hebrew in its religious schools and openly supported Zionism. At the same time, some of the most outstanding American Zionists came from the Reform movement which was becoming very pro-Zionist— including the brilliant speaker and politician, Rabbi Stephen S. Wise, who led the American Zionist cause during World War II. Only the Orthodox movements in America remained neutral, still unwilling to accept Hebrew as a spoken language and still unwilling to "force the hand of God" by declaring a Jewish state. Of course, in all three movements, there were those who were opposed to Zionism, believing that it would foster anti-Semitism in the Diaspora and that Jews outside of Palestine would be suspected of loyalty to more than one country if a Jewish state existed.

American politicians also placed a great value on the "Jewish vote," especially in states like New York, Illinois, and Pennsylvania and in cities like Boston, Baltimore, and New York which had large Jewish populations. Hadassah and the other Zionist organizations knew this, and their members were ready and willing to send postcards, telegrams, and letters to members of Congress and the government asking for support for the Zionist cause.

Dr. Stephen S. Wise

Most important of all, the new president of the United States, Harry Truman, was in favor of a Jewish state and never for a moment doubted its importance. People he trusted—like Mrs. Eleanor Roosevelt who was known for her dedication to humanitarian work and Governor Herbert Lehman of New York—were also convinced of the need for a Jewish homeland. Truman officially asked the British to allow 100,000 Jewish DPs to enter Palestine. The British government replied that Truman was pro-Zionist because it helped his political career. This reply stung Truman. From that moment on, he used his powers fully to help the Jews win their state in Palestine.

Truman agreed to send an American to be part of an Anglo-American committee to study the future of Palestine. The report issued by this committee was much like the ones before it. Even the presence of an American could not change the British interests in keeping Palestine under England's hand. The Zionists sent Ben-

President Harry Truman (left) and Dr. Chaim Weizmann.

Gurion to London, where he met with the British prime minister. Ben-Gurion offered to allow Britain to place military bases in the Negev, the south of Israel, if Britain would open the doors of Palestine and allow Jews to enter freely. The prime minister agreed, saying that he would first need approval of the Arabs. Naturally, the Arabs refused, hoping to prevent the Jews from becoming a majority in the Holy Land.

At long last, the British faced their defeat. It was just too expensive to keep 100,000 British troops in Palestine. And, beside that, the impact of world public opinion—totally against the British—turned the tide. The British were ready to place the matter of Palestine in the hands of the newly formed United Nations.

III: THE UNITED NATIONS

The United Nations was dominated by the three major Allied Powers—England, the United States, and Russia. It was now clear that England would allow a Jewish state to be formed if the UN agreed to it. It was equally clear that the United States was in favor of a Jewish state, as

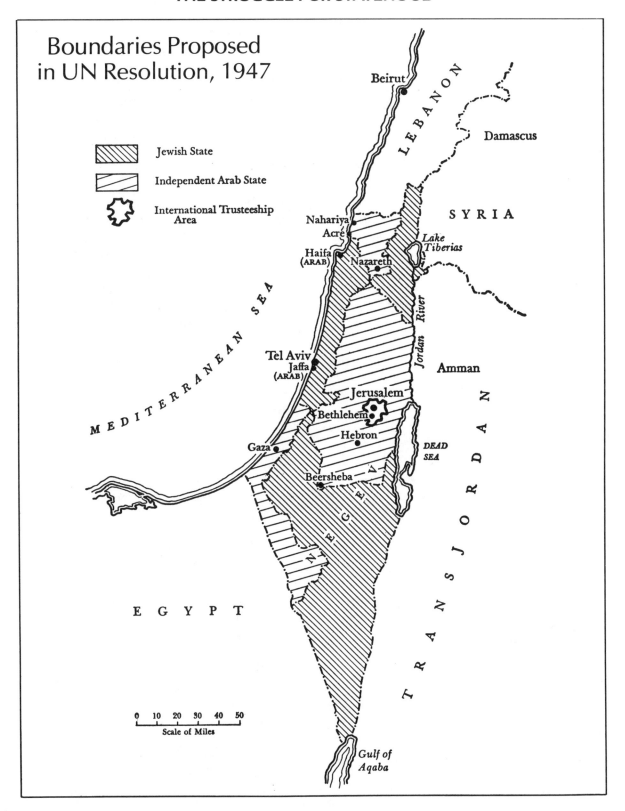

Boundaries Proposed in UN Resolution, 1947

Jewish State

Independent Arab State

International Trusteeship Area

Beirut

LEBANON

Damascus

SYRIA

Nahariya
Acre
Lake Tiberias
Haifa (ARAB)
Nazareth
Jordan River

MEDITERRANEAN SEA

Tel Aviv
Jaffa (ARAB)
Amman

Jerusalem
Bethlehem
DEAD SEA
Hebron

Gaza

N E G E V

Beersheba

EGYPT

T R A N S J O R D A N

0 10 20 30 40 50
Scale of Miles

Gulf of Aqaba

long as power could be transferred in a peaceful way from Britain to the Jews of the Yishuv. Only the Russian position was not clear.

Josef Stalin, head of the Russian Communist party and dictator of Soviet Russia, was no friend of the Jews. He hated the Zionists even more. But he saw an opportunity in the Jewish state to weaken the position of the United States and especially of Great Britain in the Middle East. He was very eager for that to happen. He was also pleased at the idea that there might be war between the Arabs and the Jews in Palestine. Such a war might allow Russia to provide weapons for one side or the other, which would be a way of Russia's gaining a foothold in the area. So the Russians decided to vote for the UN plan.

On November 29, 1947, the General Assembly of the United Nations voted 33 to 14 in favor of the partition of Palestine into two states. Everywhere, people who read in their newspapers about DPs, still shocked by the Holocaust, listened to radios as the votes were cast. For the Jews, it was not a perfect solution. The new Jewish state would be only half the area of Palestine. Jerusalem would be an "international" city, in the hands of the United Nations. Yet, the plan stated clearly that by October 1, 1948, the British would remove their troops and leave behind two free nations—one Arab, the other Jewish. And the doors of Palestine would at last be flung open for all the survivors to enter.

It was almost certain that there would be war between the Arabs and Jews of Palestine. Stalin, Truman, the British, the Jews of the Diaspora and of the Yishuv—all knew it. More Jewish blood would be spilled before the state was won.

But this was a moment for celebration. The UN decision came exactly thirty years to the month after the Balfour Declaration. In the streets of Israel, in synagogues throughout the world, in the DP camps on the island of Cyprus, Jews everywhere rejoiced, sang, and danced the *horah.*

The British were convinced that, in the coming struggle, the Arabs would win, so they did everything they could to keep the Arabs' friendship. When, toward the end of 1947, Arab rioters attacked Jewish farms and settlements, the British seized the "illegal" weapons the Jews used to fight back. They even suggested that the UN consider waiting "temporarily" and not allow the states to be independent so soon.

PREVIEW

The Yishuv rose to the challenge. Ben-Gurion made it clear that the Jews would accept no more delays, no more unkept promises. The Jew and the Land of Israel were one again; no one could stop the ancient Covenant from being reborn. Not the British, not the United Nations, not even the Arabs preparing for war. The Jews would stand and defend their Land.

Things to Consider

Imagine yourself as a reporter, waiting on the coastline of Israel to watch a ship of illegal immigrants unload. Write the story as you imagine it happening. How did the illegal immigrants feel about reaching Israel? How did the Israelis feel about greeting these refugees of the Holocaust? How do you imagine you would have felt, watching?

The chapter tells how the world leaders and the United Nations decided the fate of the new Jewish state. People like Josef Stalin and Harry Truman and Eleanor Roosevelt, all had a hand in this decision. Still, many Jews considered this a modern "miracle." Think back to your earlier definition of a miracle. Was the birth of the State of Israel a miracle according to your definition?

Jews throughout the world celebrated the day the State of Israel was born. What parts of the Covenant made Israel so important to Jews everywhere? Do you think your life as a Jew would be different if there were no State of Israel? In what ways?

FREEDOM FIGHTERS

Haganah, from the outset, adopted a policy called havlagah ("self-restraint"). They would not attack but only defend Jews against attack. They would not seek revenge, they would only protect themselves from the Arab rioters and raiders. But there were those within the Haganah who did not agree with the notion of havlagah. Many of them were members of Vladimir Jabotinsky's youth group, Betar.

Betar was first formed in Europe to train young people, before they came to Israel, in the arts of farming and self-defense. The name, Betar, was cleverly designed to mean two things: first, using the initial letters of Berit Trumpeldor, it stands for "the covenant with Trumpeldor," the Jewish soldier-hero who died at Tel Hai (see chapter fourteen); second, the name could also stand for Bethar, the place where Bar Kochba and his army fought the last battle against the Romans (see chapter six). The Betar movement in Europe was wiped out by the Holocaust, but it continued in the Land of Israel, growing into the Revisionist political party headed by Jabotinsky.

Members of Betar and others of the Haganah who did not believe in havlagah set up a new military organization called Irgun Tzevai Leumi, or by its Hebrew initials Etzel (see chapter seventeen). This group, led by David Raziel and later by Menachem Begin, studied military

Jabotinsky with Betar leaders and Menachem Begin, Warsaw, 1939.

tactics and military history and smuggled weapons into Palestine. Most of the time, the Etzel fought back in revenge against Arab attacks.

There was soon to appear another group of freedom fighters led by Avraham Stern and Yitzhak Shamir, called Lochame Cherut Yisrael ("Fighters for the Freedom of Israel"), nicknamed "the Stern gang" or Lechi. The Stern gang was even more extreme than Etzel—they were willing to assassinate British and Arab leaders, to bomb homes and offices, and to strike deep in Arab territory.

Both were small, well trained, highly secretive groups. Both were feared and hated, not only by the Arabs and the British, but by the majority of the Jews of the Yishuv. They were both made up mainly of survivors of Hitler's death camps—young men and women determined to drive the British out of Israel. Their leaders were intelligent. But even one of their early leaders and heroes, Jabotinsky himself, was opposed to these two organizations, hoping that havlagah would prove a better way to win the Jewish state.

In 1939, when the British issued the White Paper and cut off immigration, Jabotinsky and many others came out in support of the Etzel. The group fought against the Arabs openly, until both Raziel and Stern were captured by the British and thrown into prison in Acre. When they were set free in 1941, Raziel was sent by the British into Iraq to organize guerrilla fighting behind enemy lines in World War II. He was shot down in Iraq, even before he began his work. The leadership of Etzel fell to Begin.

In 1944, Lechi organized the assassination of Lord Moyne, a high British official known for his anti-Semitism. The assassination which took place in Cairo was cold and calculated; Jews were shocked by it. Immediately, the Jewish Agency announced that no official Jewish group in Palestine had been part of the plot.

As the British continued turning away one shipload of refugees after another in 1946 and 1947, the Etzel and the Stern gang continued setting fire to British military posts, shooting down British soldiers, and cutting British telephone and telegraph lines. Many people of the Yishuv felt that perhaps the Revisionists were right—that perhaps only violence would force the British to open Palestine to the refugees.

Then, in June 1946, the freedom fighters went too far. They telephoned the offices of the British Mandate government in the King David Hotel in Jerusalem, warning that a bomb had been set to go off in the King David. Perhaps the British thought the warning was a hoax, meant to frighten them. Perhaps there was never a warning call, though the freedom fighters later swore they made one. Perhaps the message did not get through. In any case, the bomb went off, destroying an entire wing. British, Arab, and Jewish lives were lost. And the losses were heavy. If the Jews of the Yishuv had any small sympathy with the so-called freedom fighters before, they now had none. This kind of bombing—killing the innocent along with the guilty—was the mark of terrorists, not freedom fighters. And the Jews of the Yishuv were, first and foremost, Jews. They wanted no part of terrorism and murder.

King David Hotel, Jerusalem, after the bombing.

UNIT FIVE

The State of Israel

19

THE WAR OF LIBERATION

The Yishuv had spent years preparing for statehood. Its leaders were well organized in a National Council, prepared to take governmental power from the British when they left. There was a strong sense of community in the Histadrut which offered health and welfare services to its worker members all over the country. And one voice stood out among the many, David Ben-Gurion. He would be the central figure in the new Jewish state.

But, as we have seen, the British wanted friendship with the Arabs more than with the Jews. They were sure the Arabs would win the war that was certain to come. In a way, they planned to leave as little behind for the Jews as possible. They stopped delivering the mail and running the railroads. They sent the funds of the Mandatory government back to Britain, except for a grant of money given to the Moslem Supreme Council, which meant to the mufti.

The Jews needed money, machinery, weapons, and more Jews. So the National Council looked for a loan, sent members of the Haganah to the DP camps to train the Jews in self-defense, and sent others in search of weapons to be bought.

Some Zionist leaders such as Stephen Wise and Moshe Shertok urged Ben-Gurion to ask the United States to protect the Jews for a while, just until the Yishuv could make ready for war. Ben-Gurion stood fast. The time was now. Ready or not, the Jews would have to fight. Any waiting might mean the end of the Jewish hopes for another generation.

Ben-Gurion pleaded with his Haganah officers—Yakov Dori and Yigael Yadin—to defend Jerusalem in case of an Arab-Jewish war. They told him how difficult it would be, how many soldiers might be lost in such a defense. Already the city was under siege; only a few shipments of food, medicine, and arms were getting past the Arab guards. Ben-Gurion saw even these few shipments as a kind of success and told them not to lose hope.

The second success for Ben-Gurion came when the Jews managed to take the port city of Haifa as the British were leaving. An Arab army had been waiting outside Haifa, ready to move in immediately. But the Jews managed to hold every important point, catching the Arabs by surprise.

I: THE DECLARATION

In December, 1947, the Arab leaders began telling the Arabs of Palestine that a war against the Jews was coming and that they should leave their homes and go to neighboring Arab countries to wait. The leaders added, Arab armies would invade from all sides and in a few days the Arab action against the Jews would be over and the Arabs of Palestine would return to their homes.

Leaving everything behind, the Arabs fled to Syria, Lebanon, Egypt, and the Gaza Strip (an Arab stronghold along the Mediterranean coast in the south). Almost at once, the Arab League sent armed troops from Egypt, Syria, and Lebanon into Palestine, calling them "volunteers." The British did nothing to stop them from entering. Nearly three hundred Jewish settlements were attacked; most of the roads fell into Arab hands. But Haifa was taken quickly by the Jews mainly because 20,000 Arabs had fled the city. Once again, the mufti led the Arabs of Palestine, this time from Cairo.

There were about half as many Jews as Arabs in Palestine, and the Arabs were supported by another thirty million in the neighboring countries. The Arab armies had tanks, artillery, airplanes, and weapons. Nevertheless, the Jews held on to almost every settlement.

Most of the time, the Haganah moved quickly and sharply. Arab forces were turned back at Tiberias, Haifa, and Tsfat in late April of 1948. In the New City of Jerusalem, the Haganah set up strongholds even as Arabs were fleeing on instructions from the Arab League. And, in the Old City, the people of the Jewish Quarter held on, in the midst of a far larger Arab population.

One day before the Declaration of Independence, the Etzion bloc—four Jewish villages near Hebron—was taken by the Arab forces. The men were sent as captives to Transjordan, while the women and children were sent to Jerusalem. Two other Jewish villages also surrendered.

The Yishuv was proud of its defense. The Haganah, filled with young and hardly-tested troops, behaved like an army.

Rumors soon spread that the Jews had slaughtered women and children in the Arab village of Deir Yassin, near Jerusalem, on April 9, 1948. The Etzel and the Stern gang had attacked, probably thinking that the village held only Arab soldiers. In the end, however, some two hundred villagers, including women and children, lay dead.

The history of war is filled with such tragedies. The Jews of the Yishuv were disturbed by what had happened. The Arabs of Palestine grew frightened. No doubt, many fled their homes after hearing of the slaughter at Deir Yassin. Ben-Gurion and other leaders of the Yishuv now swore to put an end to private armies like the Etzel and the Lechi.

Taking innocent blood was not limited to the Jews, however. Just four days later, Arabs murdered 94 Jews as they left their offices at the Hebrew University and Hadassah Hospital, both on Mount Scopus. British troops stood nearby passively as the massacre took place.

During this unofficial war, the leaders of the Yishuv were choosing a name for the new Jewish state. Many were suggested: Zion, Judea, and the Land of Israel. But the one finally chosen was Israel, the name by which the Jewish people had been known since the time of the Bible.

On May 14, 1948, in the afternoon, in the Tel Aviv Museum, just after the Tel Aviv Philharmonic Orchestra played *Hatikvah* ("The Hope"), the national anthem of the State of Israel, Ben-Gurion read aloud the Declaration of Independence. Thousands of people poured into the streets, carrying flags made of bits of blue and white cloth, the state's new colors.

Behind Ben-Gurion as he read was a photograph of Theodor Herzl. Ben-Gurion was the first to sign the declaration, followed by other leaders of the Yishuv and members of the World Zionist Organization. Spaces for signatures were reserved for those leaders who were trapped in Jerusalem.

That night, President Truman announced that the United States recognized Israel as a free and independent state. On May 17, the Russians did likewise. Then came Poland, Czechoslovakia, Rumania, Hungary, Yugoslavia, and eight other nations. Britain did not recognize Israel officially until the end of the War of Liberation in January, 1949.

The declaration included an urgent call for friendship between Arabs and Jews:

> We extend our hand in peace and neighborliness to all the neighboring states and their peoples, and invite them to cooperate with the independent Jewish nation for the common good of all.

It also sent out a call to the Jews of the Diaspora:

David Ben-Gurion reading aloud the Israel Declaration of Independence, May 14, 1948.

Our call goes out to the Jewish people all over the world to rally to our side in the task of immigration and development, and to stand by us in the great struggle for the fulfillment of the dream of generations for the redemption of Israel.

Its final note was a reminder of the Covenant, "With trust in God, we set our hand to this declaration . . . on the soil of the Homeland, in the city of Tel Aviv, on this Sabbath eve, the fifth day of Iyar, 5708. . . . "

II: THE WAR OF LIBERATION

The State of Israel had an army of nearly 40,000 trained soldiers in the Haganah and Palmach. But they lacked the material for war. They had only a few thousand rifles, about ten thousand homemade Sten guns, a few light machine guns, and two or three mortars. They had no heavy field pieces or artillery. The "air force" was made up of six or seven biplanes. Pilots had to throw handmade bombs from these while flying.

On May 15, fifty thousand Arab soldiers attacked from Egypt, Transjordan, Syria, Lebanon, and Iraq. They were not good soldiers, and they were led by inferior officers. But they were equipped with heavy artillery, tanks, and modern airplanes. In addition, their navies controlled the sea and blockaded the ports of Israel.

Ben-Gurion sent out an order that every inch of Jewish soil had to be held, and the settlers dug in on their kibbutzim and in their villages. Often the Arab armies would penetrate the fields of a kibbutz many times, only to find that the kibbutz defenders were still determined to fight on against tanks, against mortars, against heavy shellings from field cannon.

The heaviest fighting took place in and around Jerusalem. The Arab League shelled the Jewish Quarter of the Old City until it finally surrendered on May 28. Then they began working on

Signing Israel's Declaration of Independence. (Left) David Ben-Gurion, (right) Moshe Sharett (Shertok).

the New City. They controlled the important police fortress at Latrun along the Tel Aviv-Jerusalem road, and, no matter how many times the Jews attacked this fortress, they could not seize it to open the road. Inside Jerusalem, 10,000 artillery shells had exploded costing 1,200 Jewish lives and destroying 2,000 homes. The water pipeline had been cut; people were forced to line up each day for water rations. Food was running low and there was fear that people would soon begin starving.

Ben-Gurion sent his key general Yigal Allon to get supplies through to Jerusalem. When Allon saw that it would be impossible to take the stronghold at Latrun, he turned to Colonel David Marcus. Marcus was a volunteer from America who had studied at West Point. For several weeks, he had been using a footpath through the Judean Hills to lead soldiers around Latrun and into Jerusalem. Together, he and Allon agreed to widen the path and make it possible for the supply trucks and jeeps to get through. They brought hundreds of laborers from Tel Aviv and began clearing rocks and dynamiting the sides of the hills to create a bed along which the road could travel.

The Arab armies in the north and south had been held off and even forced to retreat in places. When the United Nations asked that the Arabs and Jews accept a truce for one month beginning on June 11, the Arabs accepted, glad for the break in the fighting. Ben-Gurion was nervous. Jerusalem, he said, had to be in the hands of the Jews *before* the truce began; otherwise, it might be lost forever in the negotiations.

Day and night the laborers kept at the work on the "Burma Road," which had been named after a similar road from Burma to China used by Wingate to supply the Allied troops in World War II. On June 6, the first convoys of trucks carrying water, food, and ammunition reached

Colonel David "Mickey" Marcus.

Jerusalem by the Burma Road. The New City was saved and Latrun was no longer important to the Jewish war effort.

In May, the United Nations sent Count Folke Bernadotte of Sweden to try to arrange a peace between the Arabs and the Jews. He tried to convince the Jews to give up Jerusalem, Haifa, and the Negev in exchange for peace. But the Yishuv refused to give up the lands it had won. During the one-month truce new planes and tanks were delivered to the Jews from Czechoslovakia and France; new immigrants—already trained by the Haganah—were arriving from Cyprus; the government was operating smoothly. The Yishuv felt that it could now conquer even the Negev, which remained in Arab hands.

The moment the truce was over, the Israelis took the field again. They seized the airport at Lydda, took the town of Nazareth, and sent their forces south to prepare for the battle of the Negev. It took only a week before the Arabs asked for another truce. The Yishuv agreed, unhappily. Nor were they any happier when Count Bernadotte's last report, issued after his death, suggested that they give up the Negev to the Arabs, in exchange for peace. All over Israel, Jews demanded that the Negev be taken.

The negotiation went on until September 17 when a terrorist, possibly of the Stern gang, shot Count Bernadotte as he was driving through Jerusalem. Ben-Gurion immediately ordered the Haganah to put an end to the Etzel and the Stern gang and all "private" armies. But the death of Count Bernadotte, who had helped negotiate with Germany at the end of World War II, was a stain on the Jewish nation and was mourned throughout the world.

Ben-Gurion knew that a final truce would soon be demanded by the United Nations. But there were two big problems facing the military, and it seemed there might be time and men enough to solve only one of them. The first problem was the area called Samaria which was controlled by the Arab armies and which nearly cut the territory of Israel in half. In the shape of a human ear, it jutted into the Galilee and the Negev. The

Israel after 1948

LEBANON

El Quneitra

Golan Heights

SYRIA

Tsfat

Haifa

Tiberias

Sea of Galilee

MEDITERRANEAN SEA

Nablus

Jordan R.

Tel Aviv

Amman

Ashdod

Jericho

Jerusalem

Bethlehem

Hebron

Gaza

Dead Sea

Gaza Strip

Beersheba

JORDAN

El Arish

EGYPT

N E G E V

SINAI PENINSULA

0   50

Miles

Eilat   Aqaba

Gulf of Aqaba

SAUDI ARABIA

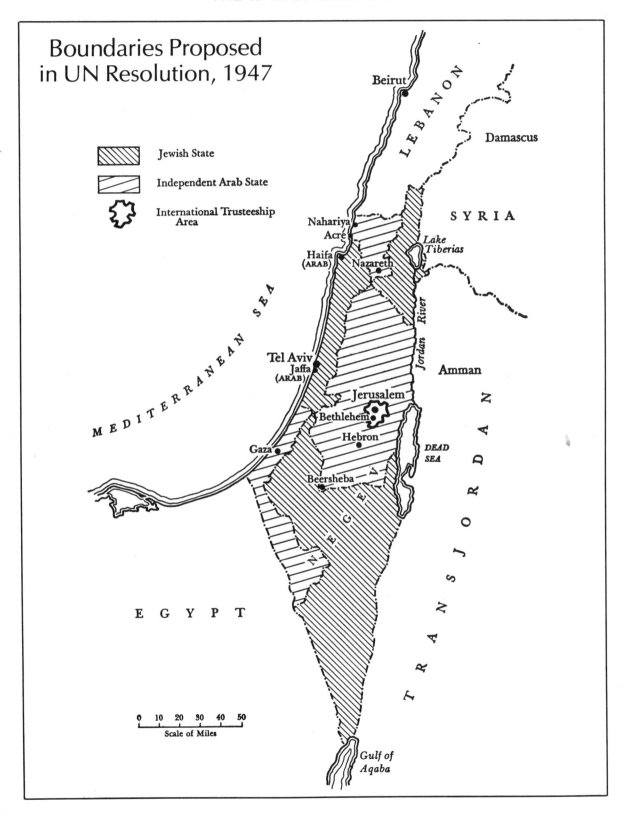

Boundaries Proposed
in UN Resolution, 1947

Jewish State

Independent Arab State

International Trusteeship
Area

Beirut

LEBANON

Damascus

SYRIA

Nahariya
Acre
Haifa
(ARAB)
Nazareth
Lake
Tiberias

MEDITERRANEAN SEA

Tel Aviv
Jaffa
(ARAB)

Jordan River

Amman

Jerusalem
Bethlehem
Hebron

Gaza

DEAD
SEA

Beersheba

N E G E V

EGYPT

T R A N S J O R D A N

0 10 20 30 40 50
Scale of Miles

Gulf of
Aqaba

other problem was the Negev itself.

Ben-Gurion was a student of the Bible. He had read of the riches of the Negev in biblical times and believed that the copper and iron mentioned in the Bible were still there to be mined. It might be the place where the future fortune of Israel would be made. He decided on the Negev.

When the Egyptian army began shelling the Tel Aviv-Jerusalem road again, ending the truce, Ben-Gurion sent the Jewish army southward. The Haganah and Palmach divided the Egyptian army by driving through it in two places. The Egyptians in January, 1949, asked for another truce and a settlement based on Israel's present military gains. But Ben-Gurion ignored this request, and the shock troops of the Palmach drove two hundred miles further south, reaching the Gulf of Aqaba. The Negev was now in the hands of the Israelis. Ben-Gurion then agreed to an armistice, ending the war.

The Israelis occupied more territory than the United Nations had given them in the partition plan of 1947. But, since the Arabs had refused in 1948 to negotiate a truce, the Israelis now insisted on settling the war at the present boundaries. Even though Truman supported Bernadotte's plan for giving the Negev to the Arabs, it was clear even to the American president that Israel had created its own borders. An armistice was signed, though the Arabs refused to meet face to face with the Israelis. But no peace treaty was ever signed.

In January, 1949, the Yishuv held its first elections. By May, the State of Israel was accepted into the United Nations as its fifty-ninth member nation. The gates of Palestine were now open to the refugees of Europe, and by the end of 1950 nearly all the refugees of the Nazi Holocaust who had not been settled elsewhere reached Haifa Harbor.

III: TWO TALES OF HEROISM

Orde Wingate, who trained the Special Night Squads, helping the Haganah learn military tactics and strategy, was killed in an air crash in 1944. But his widow, Lorna Wingate, came to Palestine in 1947–1948 to be present at the birth of the new State of Israel. She wanted to fly into one of the kibbutzim being attacked by the Arab armies, but the plane could find no place to land. So she attached a copy of the Bible to a parachute and sent it down to the people of the kibbutz below. Inside was a short note, saying: "This Bible represents a covenant between us in victory or in defeat, now and forever."

Chaim Weizmann, seventy-four years old and half-blind, was in New York on May 17, 1948, when he received a telegram saying he had been elected the first president of the new State of Israel. He was staying at the Waldorf-Astoria Hotel, which now raised the blue and white flag with its Star of David, above Park Avenue in honor of its guest's new position. Tens of thousands of American Jews crowded into the street in front of the Waldorf-Astoria to honor the new flag, to honor the man who had helped gain the Balfour Declaration, and to be present in a real way at the birth of the new nation.

PREVIEW

The work of independence was just beginning, but the miracle of independence had come to the Jewish people in our time, in our day. The Promised Land was once more in the hands of the people of Israel, the people who had come out of Egypt as slaves and into the Promised Land free and independent.

Things to Consider

The Arab nations were far stronger in men and in weapons than the Israelis. Yet the War of Liberation ended with the Israelis in control of a territory far larger than had been voted to them in the United Nations. What Jewish values were especially important to the Jews of Israel in this first test of their ability to survive?

Do you feel a special attachment to the city of

THE WAR OF LIBERATION

"Israel Liberated, 1948," commemorative coin, minted by the Bank of Israel.

Jerusalem? The text tells us that Ben-Gurion "pleaded with his Haganah officers . . . to defend Jerusalem. . . ." Why do you think he placed such an important value on this one city? (To answer this question, you'll have to review the early chapter on King David and the meaning of Jerusalem to the Jews throughout the ages.)

Mrs. Lorna Wingate delivered her message to the Jews during the days of fighting. What do you think she meant when she wrote, "This Bible represents a covenant between us in victory or in defeat, now and forever"? Who is the "us"? What did she mean by "covenant"?

TIME CAPSULES

November 23, 1947: The voice at the other end of the telephone line was excited. The professor had to meet him, he said. No, he didn't have a permit to cross the British lines from the Old City into the New. Did the professor have a permit? No. They would meet early in the morning, at the gate between the zones. They would just have to watch out for the British police. Also the Arab and Jewish police, the professor reminded him.

November 24, 1947: In the grey light of morning, Jerusalem was quiet. The professor listened to the story of the man who had called him the night before. Last spring, he said, some Bedouin goatherds lost a goat in the hills near the Dead Sea. They followed the goat to a cave, but it was too dark inside to see anything. So one of them threw a rock inside, hoping to scare the goat into running out. But the rock hit something that

made a cracking sound, like pottery being broken. So the Bedouins went in. This is what they found, the man said. He held a small piece of ancient leather and handed it to the professor.

The professor looked at the scrap of parchment. It was covered with Hebrew writing. There were three scrolls, the man said, in Bethlehem, in the hands of an Arab antique dealer. The dealer did not want to buy them if they were fakes, so he had asked the Armenian antique dealer from the Old City. The Armenian did not know if they were real, so he had called Professor Sukenik. Would Sukenik come to Bethlehem to look at the scrolls?

November 29, 1947: Sukenik knew—everyone knew—that later this day the United Nations would vote on partitioning Palestine. War was sure to come, perhaps by evening. He was on the first bus of the morning, his military pass in his

163

(Above) Area of the Qumran caves. (Opposite page) Dead Sea caves.

164

pocket. He was the only Jew among many Arabs on the bus, and he was nervous. The Armenian was waiting for him at the bus station. Together they went to the shop of the Arab antique dealer. When the three men crowded into the small attic room, the Arab brought out two large jars, taking from them the leather scrolls.

Sukenik's hand started to tremble as he unrolled them. He read a few sentences. It was biblical Hebrew! But the words were not words from the Bible. In his hands were writings that had not been seen for more than two thousand years.

The United Nations was voting to create a Jewish state. The Arab nations were preparing for war. And the professor was riding home on a bus filled with Arabs, cradling between his feet three long scrolls wrapped in paper, that looked like three long loaves of bread.

They were just the first three. A few years later, Yigael Yadin, the professor's son, arranged to buy five more in New York City. In 1951, more turned up in Jordan, leading two archeologists to study 267 caves in the Qumran area. They pieced together a picture of a long extinct Jewish sect, the Essenes (see chapter six).

The Dead Sea Scrolls were like a time capsule. They were hidden by the people who wrote them during the Great Revolt, before the Romans captured the Qumran community. In all the years that the Jews had waited for the rebirth of the Jewish state, the scrolls had waited too. It was just one more connection between past and present—the writings of the Bible and the Jews of old, waiting patiently through history for the Jews of today.

20

THE GATES OF REDEMPTION

The new Israeli parliament, the Knesset, soon passed the Law of Return. Under this law, any Jew can become a citizen of the State of Israel just by arriving in Israel and stating the intention to stay. The Knesset did this because the state had not been established just to fight wars, or even just to protect the citizens of the Yishuv. It was set up as a homeland for the Jewish people. So the 1939 White Paper, which the Yishuv had always refused to accept, was now history. The gates were finally open and the Jews began to return.

I: THE SURVIVORS RETURN

Among the first to arrive were the remnants of the once great European Jewish community from Cyprus. Some 24,000 European Jews managed to escape from the Nazis in one way or another and came within sight of Palestine, only to be captured by the British and sent to special camps set up on the island of Cyprus. During the war, members of the Haganah went to the camps to teach Hebrew, farming, and self-defense. As the British prepared to leave the country in 1948, they released the DPs from the camps and these refugees were brought to Palestine. Many of them immediately joined the army and fought in the War of Liberation.

The next to arrive were the remnants of the Jewish communities of Europe, 75,000 who had been released from the concentration and death camps and placed in DP camps all over Europe by the Allied armies. Now they were set free and brought to Israel.

In the first seven and a half months, the new State of Israel accepted over 100,000 refugees.

II: JEWS FROM ARAB LANDS

If the Jews of Europe were in grave danger before the creation of the State of Israel, a whole other group of Jews—those in Arab lands—were placed in danger because of the new state. They were threatened, persecuted, sometimes attacked—in short, they were forced by the Arab governments to flee. Some 5,000 Yemenite Jews went to the country of Aden, under British control. They were given a camp large enough for only about 1,000 people, with neither enough food nor clothing to go around. Help came from the American Jewish Joint Distribution Committee (the Joint) that was set up in 1914 to aid Jewish refugees. The first 5,000 Yemenites were brought to Israel in 1949. Later, after the rest of the Yemenite Jews fled to the camp in Aden, it held as many as 10,000 people, all fed and clothed by the Joint.

Israel sent one transport plane after another to bring the Jews out of Aden. The airlift, lasting until August 1950, was named "Operation Magic Carpet." The Yemenites, hardly knowing what to make of a modern invention like the

(Above) Displaced persons from World War II European refugee camps arriving in 1949 on the ship Atzma'ut.
(Below) New immigrants arriving at the Nathanya reception center, Jan. 27, 1949.

Yemenite Jews airlifted to safety in Operation Magic Carpet.

airplane, said they were being brought home to Israel as the prophets promised, "on the wings of eagles." Some 43,000 returned with Operation Magic Carpet. Only 1,500 remained in Yemen; of these, another 1,200 would soon arrive in the Holy Land.

Another group rescued were the Jews of Iraq. The Jewish community there was an ancient one, dating back to the destruction of the First Temple. But, as Arab persecution increased, the Jews of Iraq no longer felt safe. In the first couple of years, only 6,910 were able to escape to Israel. In the following two years, another 112,464—nearly the entire Iraqi Jewish population—arrived in Israel.

Jews came from other Arab lands, as well—from Persia, Libya, Egypt, and Turkey. They joined the European Jews from Poland, Yugoslavia, Czechoslovakia, Rumania, Bulgaria, and Germany. Nor was this all. Later, Jews fled from Algeria, Tunisia, and Morocco.

III: SETTLEMENT AND EDUCATION

In the first year of immigration, the problems of settling and educating the newcomers were hardly felt. As quickly as the men and women came, they were put into service in the military or placed on border settlements to help defend the Land during the War of Liberation. At the end of the war, however, tens of thousands of soldiers were released from active duty and jobs had to be found for them. This was no easy task.

It became even more difficult in the second year when 239,076 additional newcomers arrived. They were joined by 169,500 more in 1950; and 173,901 in 1951. There were food, housing, and work shortages. The leaders of the new state tried to settle on the land as many of the new immigrants as possible. Villages left abandoned by Jews before the War of Liberation were filled again. Kibbutzim and moshavim accepted thousands of new workers and members. When the old, empty villages were filled, the immigrants were sent out to new locations to set up new settlements. The men went first, to pitch tents, clear land, and begin the building of houses. Within a few months, they were joined by their families.

Even though most of those who came from Europe after 1949 had been merchants and craftsmen before the Holocaust, they were eager to learn farming and to work the land. During the first four years of the state, more than 270 new farm settlements were built. Of these, 85 were moshavim, the rest were kibbutzim. Where only 125,000 acres of land had been farmed by the Jews before statehood, by 1952 there were 875,00 acres in Jewish farms growing tobacco, sugar beet, flax, and cotton. In addition, the citrus groves that were damaged in Arab rioting and left untended during the War of Liberation were brought back to full life.

Women contributing their labor to the building of new settlements, 1949.

The new immigrants helped expand the olive groves and planted new fruit—figs, dates, bananas, peaches, apples, and grapes. Together with the JNF, the army, and the Ministry of Agriculture, the newcomers planted twenty-five million trees.

Nevertheless, some farm industries were in deep trouble. Vegetables were scarce. Milk, eggs, and chickens—all of which had been raised by Arabs in their villages before the War of Liberation—were now difficult to find. The Jews had been too busy fighting to take up these new areas of farming and dairy produce. Now, to solve the problems, the newcomers were put to work in these areas, as well.

There was no shortage of land, but most of the new immigrants did not become farmers. First, there were many unable to work—the lame, the blind, the aged, the deaf, those suffering from tuberculosis, heart disease, and other illnesses.

For these people, the Joint and the State of Israel together set up Malben, a social service organization to serve their needs.

Second, there were many who wished to live in the cities, but the cities had little or no available housing. So 100,000 immigrants—including many Sephardic Jews who were arriving from the Arab countries of North Africa and Asia—were placed in tent cities called *ma'abarot.* Here, they were fed and clothed at public expense. Sadly, many grew used to this, ready to live on charity forever.

Nor were there enough teachers or schools. They were desperately needed, not only for the children of the newcomers, but for the adults as well. The adults had to learn Hebrew—an educated immigrant with training in engineering, accounting, law, or medicine could not work in Israel without a grasp of the language and an ability to speak to others. For these people, and for all the other immigrants, the Hebrew language was the key to the new life. Thousands of soldiers, now free from having to fight, were trained to teach Hebrew by the *ulpan* method— in crash courses, taken for several hours each day. The *ulpanim,* or Hebrew study centers, were spread throughout the land. The Iraqi Jews were very lucky in this way. About 500 of them were already teachers. These 500 were sent out to teach the rest of their people the language of Israel. The Yemenites were lucky, too, since most of them had continued throughout the years in Yemen to receive a strong Hebrew education (the men, but not the women—since the Yemenites believed that trying to teach Torah to women was "folly"). It was the European Jews who most needed the intensive Hebrew lessons offered by the state.

In addition to language training, the state offered schools and lessons for people interested in construction, carpentry, metalwork, sewing, embroidery, and many other crafts and arts.

Once begun, the work of education continued to grow, so that education itself became one of the central concerns of the Israeli public.

The poster in the background reads (Hebrew, right-to-left):

מוסד זה משתמש במצרכים שנתרמו
על ידי אזרחיה של **ארצות הברית**
באמצעות משרד החקלאות של ממשלת
ארצות הברית של אמריקה

מלב״ן שרותי הג'וינט בישראל
מוסדות לטפול בעולים נחשלים

This institution uses commodities donated by the people
of the UNITED STATES OF AMERICA through the
United States Department of Agriculture

**MALBEN - AMERICAN JOINT
DISTRIBUTION COMMITTEE**
Services in Israel

IV: THE JEWS OF RUSSIA

In 1948, Golda Meir, an Israeli politician who came from Milwaukee during the Third Aliyah, was sent to Russia as Israel's first representative there. In those days, the Russians still hoped that their support of Israel might give them a foothold in the Middle East. Naturally, the Russians were disappointed as Israel set itself up as a democracy much stronger than anyone had imagined.

Meir decided to visit the Central Synagogue in Moscow. In a sudden outpouring of emotion, thousands of Russian Jews came from every corner of the city to greet the Israeli minister. The Russians had put an end to the Zionist movement, but it was obvious that Zionism—the love of and yearning for Israel—was far from dead in Russia.

The Communists were surprised and shocked. They struck back at their own Jewish community by forcing a Yiddish newspaper to close and by putting an end to a Jewish Anti-Fascist Committee that had become one of the best known Jewish organizations. The Communists also arrested several Jewish leaders. Later, in the 1950s, the Russians ceased to support Israel and openly began to support the Arab countries.

The Russians had offered their own Jewish population a region of Russia called Birobidjan in 1928. A few Jews actually went to this remote corner between Russia and China and, by 1951, there were about 40,000 Jews living there. But

UNIT FIVE: The State of Israel

most of Russia's Jews knew better than to go to Birobidjan. Not because it was far away, but because there was nothing Jewish about it. Like Uganda, which the British offered to Herzl (see chapter twelve), it had one great shortcoming: Birobidjan was not the Promised Land.

PREVIEW

The Jews of Russia and the Jews throughout the world found new hope in the State of Israel. No wonder the population of Israel more than doubled in its first four years! Jews were pouring in from the Arab countries, from Europe, from South America, and from North America. They were working the land, setting up businesses in the cities, teaching, planting, and building.

It was the Promised Land that called out to them. Those that did not come supported organizations like the Joint and the JNF which served the Israelis in one way or another. Support came from many who never called themselves Zionists. Something was stirring in their hearts. Call it pride. Call it satisfaction. Call it memory. It was something especially Jewish that had everything to do with the Covenant and the Bible and the promises God made to Abraham and the people of Israel. In the years to come, it would continue to rise to the surface, becoming more and more a part of the life of every Jew—in Israel and in the world.

Golda Meir, Israel's first ambassador to the Soviet Union, in Moscow.

THE GATES OF REDEMPTION

Things to Consider

The glories of the Golden Age of Judaism belonged mainly to the Sephardic Jews—those who had lived in Spain, then in North Africa and Turkey. There were also great traditions of Jewish learning and scholarship in places like Persia (the Persian Jewish community goes back to biblical times, as we know from the Book of Esther) and Yemen. Yet, in modern times, these Jews faced heavy persecution and were forced into poverty and sometimes left illiterate, as well. Like the Jews of Europe, they poured into Israel once the state was established. At first, they seemed like strangers in this new land. Can you think of a group or groups of Jews who seem like strangers to you today? What ties bind them and you to the same Jewish people?

The Jews of Russia are still trapped. Those who wish to leave are often the targets of anti-Semitism and suffer greatly when their exit visas are refused (they are known as *Refuseniks*). Today, there are organizations in the United States which work to help Russian Jews. One of their projects is to provide pen pals in Russia for Americans who wish to correspond with them. Would you like to take an active part in helping Russian Jews? Would you like a Russian Jewish pen pal?

As we have seen, our people has always placed a high value on education. In older times, education meant learning the Jewish heritage through the study of Bible and Talmud and other great Jewish writings. In the new State of Israel, it took the form of Hebrew study, the study of agriculture, and the study of modern science. Is education itself a Jewish value? Does it belong on your list of parts of the Covenant?

21

THE PEOPLE OF ISRAEL

The Jews coming from the Arab countries soon found they were entering an Israel built to suit the Ashkenazic Jews of Russia and Europe. It was a strange land to them. They came bearing with them the pride of centuries in the wisdom and scholarship of their leaders. But the Israelis they met were not, for the most part, religious. It was odd to think that these practical, strong, and idealistic Jews who were interested in farming and self-defense could possibly be the People of the Book, just as it was odd to think that this land where everyday work seemed more important than prayer and Torah study could possibly be the Promised Land.

Along with their ideals, the Jews of Arab lands (often called Oriental Jews) found challenges all around to their very way of life. In countries like Morocco, Libya, and Yemen, fathers had been supported by the work of their children, giving them time to study and pray. In Israel, elementary school was compulsory; fathers found that they were expected to work to support their children while the children studied!

In the same way, women had always been treated as the mainstays of the family. They devoted themselves totally to being wives and mothers. Now, the Ashkenazic social workers urged women to go to work, to study, to be equal in every way to their husbands. Some refused even to listen to such an idea. It seemed so very foreign to their long Jewish heritage. Others listened very carefully.

Worst of all, the Ashkenazim seemed to treat the Oriental Jews as somehow inferior. Better jobs went, of course, to the better trained European Jews. But, even though this was natural in a developing country, it seemed unfair. In fact, many of the Oriental Jews could find no work at all; and the work they did find always paid less than that available to Ashkenazic Jews. While a few European Jews were forced to live in the *ma'abarot,* the tent cities, a great many Jews from Arab lands were sent to them. And the Ashkenazic Jews began to call their darker-skinned cousins the "Second Israel."

At the same time, the leaders of the state wanted to help the Oriental Jews to become useful citizens as quickly as possible. They set up special schools, gave special tutoring to slow-learners, and offered special scholarships to the children. Slowly, they began to adjust to these new ways. Fathers grew proud even of daughters who studied hard. They began to demand more scholarships to high schools, even to colleges for their children. Even so, the Ashkenazic Jewish immigrants had a vast headstart. By the 1960s only a small percentage of Oriental Jews were in high school (which is not compulsory in Israel) or attending the universities. Few of them had become national leaders in the government; few were found in scientific laboratories or behind computer keyboards.

Both the old and new settlers wondered, "Are there *two* Israels? Is there one Israel for the Europeans and one Israel for the Jews from Arab lands?"

Jews from Arab lands. (Top) A family from Bukhara. (Center) Immigrants from Iraq. (Bottom) Immigrants from Iran. Many others came from North African countries such as Morocco and Libya.

I: ARABS IN ISRAEL AND OF ISRAEL

There was still another group of refugees whose problems the State of Israel could not hope to solve. These were the Arabs who had listened to the Arab League in the days before the War of Liberation and had left their homes behind. They were told by Arab leaders that they would return in a few days. Most could not.

An estimated 587,000 Arabs fled to the Arab countries bordering Israel—to Egypt and the Gaza Strip, to Transjordan (which later became Jordan), to Syria, and to Lebanon. They were put in camps that were supposed to be temporary. The United Nations was given the job of housing, feeding, educating, and caring for them. And the Arab states did nothing to resettle them and renew their lives. In the early years, they were called the Arab refugees. Later, they were called the "Palestinian Arabs," or just the "Palestinians."

The Arab nations chose to use the Palestinian refugees as a political tool against the Israelis. Israel tried to solve the "problem" of the refugees immediately. At the end of the War of Liberation, Israel offered to discuss the Arab refugee problem as part of the peace talks. The Arabs never came to the peace table. Israel offered to take back as many as 100,000 Arab refugees to show good will and to discuss the fate of the rest later. This offer was refused. Again, in 1963, Israel told the United Nations that the time had come to discuss the problem of the Palestinian Arabs. The Arab governments listened but were not ready to talk.

In the meanwhile, a new generation of Arabs grew up in the refugee camps. They knew no other life. They were taught that their country was taken from them by force, that the Jews of Israel were their enemies. Some were trained by Russian experts as terrorists and given weapons and explosives to carry out raids in Israel. Through the Palestinian terrorists Russia gained

a foothold in the Middle East, something it had always wanted. The terrorist activities of the Palestinian refugees have kept the Middle East—the oil-bearing territory on which Britain and Europe relied so heavily—in a state of constant unrest.

Ironically, the Arab refugees did not have to remain in the camps or remain poor. From 1948 on, the State of Israel offered to pay each Arab family for the property it lost in Israel. Israel even invited a committee from the UN to estimate the value of all the Arab properties so that the settlement would be fair.

It is unlikely that most refugees ever knew about this Israeli proposal. And, if their "friends" in the Arab nations—the nations that held them as virtual captives in the camps along the borders with Israel—ever did tell them, they probably added their opinion that Israel could not be trusted to keep the bargain.

Israel's Declaration of Independence promised the Arabs in Israel "complete equality of social and political rights." In fact, the average Israeli Arab lives a more comfortable and secure life than the average Arab citizen in the Arab nations.

But "equality" is one thing to guarantee in a written document and quite another to achieve. Arabic was made an official language of the state and can be used in the Knesset by anyone who chooses to do so. There have always been Arab representatives in the Knesset; a handful of Arabs have even reached high posts in the government. The Israeli Arabs have their own political parties, but they are also free to belong to Jewish political parties. Yet, the Israeli Arabs are not quite equal in every sense.

For a long time, especially in areas of the country heavily populated by Arabs, those who wished to travel had to apply for permits, those who wished to change jobs or move to another city had to ask permission. Arabs are not allowed to join the military or live in border towns. These differences arose because of the unrest between Israel and the Arab nations and the fear that some

Palestine Arab refugees in Alliance camp, Damascus.

Arabs might side with those nations and pose a threat to Israel's security.

For the same reason, some jobs were closed to the Arab citizens of Israel because these jobs required "security" clearances, which the Arabs could not get. And, since Jews—especially Euro-pean Jews—usually had better education, they were able to get better jobs. (To help solve this education gap, Israel spent more on education for its Arab than for its Jewish citizens.)

On the other hand, many a Bedouin Arab who once moved about from place to place in the

Refugee camp in Gaza.

Negev in search of water had found that Israeli methods of irrigation make it possible to get enough water even in the desert. The Bedouin tribes may still live in goat-skin tents, but often there is a television antenna above the tent and an electrical hook-up from the power lines along the roads.

Today in Israel, Arabs have their own school system, their own courts, and the right to govern Arab cities and villages within the Jewish state. Many go beyond high school into college. Some go to graduate schools to study engineering, law, social work, and medicine. Yet, it is only natural for Arabs in Israel to feel uneasy. Like the Jews in the United States or Canada, the Arabs in Israel are a minority. Moreover, they may have family ties with Arabs outside Israel, many of whom are unfriendly to the Jewish state.

It seems that only a full and lasting peace between Israel and its Arab neighbors will ever bring full equality to the Arabs of Israel.

II: SABRAS

Beside the Israeli Arab, the Oriental Jewish immigrant, and the Ashkenazic immigrant, there stands another kind of Israeli citizen—the Jew born and raised in the Land of Israel. These Jews were brought up tilling the soil or ready to take up middle-class life in the cities. Early on, they earned the nickname, "Sabra."

178

Sabra cactus.

The *sabra* is a desert cactus fruit, hard and prickly on the outside, sweet on the inside. So, it is said, are the Sabras of Israel. Perhaps it is because they have known little else but war for their entire lifetimes. Those born before the declaration of Israel's statehood may remember the Arab riots. Those born later may have served in the army many times since. With few exceptions, every Israeli man and woman enters the army at age seventeen or eighteen. After serving a regular term, the Israelis become part of the "citizen" army. They can be called up again to serve at any time; indeed, they must fulfill a period of *miluim* or reserve duty each year.

University students, lawyers, dock workers, printers, physicians, scientists, social workers, kibbutzniks, teachers, artists, engineers, writers —whatever their profession, they are also soldiers. Each Sabra probably has a brother, sister, or cousin, friend or neighbor who never returned from one of Israel's many battles. No wonder they are hard on the surface. Unlike teenagers in many countries, they are forced to become full adults by age eighteen.

For all this, Sabras tend to be very serious and thoughtful. Perhaps more than their elders, they are anxious for peace to come to the Middle East, for an end to the endless fighting. Their parents wanted them to be "normal," that is, never to feel inferior as Jews who knew anti-Semitism in countries like Germany and Russia often felt. Too late, these parents found their young Sabras becoming "Canaanites," people at home in the Land of Israel but who knew little or nothing of their Jewish heritage and its importance. Like the Canaanites of old, it was said, these young people had no special attachment to the ideas of Zionism and the love of Zion which come from the Jewish tradition.

This has begun to change. Israeli schools place more and more emphasis on teaching Jewish ethics and values, on the Bible as Israel's history, and even on the history of the Jews in the Diaspora. In this way, the old ideas of Israel as the Promised Land, the Covenant, and the ties between the people and the Land are becoming clearer to the new generation of Sabras.

To understand the story of modern Israel, you must know the kinds of people that make up the state. In this chapter, we looked at the major divisions—the Ashkenazic Jews of the years of *aliyah*, the immigrant Jews from Arab lands, the Sabra Jews born in the Land and belonging to it in a new way, and the Israeli Arabs who share the fate of the Jewish state even though they are a minority.

We also spoke of a problem which shaped the way Israelis and Israeli Arabs think about themselves—the problem of the Arab refugees, those who fled their homes in the shadow of the War of Liberation. Through the years—in literature and in political and social thinking—Israel has shown a real concern for the fate of these unfortunate victims of the Middle East conflict.

UNIT FIVE: The State of Israel

Infantry men going through their army basic training.

PREVIEW

The future of Israel is in the hands of its citizens; it is shaped, too, by the kind of government which they have created. It is a government as unique and complex as the people who control it. In the next chapter, we will see how this government works.

It is very different from the governments Jews in Israel had in ancient times. Yet, in many ways, it has an ancient feeling. The leaders tend to be the "elders" among Israelis. The presidents are more like the "sages" of old than they are like the heads of other nations. And leaders look back to the lessons of the past, learning from the Bible and other Jewish works, bringing the wisdom of ancient times to the service of a modern nation. And that's what you would expect in a Covenant land.

Things to Consider

For Israeli students, studying the Bible is like studying American history for Americans. Israelis are aware of the fact that they are walking where Samuel and Elijah once walked, where King David and King Solomon once ruled, where mystics studied kabbalah and sages wrote the Talmud. Perhaps that explains the great love that Israelis have for archeology. Touching the things of the past brings the past closer, makes it more alive. Consider some comparisons: Washington, D.C., is named for the "father of his country." What name does Jerusalem have that links it with a great Jewish founder? American blacks consider Abraham Lincoln the "great lawgiver" because he issued the Emancipation Proclamation, freeing the slaves. Who was the "great lawgiver" in Jewish history? In America, the easiest archeological find to make is an arrowhead. What is the most common archeological find in Israel? To what period do these finds usually date? How do our great leaders and these little artifacts serve to bind us to America? How do they bind the Jews of Israel to the Promised Land?

The Arab refugees, the Palestinian Arabs, have been taught to hate Israelis. If you met a Palestinian, what might you say to change his or her mind about Israelis and the State of Israel?

22

POLITICS AND GOVERNMENT

Israel's government may seem strange at first to an American. In the United States, for example, there are usually only two political parties (though the U.S. Constitution allows for more), voting is done by region or state, and presidents are elected nationally. There are two representative assemblies in the United States—the Senate, with equal votes for each state, and the House of Representatives, where states with large populations have more votes than states with smaller populations. Special interests are represented by lobbyists, people hired by groups and organizations to speak with members of the Congress and government about the importance of a cause or a minority.

From the very start, the Zionists created separate political parties for each separate interest group or minority. So the State of Israel has many political parties—several that represent labor, several for religious interests, several liberal parties, a Zionist Revisionist party, an Arab party, and a Communist party. Each citizen has one vote and the country is one large region for national elections.

Because the political parties stand for special interests, each person votes for a party and not for an individual (though the top party people are usually the elder political figures and are well known). The more votes a party receives, the more seats in the Knesset it can fill. It fills seats from its official "list" of party candidates. The

first seat goes to the person on top of the list, the next seat to the second person, and so on. Larger parties usually present a list of 120 candidates (there are 120 seats in the Knesset); smaller parties may present smaller lists. Any Israeli citizen, twenty-one years of age or older, may serve in the Knesset.

I: THE KNESSET

The Knesset members are elected for a term of four years, but the Knesset can vote to call for new elections at any time. Unlike the Congress of the United States, the Knesset has the sole power to make laws. No court can change these laws or declare them "unconstitutional." (Israel has no written constitution; it is ruled by the laws that are created year by year.) The president of the state has no "veto power" and must accept the laws of the Knesset as they are passed. The Knesset has the power to agree to the "government" of Israel or to vote any government out of office.

It is the Knesset that chooses the president of Israel. Unlike the president of the United States, Israel's president is mainly a figurehead. It is up to the president to greet and welcome foreign ambassadors, to sign all bills passed by the Knesset, to appoint judges (with the agreement and at the suggestion of the Knesset), and to

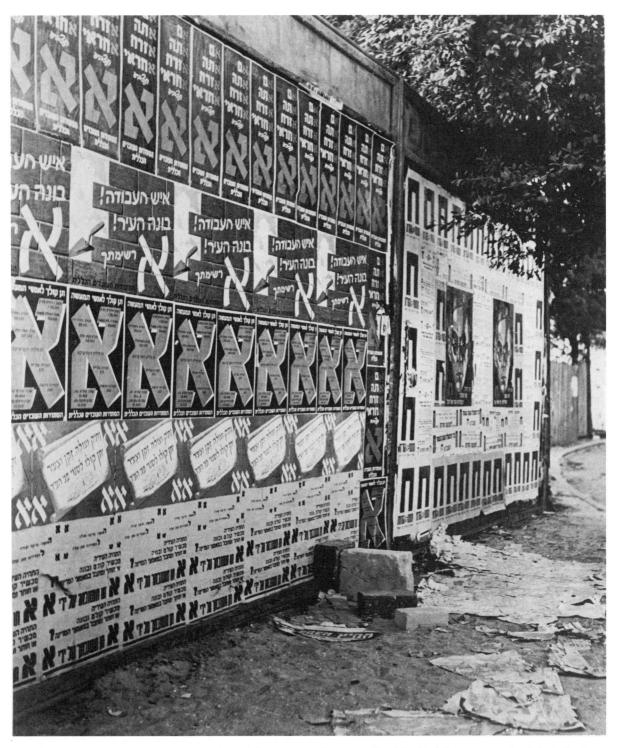

Israeli election posters. In these posters, the "alef" represented Mapai. The "chet" of the poster on the right is the first letter of "Cherut," the "Freedom" party.

Itzhak Navon (left) receiving the Founders Medal of HUC-JIR from its president, Dr. Alfred Gottschalk, Jan. 11, 1983.

invite a popular political leader to form the government of Israel.

Israel's first president was Chaim Weizmann. When he died in 1952, it was suggested that the president of Israel did not have to be an Israeli but should be one of the world's outstanding Jewish figures. Albert Einstein was asked by Ben-Gurion to consider the position, but he modestly declined. The presidency went to Itzhak Ben-Zevi, then to Zalman Shazar, Ephraim Katzir, Itzhak Navon, and Chaim Herzog. All were respected for their work in science or scholarship. Like the heads of the Sanhedrin of Temple times, they were all "sages," chosen to be honored. The president serves a five-year term and may be reelected for a second term.

II: THE GOVERNMENT

The president's hardest task is choosing who will be invited to become the next prime minister. The president speaks first to the leaders of Israel's political parties to ask who they would like as the new prime minister. Then he "invites" one of Israel's political leaders, usually the head of the political party with the largest Knesset representation, to try forming a government and choosing a cabinet. The cabinet must be chosen with care, for the prime minister and the cabinet must then be approved by the Knesset.

Since no political party in Israel has ever had a clear majority of the seats in the Knesset, Israel has always had a "coalition" government. That is, the cabinet is made up of leaders from more than one political party, so that these parties will approve the government in the Knesset and a majority vote in favor of the new government can be achieved. The major problem arising from this situation is that a small, minor party can exert disproportionate control over government policy by making its demands the price for entering and supporting a coalition.

Under the leadership of the prime minister, the cabinet makes government policy and carries on the business of the government. It suggests laws to the Knesset and enforces the laws which the Knesset passes. It runs the day-by-day affairs of the nation.

If the Knesset does not like the government or the actions of the government, it can vote for "no-confidence" in the government. If this vote passes, the entire cabinet must resign and the president must begin again, looking for a new prime minister.

III: THE COURTS

Israel's system of law is based on Jewish law as well as two other systems—the Ottoman Turkish legal heritage and British law from the time of the Mandate. Judges are nominated by the Knesset, then appointed by the president. A judge is appointed for life but can retire at age seventy (or younger, for health or other reasons).

There are civil courts, religious courts—Jewish, Moslem, Christian, and Druze—and special courts like the Tax Tribunal. In Jerusalem there is a ten-member Supreme Court. There is no capital punishment in Israel except for cases of treason in wartime and for Nazi criminals and those who helped Nazis during World

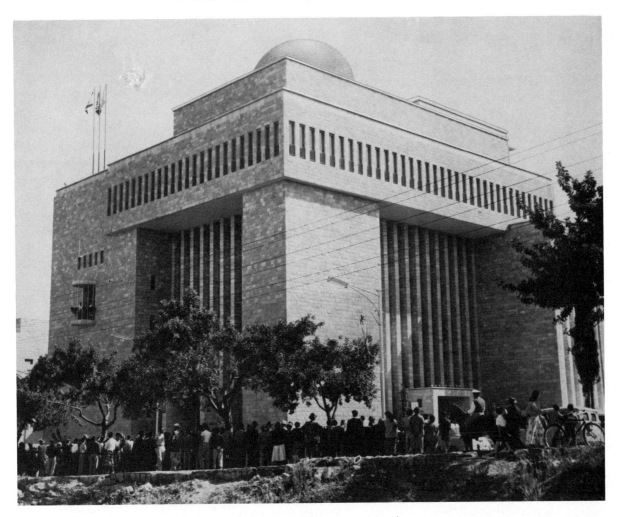

Jerusalem Chief Rabbinate building.

War II. In capital cases, a Supreme Court judge must be one of the three judges present. There are national courts for all national cases, and regional and local courts, as well.

IV: LOCAL GOVERNMENTS

Just as in other nations, cities and regions in Israel have local governments. In fact, on the local and regional level, the Oriental Jews and the Arab minorities have been successful in entering politics. Many of these regional and city officials will later rise to leadership of their

parties and then to the leadership of the country. In the future, then, it is likely that more non-Ashkenazic Jews as well as more Arabs will become members of the Knesset and government.

V: ANCIENT AND MODERN

If the presidents of modern Israel are like the sages who headed the Jewish Sanhedrin, the rest of the government is somewhat like ancient Israel's government, too. The court system is much like the court system created by Moses.

UNIT FIVE: The State of Israel

וַיִּבְחַר מֹשֶׁה אַנְשֵׁי־חַיִל מִכָּל־יִשְׂרָאֵל וַיִּתֵּן אֹתָם רָאשִׁים עַל־הָעָם שָׂרֵי אֲלָפִים שָׂרֵי מֵאוֹת שָׂרֵי חֲמִשִּׁים וְשָׂרֵי עֲשָׂרֹת: וְשָׁפְטוּ אֶת־הָעָם בְּכָל־עֵת אֶת־הַדָּבָר הַקָּשֶׁה יְבִיאוּן אֶל־מֹשֶׁה וְכָל־הַדָּבָר הַקָּטֹן יִשְׁפּוּטוּ הֵם:

Moses chose capable men out of all Israel, and appointed them heads over the people—chiefs of thousands, hundreds, fifties, and tens; and they judged the people at all times: the difficult matters they would bring to Moses, and all the minor matters they would decide themselves. (Exodus 18:25–26)

The Knesset, too, resembles the Sanhedrin of old, in that it is the elders of each political party who are elected to the Knesset. In Israel, old age is seen as a time of wisdom, rather than as weakness as it is seen by many nations where elderly people are not voted into office because of their age.

The government is similar to the government in ancient times. But only in some ways. In many others, it is very different. There are no tribes today, and no family clans to appoint their own elders. Voting is now done by men and women equally, not by the heads of families alone, as in olden days. Ancient Israel's government was designed for a farming people, and many of the laws of the Torah and Talmud are concerned with farms and farming, but today's

Inside the Knesset.

LE SANHÉDRIN OU GRAND CONSEIL DES JUIFS.

Inside the Sanhedrin, the great council of Jews which flourished during the latter part of the period of the Second Temple.

Israelis are mainly city-dwellers and factory workers. Today's government is, after all, a government for a modern state—it is more democratic and more representative than any Jewish government before it.

PREVIEW

From the moment that the government was set up, it was forced to deal with the problems of the new Jewish state. And the greatest of those problems was defense. How the government faced this and other problems, how these problems changed and shaped the Israel we know today is the subject of the next chapters. As we shall see, the government has served Israel well.

Things to Consider

The government of modern Israel is not based directly on the Torah. It is based on the laws of the Ottoman Turks and the British Mandate. But, in many ways, it is also very Jewish. From the chapter, what Jewish values would you say can be found in the way the modern Israeli government works?

The Knesset of Israel is somewhat like the Congress of the United States or the Parliament of Great Britain. But the Congress is divided into two "houses," the Senate and the House of Representatives, so we call it "bicameral." The Knesset is "unicameral," since it is only one "house." Can you compare the cabinet and prime minister of Israel with the president and the presidential cabinet of the United States? How are they the same? How do they differ?

What parts of your definition of the Covenant are at work in the Knesset, in the cabinet, in the office of the prime minister of Israel? In the way the president of Israel is chosen? In the courts?

23

SINAI AND THE SIX DAY WAR

Israel's most popular political parties have always been those with long Zionist histories. Of these, the largest was Mapai (see chapter sixteen), the Israel Labor party which ran the Histadrut. Mapai, as the central party, ruled every coalition government for the first twenty-nine years of the state. And, for most of that time, its foremost leader was David Ben-Gurion, Israel's first prime minister.

Spry and lively despite his years (he was 62 years old in 1948), Ben-Gurion met challenges head-on. He had a clear vision of the kind of state he wanted to create—moral and tough and Jewish. He arrived in the Second Aliyah, was a member of Ha-Shomer, and later in the Haganah command. He was also a devoted student of the Bible, a good husband and father. Yet, he placed the state above all else. He demanded unity of thought and unity of purpose in the State of Israel.

In 1948, for example, when news came that the ship *Altalena* was sailing into Haifa Harbor loaded with weapons bought by the Etzel in France, Ben-Gurion agreed to allow the ship to land. But, when Menachem Begin and the Etzel demanded that at least 20 percent of the weapons be given to Etzel soldiers, Ben-Gurion refused. There should be only *one* army in Israel, he said. He would not let the weapons be unloaded. When the *Altalena* tried to send weapons ashore, the Israel Defense Forces fired on it. It went up in flames and eighty-two people died. Part of the precious arms shipment was lost. Ben-Gurion then demanded that several of Etzel's leaders be arrested, and he put an end to all private armies.

Again, in 1951, he met Begin head-on. This time, Ben-Gurion was prime minister and Begin was the head of the Cherut (Revisionist) party. The issue was how to answer West Germany.

Chancellor Konrad Adenauer of West Germany announced that his country was ready to make payments to those Jews who suffered losses in the Holocaust. This included a very large number of Israelis. Most of the political parties were in favor of these "reparation" payments. But, a few hours before the debate in the Knesset, Begin spoke to a street crowd in Jerusalem, saying, "This will be a fight for life or death!" He incited the crowd which attacked the Knesset, striking at police with sticks, and throwing stones at the assembly. More than a hundred policemen were injured. Troops were called to bring order.

In the debate, Begin argued that reparations were "blood money." But the decision went to Ben-Gurion, and by 1963 the Israeli government had received almost 780 million dollars from West Germany, and many Israeli citizens also received payments. Ben-Gurion saw this as a way of allowing Germany to "atone," if not totally, at least in part, for what was done in the Holocaust. In later years, West Germany became a strong ally of Israel.

At the age of 67, in 1953, Ben-Gurion decided

Ben-Gurion at Sedeh Boker.

to retire. He left Jerusalem to work on Kibbutz Sedeh Boker in the southern Negev. If other Jews needed to be shown the importance of working on the land, he said, he was willing to show them. But a new challenge to Israel's morality brought him out of retirement a short while later.

I: THE LAVON AFFAIR

Moshe Sharett, foreign minister in Ben-Gurion's cabinet, was chosen by Mapai to be the next prime minister. He appointed Pinhas Lavon as minister of defense. It was his only real change in the government, but it was a fateful one. Lavon proved a hard man to work with, and headstrong, too.

Lavon was accused of sending Israeli spies, dressed as Arab terrorists, to bomb American offices in Cairo and Alexandria. The plan was to make the Arabs look bad. Unfortunately, one bomb, strapped to the leg of an Israeli spy, went off before he reached his target. The Egyptians quickly rounded up the rest of the saboteurs before any damage could be done. The operation was a terrible idea from start to finish, and Israel paid a high price in world embarrassment. Lavon was forced to resign. The "Lavon Affair," as it was called, became a scandal of major importance.

Sharett called on Ben-Gurion to return to the government as the new minister of defense—to bring unity—and Ben-Gurion agreed.

It was an important year for Israel. A program of aid for young African nations began. And Israel made an agreement with the United States to set up an atomic reactor in Israel for research on the use of atomic power for peaceful purposes. In the elections of 1955, Mapai again won the largest number of seats in the Knesset and the president invited Ben-Gurion to head the new government.

II: THE SINAI CAMPAIGN

The new government had to spend much energy on defense matters. Egypt signed a treaty with Czechoslovakia and received Czech tanks, jet planes, submarines, and artillery in exchange for Egyptian cotton and rice. Cairo's radio station announced, "The day of Israel's destruction approaches—there will be no peace on the borders, for we call for vengeance—death to Israel!" In his first speech to the Knesset, Ben-Gurion offered to meet with Egypt to bring peace to both countries. The answer came in Jewish blood.

Arab raids from Egypt and Jordan increased.

In the Arab refugee camps of Gaza and Sinai, Egyptians trained young refugees as *fedayin*, terrorist raiders, and sent them into Israel to murder. From 1950 to 1955, 884 Israelis were wounded or killed by terrorists. In some cases, the Israelis struck back, raiding Arab territory and destroying hotbeds of terrorism. But the Arab raids increased in 1956.

Late in 1956, Egypt moved troops into positions along the southern border of Israel; Jordan and Syria agreed to set up a joint command of Arab troops with Egypt. After trying to settle the trouble peacefully, Israel decided to strike first. On October 29, 1956, Israeli troops entered the Sinai and the Gaza Strip to clear out the nests of *fedayin* and to force the Egyptian army back.

There were fierce air battles between the Israelis and the Egyptians over the desert. Nevertheless, the Sinai Campaign was successful; seven days later, Israel's troops forced the Eyptians back across the Suez Canal. An Egyptian destroyer, sent to attack Haifa, was captured by the Israeli navy. At the Suez Canal, the Israeli troops joined the French and the British who had helped plan the Sinai Campaign to defeat Nasser.

The UN called for a cease-fire, demanding that Britain and France remove their troops and Israel withdraw to its former southern border. To keep the peace, the UN sent an international force to patrol the border on the Egyptian side.

Once again, oil tankers were able to reach Eilat from the Red Sea through the Straits of Tiran that Egypt blocked before the Sinai Campaign. Israel now built a pipeline from Eilat to Beersheba and another, larger one all the way to Haifa. Despite artillery fire from Syria, Israel managed to reclaim over 15,000 acres of land by draining the swamps called "Lake Huleh." A new water pipeline was laid to bring the precious liquid south for irrigation. Then oil was discovered in the Negev. On the shores of the Dead Sea, where once Sodom and Gomorrah stood in biblical times, Israel set up a factory to take chemicals from the mineral-rich waters. The desert was beginning to bloom in many ways.

The Huleh Valley. Before reclamation, the valley was swampland. After draining, the valley was turned into fertile farmland. (Below) Fish ponds.

Israel's population by 1963 was 2,219,000 Jews and nearly 301,000 Arab citizens.

III: CULTURE

Together, the *ulpanim* and the army had taught Hebrew to the majority of Israel's adults. The Hebrew theater, *Habimah,* which started in Russia and was later brought to Israel, became a national institution, presenting plays written in Hebrew or translated into Hebrew. Elementary education for all young people between ages five and fourteen was guaranteed; from 1955, poor pupils were given scholarships to high schools and colleges; some special schools and clubs were set up to help Sephardim and Arabs to get a

better education; sciences were given special attention at the Technion University in Haifa and the Weizmann Institute at Rehovot. The Hebrew University was joined by many additional schools of higher learning, and the number of *yeshivot* increased.

Sabras, the young people of Israel, along with their elders and the rest of the world witnessed an event of international importance in Jerusalem—the trial of Adolf Eichmann. In 1960, Israel's secret service located and arrested Eichmann in Argentina and smuggled him to Israel. Eichmann, the man chiefly in charge of the Nazi murder of 6,000,000 European Jews during the Holocaust, was brought to trial the following year.

Until the trial began, many of Israel's young

A young Russian immigrant in an ulpan.

The Technion, Israel Institute of Technology, in Haifa.

people believed that Europe's Jews had gone to the gas chambers as lambs are led to slaughter. The military-minded Sabras were ashamed of this and had little respect for the Jews of Europe—which meant, for many, little respect for their own parents! Now, as the testimony in the Eichmann trial continued and the truth unfolded daily, all Israelis learned of the bravery of those who died and those who survived, of the horrors of the concentration and death camps, and of the Jewish resistance.

Through the miracle of modern telecommunications, the rest of the world learned along with them. Eichmann was sentenced to death under

the special law for Nazi criminals and was executed at the end of May, 1962. His ashes were scattered in the Mediterranean.

IV: THE SIX DAY WAR

In 1963, after a new argument about the Lavon Affair, Ben-Gurion resigned again. He was replaced by Levi Eshkol, a long-time Mapai politician. Eshkol had little of Ben-Gurion's fire. Nor was he a lover of Ben-Gurion's young corps of leaders, people like Abba Eban, Moshe Dayan, and Shimon Peres. From retirement, Ben-Gurion

Levi Eshkol.

continued to cause Eshkol trouble, especially since the "Old Man" (Ben-Gurion's nickname) demanded a final decision on the Lavon Affair, while Eshkol preferred to forget about it. For Ben-Gurion, the Lavon Affair was a question of Israel's morality. Should Israel's secret service be allowed to commit murder, even for political reasons? He would not let it rest.

Along with Peres and Dayan, the Old Man started a new political party (Rafi) just before the 1965 elections. But the Israeli public, like Eshkol, preferred to forget about Lavon and Eshkol stayed in power.

The Russians, meanwhile, were shipping more weapons to Egypt and Syria. A pro-Communist party took control of Syria in 1965, and a new group, the *Al-Fatah,* began raids into Israel the same year. Gunfire along the Syrian border grew heavier until the situation became explosive. The Syrians promised "a final resting place for Israel."

In May 1967, the Egyptians moved troops to the southern border of Israel again. On May 16, they demanded that the United Nations remove

its peace-keeping force. To the shock of the Israelis, the UN agreed and sent its troops home, thus setting the stage for another war.

On May 22, Egypt closed the Straits of Tiran, cutting off the port of Eilat. Jordan and Iraq agreed to place their troops under Egyptian command, and more troops came from other Arab states. There were 250,000 Arab soldiers surrounding Israel. They had 2,000 tanks and 700 bombers and fighter planes. The State of Israel was in serious danger.

The Jews of the world awoke suddenly to this threat. Vast sums of money poured in from America and other Jewish communities; thousands of Jewish volunteers flew to Israel to take over civilian jobs as the army was called to active duty. Even after the war was over, the volunteers kept coming to help out.

The morning of June 5, 1967—after a last-minute attempt to negotiate a peace failed—Israel's air force attacked. In less than three hours, 391 Arab planes, most of them caught on the ground, were destroyed. Only nineteen Israeli jets were lost. For the next five days, Israel controlled the air, using its planes to help the Israeli combat troops below.

On the night of June 5, Israel captured Latrun—the fortress near Jerusalem held by the Arabs through the War of Liberation and since (see chapter nineteen). On the third day, June 7, after heavy fighting, the Old City of Jerusalem fell to Israel, and Sharm el-Sheikh in the extreme south of Sinai was taken. On the fourth day, the mass of Israel's army reached the Suez Canal, forcing the Egyptians to retreat to the western side.

Freed from fighting in the south, the air force attacked the Syrians on the Golan Heights. From these hills, they had shelled and fired on Israel's villages for many years. On the last two days of fighting, the Golan Heights fell to Israel. The Israel Defense Force stopped on the road to Damascus.

In six days, as the world and Jews everywhere watched and waited, Israel destroyed the armed

Levi Eshkol (right) with Moshe Dayan (left) and Chief-of-Staff General Haim Bar Lev (front center), 1967.

strength of the Arabs. Nearly 6,000 Arab prisoners were taken, another 15,000 lay dead or wounded, and Israel had captured huge amounts of Arab weapons and tanks. In all, 777 Israeli soldiers died; 2,586 were wounded. The Arabs managed to take a handful of Israeli prisoners, mostly pilots whose planes had been downed. These few were exchanged for the Arab 6,000. The prime minister of Egypt, Abdel Nasser, resigned on June 9, telling the world that the Russians had forced him into the war.

V: AFTER THE WAR

In the days of fighting, 200,000 Arabs fled from the West Bank of the Jordan across the river to the East Bank. After the war was over, Moshe Dayan announced an "open-bridges" policy, allowing Arabs to cross back and forth from Jordan freely. In the meanwhile, the Russians visited Egypt and promised to rebuild the Egyptian army. Nasser once again ruled. A Soviet airlift began to replace the millions of dollars worth of equipment Egypt lost to Israel. It was clear that Russia did not want peace in the Middle East.

Russia also helped the Arab terrorists to go back into action. Bombs were placed in the Tel Aviv bus station, the Hebrew University cafeteria, and the American consulate in Jerusalem—each killing innocent men, women, and children. Busses were attacked on Israel's roads.

In 1969, the Egyptian navy sank an Israeli destroyer off the coast of Sinai. In the following

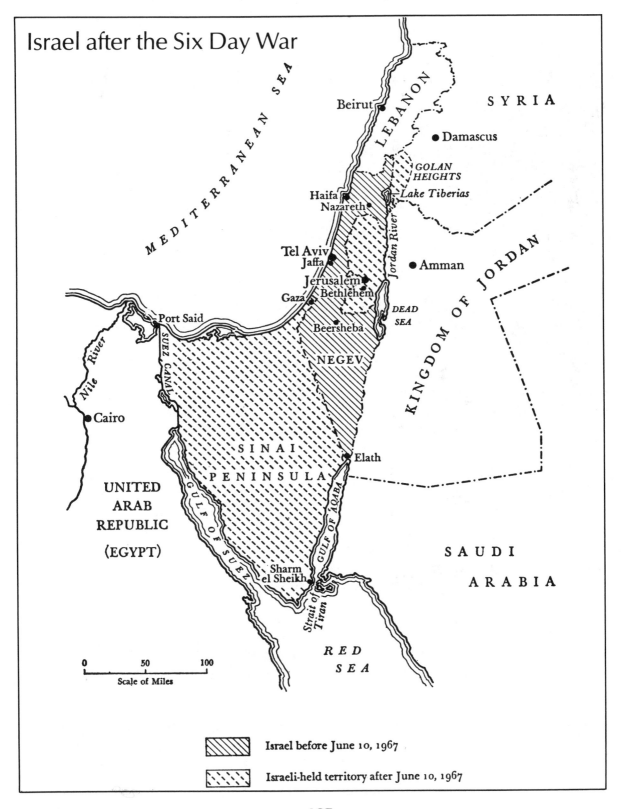

Israel after the Six Day War

MEDITERRANEAN SEA

SYRIA

Beirut

LEBANON

● Damascus

GOLAN
HEIGHTS

Haifa
Nazareth

Lake Tiberias

Jordan River

Tel Aviv
Jaffa

● Amman

Jerusalem
Bethlehem

Gaza

KINGDOM OF JORDAN

Port Said

Beersheba

DEAD
SEA

SUEZ CANAL

Nile River

NEGEV

Cairo

SINAI
PENINSULA

UNITED
ARAB
REPUBLIC

(EGYPT)

GULF OF SUEZ

Elath

GULF OF AQABA

SAUDI

ARABIA

Sharm
el Sheikh

Strait of
Tiran

RED
SEA

| 0 | 50 | 100 |

Scale of Miles

Israel before June 10, 1967

Israeli-held territory after June 10, 1967

Egypt's Russian-built tanks captured by Israel in the Six Day War.

few years, Egypt began the "war of attrition," hoping to whittle the Israelis down and wear out their strength little by little. There were artillery attacks from across the Suez Canal and minor air battles over the Sinai.

Against these attacks, Israel held its ground, sending raiding parties to punish the Arab terrorists and the Egyptian forces. The Arab countries paid a high price for the Six Day War. There were revolutions or attempted revolutions in Iraq, South Yemen, Sudan, Libya, and Saudi Arabia. The terrorists, finding Israel a hard target, turned on their own people, becoming a serious problem in Jordan and Lebanon.

Jerusalem was reunited, Old City and New. The old gates and stone barricades were removed. The barbed wire was taken away. Jews could again visit the holiest of Jewish religious sites, the Western Wall of the ancient Temple. The Jews, Arabs, and Christians of Jerusalem were now citizens of one city.

VI: JERUSALEM OF GOLD

The Arabs defending the Old City took aim through niches high in the walls built by Suleiman the Magnificent, niches that were meant for archers to use. Machine guns were placed in low spots on the wall, which in Crusader times were used to pour boiling oil on the enemies below. The Israelis fought from behind sandbags and from rooftops and windows until the time came to storm the gates of the Old City. Then there was no choice but to run out into the open and face the Arab guns with little or no protection. The battle fought in Jerusalem was a bloody and vicious one. To this day, it is possible to see the deep holes gouged in the outer wall by fire from machine guns and rifles.

Both sides were well aware of what was at stake. The Arabs call Jerusalem *Al-Quds,* "The Holy." It is the third most important site in the Islamic religion. According to Islamic teaching, Mohammed stood on the rock enclosed by the Dome of the Rock, just before he was taken up to heaven. The Jewish name Jerusalem means "the City of Peace," and part of that same rock so holy to the Arabs may have been the *even sha-tiyah* on which the Holy of Holies was built—the very center of the Temple, the holiest place on earth for the Jewish people. According to Jewish legend, this is the rock that God used as a cornerstone of creation—the center of the world itself. Jerusalem is central to the Christian religions, too, for it was the scene of the crucifixion of Jesus.

For observant Jews, the Temple mount is so holy that they will not climb the steps to the platform on which it once stood (where the Dome of the Rock now stands). The closest these Jews will come is the Western Wall, the last remnant of the huge stone wall built in the time of Herod that encircled the Temple (see chapter six).

From 1948 to 1967, the Old City was ruled by Jordan. Jews were not allowed to enter it to pray at the Western Wall. Guards—Arab and Jewish—stood across from one another, separated by the Old City wall and a street on which children played beneath the shadows of cannon and barbed wire. Everyone fighting in the brutal sun of those critical summer days of 1967 knew what was at stake.

When Israeli soldiers finally took the Old City, many rushed directly to the Western Wall—to gaze on the ancient stones, to touch the cool

rocks for the first time in twenty years, to write prayers on paper fragments and slip them into the crevices between the stones. Prayers were offered that day, just as they continue to be offered at the Wall every day ever since, just as Jews come from around the world to stand and stare at these stones laid by their ancestors—to touch history, to feel the past standing firmly in the present.

What the Israelis discovered was disturbing. Twenty-two of the twenty-seven synagogues in the Old City had been destroyed by Arab troops in the war of 1948. The last five were demolished by the Jordanians when they took over. Hundreds of Torah scrolls, holy books, and treasured manuscripts had been burned. The ancient cemetery on the Mount of Olives—a cemetery so holy that Jews from the Diaspora through all the generations had asked to be buried there—had been desecrated. Many of the tombstones had been uprooted and overturned; others had been broken and removed. Some were used as

building blocks for latrines and barracks in Jordanian army camps. Ten yards away, a new hotel had been built and a whole section of the graveyard had been bulldozed to build a road to it.

Since Israel annexed the Old City, the holy places of three religions have been open to all. Along the Via Dolorosa, Christians carry crosses in Easter processions, walking the path Jesus walked to his crucifixion according to their Scriptures. Arabs come and go, free to visit and pray in the Dome of the Rock and the mosque nearby. And Jews visit the Western Wall. A modern Israeli song says, "There are people with hearts of stone; there are stones with human hearts."

Jerusalem is a city that calls out to the soul. Could modern Israel have any other capital city? Could Israel truly be a Jewish state without Jerusalem? It is as if a vast sigh of relief and a small cry of joy went up from every Jewish soul on the day the walls of the Old City gave way before the brave young soldiers of Israel's army. Somehow, it seemed, the Jewish people was just not whole so long as the City of David was divided. Every feeling and every emotion about Jerusalem is like the stones of the Western Wall, bound up in history and family, in religion and identity, in the roots of the Jewish people.

Jordanians desecrated Jewish cemeteries. Tent emplacement in an Arab Legion camp built partly from tombstones taken from the Jewish cemetery on the Mount of Olives.

Israeli parachutists at the Western Wall, June 7, 1967.

SINAI AND THE SIX DAY WAR

PREVIEW

Most importantly, the Jews of the world now knew how much Israel meant to all Jews and to Judaism. Zionism was no longer a political movement to join or reject, it was a Jewish way of feeling. As Achad Ha-Am dreamed (see chapter twelve), Israel was becoming a world center for Jews, the beating heart of the Jewish Covenant.

Still, peace seemed distant. Perhaps that is why, in the following few years, the quiet which set in between Israel and its neighbors almost lulled Israelis to sleep—and, very nearly, to destruction.

Things to Consider

In this chapter, you read how David Ben-Gurion and Menachem Begin often came head to head against one another, as leaders of their separate causes within Israel. Consider the *Altalena* incident, the question of West German reparation payments, and the struggle for leadership in which Begin headed the Revisionist party and Ben-Gurion the Mapai party. It is important to remember that *both* these men were important leaders. Though Ben-Gurion headed the Jewish state for many years, later Menachem Begin also became prime minister of Israel. Both were strong-willed and determined people. Both

showed extraordinary courage. Look up both men in a Jewish encyclopedia, then write a short essay telling the ways in which each helped in building the new State of Israel.

A few days after the capture of Adolf Eichmann, Ben-Gurion wrote to a member of the Knesset, "I see the importance of the [Eichmann trial] that it has made it possible for an Israeli court to reveal in detail the tragedy of the Holocaust . . . so that Israeli youths who grew up and were educated after the Holocaust will know the facts. . . . '' One thing which made Sabras different from all Jews of the Diaspora was that they grew up never knowing what it meant to be part of a minority and having no experience with anti-Semitism. The Eichmann trial was especially important in changing their attitudes toward the Jews of the Diaspora. Looking back at your definition of the Covenant, what parts of that definition do you think the Sabras might have learned from hearing the story of the Holocaust during the Eichmann trial?

The Six Day War changed the attitudes of many Diaspora Jews toward Israel. In a way, it was a turning point for the Jewish people in our times. Ask your parents where they were when the war in Israel broke out in 1967, what their feelings were when they first heard the news that Israel was fighting for its survival, and how they felt when the war was over six days later.

24

THE YOM KIPPUR WAR

In November, 1967, the United Nations Security Council passed Resolution 242, asking Israel to remove its troops from areas conquered in the Six Day War, and "to work for a just and lasting peace." This same resolution asked Arab states to give up all claims to the land of the State of Israel and for all peoples in the area to live in peace. It called for the reopening of the Suez Canal and Straits of Tiran, "a just settlement of the refugee problem," and a new degree of safety on all borders. Israel accepted this resolution, saying that the issues raised in it could be the starting point for a new peace settlement. Egypt and Jordan also accepted the resolution but said that, before any negotiations, Israel would have to retreat to the original boundaries of 1949.

In April, 1968, with the new weapons given to Egypt by the Russians, the "war of attrition" began. Egypt bombarded the Israeli side of the Suez Canal and sent its airplanes to attack the Israelis. In 1969 alone, Israel shot down forty-seven Egyptian planes. In March of 1970, the Israelis learned that Russia was giving new missiles and planes to Egypt of a kind that only Russian soldiers and pilots could handle. Israeli pilots now faced Soviet pilots. The war was also continuing in the north, where *Al-Fatah* terrorists shelled Israeli villages from Lebanon.

A new, more extreme terrorist group, the Popular Front for the Liberation of Palestine (P.F.L.P.) waged war in another way—by hijacking regular airplane flights and attacking offices of El Al and the government in foreign countries. In 1968, the P.F.L.P. attacked an El Al plane on the ground in Athens Airport. Two days later, the Israelis sent a commando unit to destroy fourteen Arab planes on the ground at Beirut Airport, where the P.F.L.P. had its headquarters. Nonetheless, the hijackings continued. There were five in August 1970; innocent passengers were held for ransom in Switzerland, Germany, and Britain.

I: THE REFUSENIKS

In the meanwhile, growing numbers of Russian Jews went to the visa offices in the Soviet Union to ask for permits to leave Russia in order to go on *aliyah* to Israel. At the end of 1970, a family of Refuseniks (the name given to those who were refused exit visas) was put on trial in Leningrad for trying to hijack a Russian plane to fly them to Israel. News of this proved to the Jews of Israel and the West just how desperate the Soviet Jews were becoming. During the trial, Israelis held mass demonstrations at the Western Wall to show solidarity with the Refuseniks.

In 1971, suddenly and without explanation, the Russians allowed a mass emigration of Jews. It was the beginning of a new *aliyah:* 13,000 came in 1971; 31,500 in 1972; 32,920 in 1973. This flow of immigration continued until the end of the 1970s when, again without explanation, it slowed down to a trickle and the problem of Refuseniks once again became serious.

Through the years, the Russian Communist

Heavy damage at a Kibbutz Masada chemical storage shed hit by a "Long Tom" shell from Jordanian positions.

government continued to arrest, try, and imprison many of the leaders of Soviet Jewry. Some, like Anatoly Shcharansky, have spent most of their lives in prison camps in Siberia or prisons in the major cities. Shcharansky's hunger-strike brought international attention to the tragedy of these Refusenik leaders.

II: THE TERRORISTS

The *fedayin* and the *Al-Fatah* members living in Jordan became difficult to control, and King Hussein of Jordan soon felt they were challenging his power. He struck suddenly, forcing the terrorists to fight back in what became a civil war in Jordan. While the war continued, the terrorist raids into Israel nearly stopped. The Israelis began to feel sure that the Arabs, fighting amongst themselves, would become weaker,

perhaps even too weak to threaten Israel. In July of 1971, Hussein succeeded in forcing the terrorists out of Jordan. But, though the situation shifted, it did not change greatly. The terrorists took control of Lebanon and set up their camps to the north of Israel.

Terrorist attacks continued, especially from a new group called Black September. Letter bombs, assassinations, and kidnapings occurred in Europe against Israelis and against Russian Jews traveling to resettle in Israel. In these attacks, 116 people were killed and 102 injured. Israel struck back at terrorist bases deep in Lebanon.

III: NEW GOVERNMENTS

In Egypt, Abdel Nasser died and was replaced by Anwar Sadat. Sadat continued to talk of war against Israel, but the firing along the Suez Canal stopped and, by the early 1970s, the Israelis were feeling certain that Sadat had given up as too dangerous the idea of making war.

In the meanwhile, Levi Eshkol was replaced by a new prime minister, Golda Meir (see chapter twenty). This soft-spoken grandmother had a will of iron. She was a long-time member of the Mapai party, and in 1969 she managed to bring all the labor parties of Israel together in a new coalition which won 55 seats in the Knesset. It was not enough for a clear majority, but, with the addition of a few non-labor ministers, she organized a new cabinet and took over the country's leadership. At the end of 1972, Meir learned that the Egyptian troops were massing along the Suez Canal. She called up Israel's troops and secretly invited Sadat to a peace conference. Weeks passed quietly, and finally she allowed the troops to go home. Her defense minister, Moshe Dayan, even announced that the government was thinking about shortening the length of military service in Israel. "Three years is a very long term to serve," Dayan said, "in a time of tranquillity."

The government spoke more often about the

Golda Meir.

chances for peace. Only one general spoke out, reminding the Israeli public that Russia was sending new weapons to Egypt, Syria, and Jordan.

IV: THE YOM KIPPUR WAR

The Arab countries took Israel by surprise. On Saturday, October 6, 1973, at 2 p.m., the Egyptian and Syrian armies attacked. It was Yom Kippur, the Sabbath of Sabbaths, the holiest day of the Jewish year. Israel had little warning. News that the attack was about to begin reached Golda Meir at 4 a.m. that morning. The army was first called up at 10 a.m. Actually, it was very fortunate for Israel that the Arabs had chosen to strike on this holy day, for almost all of the Jewish soldiers could be found either in the synagogue or at home. On any other day, it might have taken many more hours to assemble all the troops.

Even so, Israel had lost the chance to strike first, as had been the case in former wars. It took several days for Israel to gain the advantage; during these days there were heavy losses to the armed forces. The Syrians seized Mount Hermon and the Golan Heights, and it was not until October 22 that Mount Hermon was recaptured by the Israelis. The Egyptians crossed the Suez Canal and it was not until October 19 that the Israelis were able to cross to the western side of

The Yom Kippur War, October 1973.

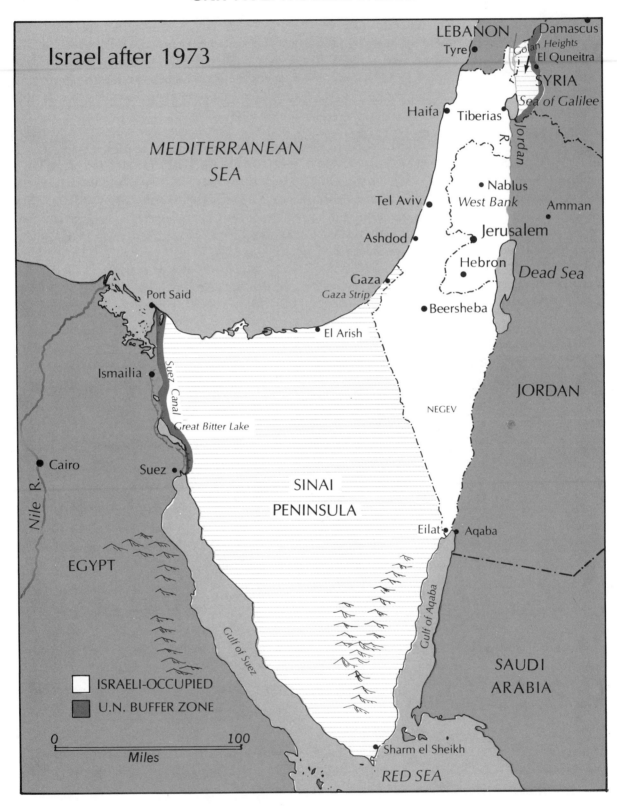

Israel after 1973

LEBANON
Damascus
Tyre
Golan Heights
El Quneitra
SYRIA

MEDITERRANEAN
SEA

Haifa
Tiberias
Sea of Galilee

Jordan R.

Nablus
Tel Aviv
West Bank
Amman

Ashdod
Jerusalem

Gaza
Hebron
Dead Sea
Gaza Strip

Beersheba

Port Said
El Arish

Ismailia
Suez Canal

Great Bitter Lake

NEGEV

JORDAN

Cairo

Nile R.
Suez

SINAI
PENINSULA

Eilat
Aqaba

EGYPT
Gulf of Suez
Gulf of Aqaba

SAUDI
ARABIA

ISRAELI-OCCUPIED
U.N. BUFFER ZONE

0   100
Miles

Sharm el Sheikh
RED SEA

THE YOM KIPPUR WAR

the canal to threaten Cairo, and not until October 24 that Israel was able to take the entire canal.

In the northern battle, the Syrians lost almost their entire air force and nearly 1,100 tanks, some the latest Russian models. In all, 3,500 Syrian soldiers had been killed and another 370 taken as prisoners.

In the battle with Egypt, Israel destroyed 1,000 Egyptian tanks and took nearly 8,000 prisoners.

The Israeli navy was very successful. Equipped with Israeli-built missiles, the navy managed to destroy the Syrian navy and part of the Egyptian fleet. Israel gained control in both the Mediterranean Sea and the Red Sea. It was the first time in history that naval battles were fought with missiles.

Compared with the Egyptian losses of 15,000 soldiers, Israel suffered the loss of only 2,522 soldiers. But even this number was too many. There was hardly a family in the entire State of Israel that had not suffered a loss—sons, daughters, fathers, mothers, uncles, aunts, cousins, friends, neighbors, companions, acquaintances. People sat and wept in the streets as they read the lists of those who died in the fighting.

Naturally, many blamed the government for being blind to the Arab threats. News that Golda Meir and Moshe Dayan had been warned in advance but had not acted by calling up the military in time brought loud protests and even a demand that both resign.

In the Six Day War, the world had sympathized with Israel and hoped for Israel's victory.

Israelis weeping in the streets over their casualties.

This time, Israel was strangely alone. The Arabs used their greatest weapon to control world public opinion—oil. They began an embargo by not shipping oil, a move that caught the major countries of the world by surprise. European nations and almost all the black African nations took the Arab side to avoid losing their oil shipments. All the good that Israel had done for the new states of black Africa was set aside as one nation after another cut off all contact with Israel.

Israel was scarred deeply, not just by the loss of many of its citizens, but by the economic losses caused by the war itself. Huge amounts of money were needed to pay the soldiers, to help them support their families, to save factories that lost nearly all their workers during the war, and to save businesses that had been temporarily abandoned in order that owners and employees could fight. The Israeli public was asked to take cuts in pay and to allow for a national loan of one billion Israeli pounds. Once again, world Jewry, especially the Jews of North America agreed to help, promising twenty billion dollars to aid in Israel's recovery.

But for the first time, through the efforts largely of the United States secretary of state, Dr. Henry Kissinger, a German-born Jew, peace talks began between Israel and Egypt. The early talks led to Israel's exchange of 8,000 Egyptian prisoners for 240 Israelis who had fallen into Egyptian hands.

The Yom Kippur War was the hardest and longest that Israel had fought since 1948. It was the costliest, too. The government agreed to allow a committee to inquire about the responsibility for the heavy losses, and both Golda Meir and Moshe Dayan were called to answer. In the end, both were declared innocent, but the weight of public opinion was against them and, in 1974, Golda Meir resigned.

In the new government, Mapai was still the strongest party, though the number of votes cast for it was lower than before. When Yitzhak Rabin was chosen as the new prime minister, he brought together a new coalition cabinet; but it was a weaker coalition than ever before.

Yitzhak Rabin.

At long last, in 1977, after trying eight times before to win the government, Menachem Begin, founder and leader of Cherut, was invited to become the prime minister of Israel, heading the Likud coalition party. For Begin, who had waited so long, it was a moment of personal triumph. The man who had been defeated so many times by David Ben-Gurion (who had died in 1973) had his victory, at last.

PREVIEW

Menachem Begin would remain in power for six years, until his resignation in 1983. Under his leadership, Israel would see major changes in policy and in action. Begin was now the old man of Israeli politics, beloved especially by the Oriental Jews and even by many of the religious parties.

And, ironically, it would be Menachem Begin

THE YOM KIPPUR WAR

Menachem Begin.

Most American Jews—and Jews throughout the world—were in their synagogues on the Yom Kippur day when the Arab nations attacked Israel in 1973. Many rabbis stopped the regular services to insert a special prayer. If you were a rabbi, what prayer would you have offered that day? Try writing a prayer in your own words that you might have spoken on that occasion.

The "war of attrition" in the years following the Six Day War and before the Yom Kippur War interrupted the daily life of many Israelis, especially those who lived along the borders. In those days, many schoolchildren on the border kibbutzim and in border villages spent whole days and nights in air raid shelters, while artillery shells struck and exploded all around them. Yet their school lessons went on, even inside the shelters. What part of the Covenant list that you have made was being enacted by the teachers along Israel's borders?

What kind of leader was Golda Meir? To find out more about the life story of this extraordinary woman, look up her biography in a Jewish encyclopedia.

who would finally sit at the peace table to sign Israel's first peace agreement with one of its Arab neighbors.

THE FIRST PEACE AGREEMENT

In 1977, President Anwar Sadat agreed to come to Israel to speak publicly to the Israeli Knesset. It was a historic moment—the first time any Arab leader had entered Israel in peace. It led to Israeli visits in Cairo and further talks between the two countries. The greatest sign of hope, however, was the fact that Sadat himself had begun the discussions, willing to take the first step.

A year and a half later, President Jimmy Carter of the United States invited both Sadat and Begin to discuss a treaty of peace. The historic meeting took place at the U.S. presi-dent's retreat near Washington, D.C., Camp David. In the privacy of Camp David the three leaders discussed the problems of the Middle East face to face. All agreed that the time had come for reason and wisdom to replace weapons and hostility.

The agreement they reached was called the Camp David Accords. It did not settle the burning questions entirely—there remained the problems of the territory Israel held, the Arab refugees (now called the "Palestinians"), and the fact that other Arab states refused to take part in the meeting. But all three leaders saw it as a

The Camp David Accords. The historic meeting and peace treaty signing by Egyptian President Anwar Sadat (left), Israel Prime Minister Menachem Begin (right), and American President Jimmy Carter at Camp David.

beginning, a chance for peace to develop in the war-torn countries of the Arabs and the Jews.

Israel agreed to leave the Sinai Desert and return it to the Egyptians. Egypt agreed to keep the Straits of Tiran and the Suez Canal open. Both agreed to go on talking. Israel also agreed to allow the Arabs of the West Bank and Gaza to be "autonomous," that is, to govern themselves.

As the treaty of peace was signed by Carter, Begin, and Sadat, the Jews of the world watched their television screens. Americans watched. Arabs watched. Carter (a Christian) had succeeded in bringing together Sadat (a Moslem) and Begin (a Jew). It seemed almost too good to be true. Perhaps it was. Other Arab nations called Sadat a traitor, and, soon after the Accords were signed, he was assassinated by Arab extremists.

Begin also seemed to forget the promises of Camp David—or, to put it another way, he read the words differently. The Accords called for "full autonomy" for the Palestinian Arabs, but Begin and his government continued to rule the West Bank. The government also continued to encourage and allow new Jewish settlements on the West Bank.

The effect of this was already seen in the Sinai, where Begin had allowed large Jewish settlements to grow in the years of Israel's rule. When he agreed to give back the Sinai to Egypt, he was agreeing to give up these Jewish settlements. He waited to the very last minute before asking the Jews to leave the city of Yamit in Sinai; and, after the settlers were forced to leave, he ordered the town destroyed before returning it to the Egyptians. Could the Egyptians possibly see this as the act of a friend? Would this hurt the good work done by the Israelis in the West Bank and in Gaza?

To the end of his term in office, Begin and his party continued to see the West Bank as a part of the "full Israel." This had always been the view of the Revisionists (see in Unit Four "Freedom Fighters"), whose slogan was "Both banks of the River Jordan," meaning that the Jewish state should occupy all of what had once belonged to the Jews. The Begin government refused to call this occupied area the "West Bank" because this name meant that it was really a part of Jordan. Instead, they referred to it as "Judea" and "Samaria," using older, biblical names that seemed to attach it to the Jews. In this, the government was supported by many of the religious parties which also wished to keep the West Bank as Israeli territory forever. But how could Begin promise "autonomy" and "legitimate rights" to the Palestinians at Camp David and still control the West Bank? This question remained unanswered, even as Begin resigned in 1983.

Camp David was a beginning for the peace process. But the many open sores still kept the other Arab nations from being friends with Israel. Moreover, they isolated Egypt, shunning it because it had gone to the peace table. By the early 1980s, Egypt seemed more to want to rejoin the other Arab nations than to continue the peace process with Israel. Nevertheless, Israel and Egypt now live on friendlier terms, proving that it is possible for the Arabs and the Jews to share the Middle East. Camp David was, indeed, a turning point.

25

ISRAEL AND THE PALESTINIANS

The last two chapters told of the official wars between Israel and its Arab neighbors. To tell of the unofficial war between Israel and the Palestinians, it is necessary to turn back the clock.

One day in May 1972, three Japanese travelers got off a plane in Israel's Lydda airport, picked up their luggage, took machine guns and hand grenades from their suitcases, and murdered twenty-six people, wounding another seventy-two before they could be stopped. They were members of a Japanese terrorist organization, the Red Army. They were just "helping out" their friends, the Palestinian terrorists.

International terrorism was a serious danger to all the nations of the free world. Yet only the Arab nations and Israel took strong measures to stop it. The Jordanians drove the Palestinians northward out of their country beginning in September of 1970 (this was the "black" September from which one terrorist group took its name). The Israelis put an end to most terrorist raids coming from Lebanon by setting up a two-mile wide demilitarized zone along the Lebanese-Israeli border and patrolling it constantly.

Border patrols on all Israel's boundary lines, as well as searches and arrests of Arabs possessing weapons or explosives in the occupied West Bank and Gaza, brought a measure of safety to the Jews in Israel. But it did not bring safety to Israelis traveling outside of Israel, or to Jews throughout the world. Nor was terrorism just an Arab or Israeli problem.

In one case, terrorists hijacked four planes—two American, one Swiss, and one British—flying them to a landing strip in the Jordan's desert. Here, they held 310 passengers and crew captive, threatening to kill them. The terrorists demanded the release of some hijackers who had been captured and imprisoned in Europe. The governments of Europe freed the hijackers, and the prisoners were released.

This was blackmail and the lesson the terrorists learned was that blackmail worked. Lufthansa, the West German airline, made regular payments for some years to the Palestinian terrorists who promised in return not to hijack Lufthansa planes. The French government secretly agreed not to give political support to Israel as long as French planes were not hijacked.

In 1972, Palestinian terrorists invaded the site of the Olympic Games in Munich and took eleven Israeli athletes hostage. News of the capture, the strange conversations between the police and the terrorists, and the final murder of the eleven Israelis were broadcast by satellite to the far corners of the earth. When it was over, the rest of the Israeli Olympic team went home, heartbroken and in mourning. The Olympics, however, went on almost as if nothing had happened. Didn't the world care?

Israel alone stood up to the terrorists, refusing to negotiate with them, refusing to give in to blackmail. In 1976, Palestinian terrorists hi-

A school bus attacked by P.L.O. bazookas, Israel-Lebanon border.

jacked a plane on its way from Israel to Greece. This time, most of the passengers were Jews and Israelis. The terrorists flew the plane to Uganda, where the government led by Idi Amin, not only allowed them to land, but joined in their blackmail scheme. Amin and the terrorists announced they would kill the hostages unless Israel and other nations gave them millions of dollars and released more terrorists from prison. Israel pretended to negotiate, buying time.

Suddenly, some 2,500 miles from home, Israeli planes landed in Uganda's Entebbe Airport. A lightning fast surprise attack by Israeli commando troops resulted in the death of most of the terrorists and the Ugandan soldiers guarding them and the rescue of more than one hundred hostages. This daring rescue gave new hope to the Israelis, in part because it showed the other nations of the world that it was possible to defeat terrorism without giving in to terrorist demands.

I: THE P.L.O.

Hijacking and assassination were only part of the Palestinian program which also included organization, influence, and propaganda. The many small groups of terrorists joined together as the Palestine Liberation Organization (P.L.O.) and issued a "Palestinian National Covenant," which called for the world to accept the rights of Palestinians and for the destruction of Israel.

The Arab nations, at their summit meetings, declared this new organization "the sole representative of the Palestinian people." Yassir Arafat became the new leader of the Palestinians. Wearing his *kaffiyeh* (Arab headdress) and sunglasses, he became a popular figure first in Arab newspapers and then for reporters around the world.

Arafat promised to create a new Palestinian state where the "Zionist invaders" now had the "illegal" State of Israel. In his new state, Arafat declared, there would be room for all Jews who lived in Palestine, as the P.L.O. called it, "before the Zionist invasion" (that is, before the State of Israel was declared). In the old days, Arab leaders spoke mainly of the "plight of the Arab refugees." Arafat concentrated on the "rights of the Palestinians." Parts of Lebanon now were called "Fatahland." By 1975, the P.L.O. was officially accepted by more than a hundred governments—not all of them Communist.

Israel took a firm stand in this political game.

It would not negotiate with the terrorists in any peace conferences, just as it would not negotiate with them when it came to blackmail or ransom. The Jews of America spoke of Arafat as a "murderer of women and children," hoping to turn world opinion away from the Palestinians. This did not work. The world was seriously concerned, even as most Israelis were, about the problem of the homeless Arab refugees. In November 1974, Arafat was welcomed to the United Nations General Assembly to speak on behalf of the Palestinians. This time, Arafat made a blunder in judgment, for he appeared

Yassir Arafat, P.L.O. leader, at the United Nations General Assembly.

before the assembly with a pistol strapped in a holster at his side. How could anyone believe this man came in peace. Before this visit to the UN, many groups in America—especially journalists and students—supported Arafat, believing he was leading a moderate, peaceful movement toward creating a state for the Arab refugees. But Arafat, in his speech, made it clear that he wanted all of Palestine for his people and that the State of Israel would have to be dismantled or destroyed. Many who placed their hopes for a settlement on Arafat and the P.L.O. now understood that he was not to be trusted as a peacemaker.

Something else could be seen after Arafat's appearance in the UN. The United Nations itself had changed greatly. Many of the smaller nations were willing to support Arafat in exchange for the material support of the oil-rich Arab nations. In fact, in 1975, the UN passed a resolution stating that Zionism is a kind of "racism." Jews everywhere were shocked by this statement. They never believed that Zionism was aimed at harming the Arabs in any way. It was a movement to create a Jewish state; that, and nothing more. Many Jews who had been among the greatest supporters of the UN now turned their backs on it, calling it "morally bankrupt."

That same year, the Arab nations in the UN asked for the international organization to remove Israel entirely from the United Nations. Only the strong opposition of the United States kept this from happening. The Israelis, for their part, no longer trusted the United Nations at all.

Demonstration in Haifa against the UN resolution equating Zionism with racism.

In time, the UN proved itself less and less a friend to Israel, more and more a puppet of Russia, the Soviet bloc of nations, and of the Arab countries. In 1983, the UN even held an international conference on the question of Palestinian rights. The United States and Israel refused to attend this conference.

The conference itself was a great failure, but it pointed again to the fact that the United Nations had become a political ballpark in which Israel always began the inning with three outs against it.

II: ARABS IN THE OCCUPIED TERRITORIES

Clearly the chances for peace between Israel and the Arab countries are tied at least in part to the problem of the Palestinians, and the problem of the Palestinians is tied to the West Bank and the Gaza Strip. Nearly all Israelis say that returning to the pre-1967 borders of Israel is too dangerous. The West Bank and Gaza can easily return to being a base of operations for terrorist raids against Israel, or a base for invasion forces coming from Jordan and the south. The Russians, who already have installed rocket launchers in Syria, Egypt, and Lebanon, could easily install such rockets in Gaza and the West Bank, both of which are far closer to Tel Aviv, Beersheba, and Jerusalem. And there is even the possibility that, if Israel left these two regions, the Russians might be invited to install whole military bases there. Those are the dangers that worry many Israelis.

But there may be dangers in Israel's holding on

Dera'a emergency camp in southern Syria, part of the United Nations Relief and Works Agency for Palestine refugees.

The West Bank.

to these territories, too. For example, the Arab population in these areas is already growing at a much faster rate than the Jewish population in Israel. At present, throughout the country, there are five Israelis for every three Arabs, but, if the Arab birthrate continues to grow and new Arabs enter the West Bank and Gaza, the shift in population could be dangerous for Israel's political future. The Jewish state might soon become a Jewish-Arab state. If that happened, the Palestinian program of creating a "secular, democratic Palestinian state" could become a reality without any fighting at all.

To keep this from happening, the Jews of Israel may be forced at some point to give up the democratic principle of "one person, one vote." They would have to take the right of voting away, not just from the Arabs of the West Bank and Gaza, but probably from all Arabs in Israel. The Jewish state would no longer be a democracy, and the Arabs of Israel would surely rise up against it.

Meanwhile, Israel's government has been allowing and even encouraging new Jewish settlements and towns to grow up in the West Bank.

Most of these were established by the Orthodox religious groups who hold to the idea of the "full Israel." These settlers will not be easily removed from their new homes. Indeed, a good number of Israelis who are not Orthodox agree with the argument made by the religious settlers that these villages and towns are needed for the defense of the West Bank if Israel should ever fight there again. Other Israelis are convinced that such a policy makes peace all but impossible and that in the event of another war the defense of these settlements would weaken, not strengthen, Israel's total effort.

This is a dilemma. On the one hand, it is dangerous for Israel to continue to hold the West Bank and Gaza. On the other hand, it is dangerous for Israel to allow them to become a Palestinian state, or to return them to Jordan and Egypt.

The only workable solution proposed has been the so-called "Jordanian option." The West Bank Arabs need to meet and trade with their Arab neighbors, so an agreement between Israel and Jordan, allowing Jordan a hand in ruling the West Bank, might be the key to some kind of peaceful solution. Israel would still have to keep soldiers around the borders of the West Bank, even with this plan. But that is not the only problem. What would happen to the Jewish settlements in this case? Would they be dismantled by military force as was the settlement of Yamit in the Sinai before the Egyptians returned?

Another possibility is that Israel could allow the West Bank to become a Palestinian state, independent of Jordan. In this case, Israel would just have to face the dangers that such a state might pose. Even so, the Palestinians in the past have felt that the West Bank was just not enough for them. Would they now agree to accept only that much of the Middle East for their state?

PREVIEW

Israel's problems are the problems of world Jewry, as well. The Jewish state is precious to all of us, whether we live in Israel or remain in the Diaspora. The Palestinian problem, as we shall see, is just one of the issues that we face in the years ahead. Whatever wisdom we bring to it, we shall have to look to the past as well as to the present for guidance. We will have to draw strength from the Torah and the Covenant. At least one piece of advice stands out clearly:

הַקָּהָל חֻקָּה אַחַת לָכֶם וְלַגֵּר הַגֵּר חֻקַּת עוֹלָם לְדֹרֹתֵיכֶם כָּכֶם כַּגֵּר יִהְיֶה לִפְנֵי יְהֹוָה: תּוֹרָה אַחַת וּמִשְׁפָּט אֶחָד יִהְיֶה לָכֶם וְלַגֵּר הַגֵּר אִתְּכֶם:

. . . There shall be one law for you and for the resident stranger; it shall be a law for all time throughout the ages. You and the stranger shall be alike before the Lord; the same ritual and the same rule shall apply to you and to the stranger who resides among you. (Numbers 15:15–16)

Things to Consider

In many ways, it was because of the Covenant that Israel decided never to make deals with terrorists and not to deal directly with the P.L.O. in any peace settlements. On the other hand, Israel also wanted to live in peace with its Arab neighbors. Is the idea of *shalom,* "peace," a part of your Covenant definition? Should it be?

Imagine that you are a peacemaker for the State of Israel, sitting down to talk with Arab peacemakers from Jordan, Syria, and Egypt. Would you be willing to divide Jerusalem again—giving half back to Jordan and keeping half for Israel? Why? Why not?

The chapter closes with a quotation from the Torah regarding the rights of strangers who live among the Jewish people in the Land of Israel. Now that the territories of Gaza and the West Bank are occupied by Israel, the Arabs living there are "resident strangers." Divide a piece of paper into two halves with a line down the center. On one side, list those rights which you think Israel can give to the "resident strangers." On the other side, list those rights which you think cannot be given to the "resident strangers." Do you think, as the Torah recommends, that there can be one set of laws for all peoples—Arabs, Jews, and Christians—in Israel today?

26

THE WAR IN LEBANON

In 1970, the Jordanians drove the Palestinian terrorists out of Jordan. A few years later, the Syrians, who also learned that the terrorists could not be controlled, drove them out of Syria. The Palestinians then moved into Lebanon.

Up to that time, Lebanon had been a nation walking a tightrope. It was made up of both Arab Moslems and Arab Christians; there was a carefully constructed balance in the government which had kept Lebanon one of the most peaceful and stable countries in the Arab world. In 1975, when the Palestinian terrorists upset that balance, a civil war broke out in Lebanon. The war-torn country fell mainly into the hands of the Palestinians who treated the Lebanese cruelly.

The terrorists also opened up camps along the Israel-Lebanon border and raided Israel from these camps. When the Israelis put an end to the raiding by patrolling a two-mile wide no-man's land along the border, the Lebanese government did not complain. They were somewhat pleased to see the Israelis putting an end, even temporarily, to the terrorist campaigns. But the P.L.O. received new weapons from Russia—Katushya rockets—with which they bombarded the villages in the north of Israel, forcing the villagers to live in bomb shelters much of the time and bringing tourism to a halt in the north.

I: THE WAR BEGINS

In June 1982, after the attempted assassination of an Israeli diplomat in London, Israel attacked the P.L.O. in Lebanon. The war began as a limited action. The Israeli government announced that it would send the army only part way (40 or 50 kilometers) into Lebanon—just far enough to clear away the rocket launchers and military bases. The rockets, especially, were a serious threat to Israel, even though the Palestinians had been using them less in 1981–1982 than before. No one in Israel doubted the worth of removing these rockets, no matter what the risk taken by Israeli soldiers, particularly because this first part of the war was quickly completed.

Israel was shocked by what was discovered in southern Lebanon. The army captured huge stockpiles of Russia's most advanced weapons and arms. There were surely enough supplies for the P.L.O. terrorists to plan a full-scale invasion of Israel from the north. General Arik Sharon and Prime Minister Begin decided to continue the war, to press further north into Lebanon. They hoped to force the P.L.O. out of Lebanon entirely, to help the Lebanese set up a new government that would be more friendly to Israel, and then to bring the Israeli troops home to a safer state.

It was this decision which was critical. Continuing the war brought the Israeli soldiers into the heavily-populated city of Beirut. The Israelis suffered heavy losses because they were forced to fight hand to hand in the city. Ultimately, the Israelis managed to gain control of Beirut and to corner Arafat and a few of his top officials and staff members. It would have been easy to kill Arafat and the staff of the P.L.O. then and there,

The "Good Fence" at the Israel-Lebanon border.

but the Israelis took a different path, hoping again that it might bring peace. The Israelis chose to force Arafat and all of his fighters to leave Lebanon.

While this second part of the war was being fought, the Syrians joined the conflict in Lebanon's Beka'a Valley, posing a new and greater danger to Israeli troops. Arafat took full advantage of this situation by speaking freely with reporters from the world press and posing as the little David on whom the great Goliath (by which he meant Israel) had chosen to make war. It did not matter whether the people of the world believed what he was saying, the fact was that Israel had made the Lebanese nation into a battlefield, and Israel's presence had made it possible for Syria to attack with the excuse that it was coming to "save" the Lebanese people.

The P.L.O. forces were damaged greatly by Israel's army, but the P.L.O. continued to claim that it was the single voice for the Palestinians. And, in their moment of crisis, the Palestinians turned for help to the most extreme of all Arab leaders, Colonel Qaddafi, the dictator of Libya. With his help, Arafat kept control of the P.L.O. and, as the days of Israeli occupation wore on, even managed to return the Palestinians to northern Lebanon—until he and those loyal to him were forced out by a rival group of Palestinians in 1983.

The Israelis were forced to pull back out of

Beirut to southern Lebanon as it became clear that the Lebanese could not agree on a unified government and fighting broke out between the various religious and political groups of Lebanon's Arab population. Even greater damage was done to Israel's image in the world when the Israeli army allowed a group of Christian Lebanese to enter the refugee camps of Sabra and Shatila near Beirut, resulting in the massacre of Palestinian civilians. Israelis demanded to know who was responsible, and, less than a month later, a special commission was set up to investigate what happened at Sabra and Shatila. The whole world watched, expecting that the Israelis would lay the blame entirely on the Lebanese Christians who had actually committed the murders. But the commission's report did not excuse Israel's leaders. Minister of Defense Arik Sharon and two army generals were forced to resign when the report was released. Israel proved to the world—and what was more important, to itself—that the nation respected morality and treasured its honesty. A mature nation, Israel took responsibility for its mistakes.

In this war, Israel showed the might of its armies, but it also showed a lack of ability to forcibly alter conditions in the Arab world. The occupation dragged on. Peacekeeping forces

Concrete wall facing the Syrian border, protecting a kibbutz dining room. The Syrian border is approximately 200 yards away from Kibbutz Shaniv, at the top of a hill.

from the United States and other countries arrived; they too were dragged into the conflict. In surprise terrorist bomb attacks, the U.S. Marines and the French army suffered heavy losses. They were forced to fire back, damaging their image as peacekeepers.

At the same time, the new Lebanese government seemed to grow weaker and the danger posed by the Syrians grew stronger. Israel was forced to do something which it had never done before, which it was not really equipped to do—it had to continue occupying the south of Lebanon for a great length of time.

For some armies, occupation of land is not a major problem. Soldiers are stationed. Temporary or permanent forts are set up. Artillery is put into place. But Israel's army is made up of citizens—even its officers come to battle by leaving civilian jobs. So keeping an Israeli army in place outside Israel for any length of time means that vital industries lose many people from the work force, putting a strain on the already weak economy.

Many in Israel began to question the war as soon as it entered the second phase. They continued questioning and protesting it for some time. Yet they agreed that it would be too dangerous for Israel to just pull out its forces. Syria, armed heavily by the Russians, and perhaps even directed by the Russians, had moved into place, ready to take over whatever parts of Lebanon it could. And Syria was the most dangerous of Israel's Arab neighbors. So the Israeli armies were forced to remain, hoping as the United States hoped, that the new Lebanese government could soon unite its people and control its own country.

II: THE WAR IN LEBANON AND WORLD JEWRY

The war sparked a series of anti-Semitic attacks in unexpected places like Los Angeles and New York—and some very brutal ones in Europe. These were planned and carried out by terrorists.

But there was little sympathy for the Jews in the world press. Israel was portrayed as a warlike country in a way that it had never been before. Repeatedly, it was pointed out that Israel *started* this war.

The Israelis answered that Lebanon before the war had been a nest for terrorist activities and that the P.L.O. had been cruel rulers, oppressing the Lebanese and very nearly enslaving them in their own country.

The real question brought home by the war in Lebanon was the moral question: Did Israel have the right to take lives before it was actually forced to do so? On the positive side, it could be argued that removing the terrorist P.L.O. from Lebanon meant saving the lives of Israelis. On the other side, it could be argued that the war should only have been fought if real change was possible. But, of course, no one could tell in advance what was and what was not possible. As it turned out, the situation in Lebanon was more complex than anyone could have predicted.

In the midst of the crisis, Menachem Begin resigned as prime minister in 1983 for personal reasons. Yitzhak Shamir, a long-time supporter and follower of Begin, became the new prime minister, inheriting the problems of ending the war and the problems of what to do about the West Bank and Gaza. But Begin's party, the Likud, had lost only some of its popularity in Israel, as the 1984 elections showed.

PREVIEW

The Covenant of Isreal has been given many meanings throughout Jewish history. You have seen it grow and change, as you have studied the history of our people in its Land. One thing, however, is sure: the Covenant is not just a gift of the Land of Israel to the Jewish people, it also requires our people to act justly and to become a "light to the nations." As the Lebanese crisis continued, the world watched and waited. Could Israel find a way to be both a secure and Jewish state?

UNIT FIVE: The State of Israel

Things to Consider

As this book is being written, the war in Lebanon is still not over. Yet, things change rapidly in the world. What is happening in Lebanon as you are reading this book? What part is the P.L.O. playing now?

In his years as prime minister and as the leader of the Jewish state until his death in 1973, Ben-Gurion stressed the importance to Israel of acting morally. The report issued after the massacres at Sabra and Shatila showed that Israel was truly acting according to the Torah's laws of morality. But many people believe that Israel should not be "more moral" than any other nation. On which side are you? Should Israel behave just like all the other nations of the world? Should it be more concerned with justice than any other nation? Why? In what ways?

What do you think about the question raised after the war in Lebanon? Did Israel have the right to start that war? Does a nation always have a right to protect its citizens against attack?

UNIT SIX

Judaism and the Jewish State

27

RELIGION IN ISRAEL

Many visitors to the Holy Land, expecting to find a place where religion is paramount, are confused by what they see. On holidays like Sukot, Pesach, Chanukah, and Shabbat, more Israelis can be found driving to the seashore, drinking tea and espresso coffee at the open air cafes, and relaxing than in the synagogues praying.

In part, this is because Israel's weekends and holidays are short. The working week in Israel begins on *Yom Rishon,* the "first day" or Sunday, and ends on *Yom Shishi,* the "sixth day" or Friday. Jews take only Shabbat as their weekend rest. And, in Israel, according to Jewish law, the major holy days (except Rosh Hashanah) are celebrated for only one day, even by the Orthodox. So the number of days off from work are few. True, they are all *Jewish* holidays (the minority religions are permitted to rest on their holy days, also, but these are not national holidays, and Jews do not observe them.)

Those willing to devote their *only* days of relaxation to religion do so because religion is very important to them. But they are a minority because the Orthodox Judaism familiar to most Israelis is not very attractive to them. In many ways, it has become more difficult to be a committed and religiously sincere Jew in Israel than in the rest of the world.

I: ORTHODOXY AND ZIONISM

Theodor Herzl, in his book *The Jewish State,* called for the separation of religion and politics in his dream of what Zion should be like. "We shall keep our rabbis in their synagogues," he wrote, "just as we shall keep our army in their camps." But, when it came to organizing the Zionist movement, Herzl found that the observant Jews of Eastern Europe supported and gave strength to it. So, at the Second Zionist Congress in 1898, he tied his political goal—the creation of a Jewish state—to their religious goal—to create a spiritual center for Judaism in the Holy Land.

Even so, most Orthodox Jews and nearly all their leaders and rabbis rejected Zionism entirely, saying that the messiah alone could lead the Jews back to Israel; human beings should not try to play God. Today, in Israel and in the Diaspora, small groups of extreme Orthodox Jews refuse to support the modern State of Israel and continue to act as if it did not exist!

Yet, some Orthodox Jews from Eastern Europe did join the Zionist movement. In 1902, they set up their own party in the World Zionist Congress, naming it Mizrachi, an abbreviation of *Mercaz Ruchani* ("Spiritual Center"). The Mizrachi party motto was "The Land of Israel for the people of Israel, according to the Law of Israel." They dreamed of a Land where the laws of the Torah would be the laws of the government. They sent settlers to Israel in the many *aliyot,* setting up businesses, kibbutzim, a Mizrachi newspaper, and a religious school system for their children. In doing so, they found that many of the Orthodox Jews of the old Yishuv were opposed to them.

225

Praying at the Western Wall. Religion plays an important role in the lives of many Orthodox Jews.

II: THE DATI ESTABLISHMENT

A part of all taxes paid by Israelis—religious or not—is set aside for the official religious groups of Israel. This money goes to pay salaries of officials among the Moslems, the Christians (except for some Protestant groups), the Druze, and the Orthodox Jews. So the separation between religion and state that Herzl hoped for has not come to pass in Israel. And this has caused problems resulting in arguments between *dati'im* and other Jews in Israel.

To be legal, a marriage must be performed by an Orthodox rabbi. But Orthodox law does not allow marriages between Kohanim (descendants of the priestly line of Judaism) and divorced women. Nor does it allow marriages between those born of non-Jewish mothers and born Jews. Moreover, children born of such marriages are not allowed to be buried in a Jewish cemetery. This means that even the nonreligious labor

(Above) A devout Jew kissing the tombstone of Shimon Bar Yohai, Meron, on the holiday of Lag Ba'omer.
(Below) Orthodox Jews lighting candles at the tomb of King David, Jerusalem.

When the State of Israel was declared, all citizens were granted freedom of religion. No one outside the circle of the very Orthodox even considered the idea that the laws of the Torah should be the laws of the new state; yet the religious parties still think that this is the ideal; they still try to change Israeli laws to make them conform to Orthodoxy. And they have managed to gain some of their political goals. In 1953, for instance, the Knesset voted that all marriages and divorces in Israel were to be ruled over by the *bet din,* Israel's religious court.

The Orthodox of the old Yishuv continue to live apart from the rest of Israelis to this day, but the newer modern Orthodox Israelis, calling themselves *dati* or "religious," belong to Israel's several religious political parties. (Though many of the *dati'im* have joined labor parties or other political parties to meet other needs they feel are important.)

227

and socialist kibbutzim must bring in Orthodox rabbis to make their marriages official under Jewish law.

On Shabbat, most shops, theaters, and restaurants are closed and busses and trains do not run, except in Haifa. Women are separated from men in nearly all Israeli synagogues, and the synagogues are very different from what Jews in the Diaspora are used to. There is no synagogue membership, as Diaspora Jews know it. Since almost all Orthodox synagogues receive support from taxes, through their local religious district offices, synagogues are open to anyone. They tend to be small in size, not very well decorated, and have rabbis who are not usually paid by the synagogue but who serve as judges or local, regional, or national religious officers, paid by the state.

Most Israeli rabbis are trained in *yeshivot,* where they study Talmud and Torah but seldom any secular subjects. Almost no rabbis attend regular universities. So they rarely take part in Israel's cultural life, and they generally do not make themselves heard publicly in even spiritual matters. For instance, they do not deliver sermons, nor do they serve their congregations as teachers or visit sick congregants regularly. Neither do they speak out, as rabbis elsewhere do, on the moral issues facing society.

All religious affairs fall under the Ministry of Religion, which divides the tax monies to national, regional, and local religious councils. In addition, there is the religious court, the *bet din,* which makes decisions on all matters of Jewish law and on cases brought to it by Orthodox Jews. Under the British, two rabbis—one Sephardic and one Ashkenazic—were made "chief" rabbis of Israel. They are elected for a term of ten years by the Chief Rabbinical Council. They cannot be reelected. Naturally, having two "chiefs" equal to one another causes serious problems and arguments. They seldom agree, since they come from very different traditions of Jewish law.

When a mother in Great Britain had a baby by artificial insemination, for example, the Sephar-dic chief rabbi said such a procedure was permitted by Jewish law. The Ashkenazic chief rabbi said it was forbidden. The Ashkenazic chief rabbi wants a new army prayer book; the Sephardic does not. The Ashkenazic chief rabbi says it is forbidden for Jews to give back the occupied territories since they were given to Israel as part of the Covenant. The Sephardic chief rabbi says that, by Jewish law, peace is more important than territory, since peace preserves life. The Ashkenazic chief rabbi says it is permitted for Jews to pick and eat capers growing on the Western Wall; the Sephardic chief rabbi says it certainly is not. The debates and arguments go on all the time.

There is a larger issue: Is it really in the spirit of Judaism for there to be "chief" rabbis?

III: WHO IS A JEW?

The Law of Return (see chapter twenty) states that any Jew who wishes to claim Israeli citizenship can do so immediately on arrival in Israel. To put this law into practice, it became necessary for the Israelis to define the word "Jew," and the question of "Who is a Jew?" became a burning issue in the Land of Israel.

The *dati'im* claim that only a person born of a Jewish mother or one converted to Judaism under Orthodox supervision is truly a Jew. But Reform Judaism also includes as Jewish those born to a Jewish father and raised as Jews; both Conservative and Reform rabbis believe that people converted according to Reform and Conservative practices are authentic Jews.

The Orthodox political parties, which have been members of coalition governments, have often threatened to resign and force the rest of the government to resign, if this question is not settled according to Orthodox law.

Nevertheless, two cases decided by the Supreme Court of Israel challenged the Orthodox definition of a Jew, at least insofar as the State of Israel is concerned. One was the case of Brother

Daniel, a Catholic monk who had been born Jewish then converted to Christianity during World War II. He arrived in Israel in 1958 to join his order of monks there, claiming to be a citizen under the Law of Return.

Brother Daniel argued that, since Orthodox Jewish law teaches that conversions do not change one's birthright as a Jew, he was still a Jew under Orthodox law and should be allowed to become a citizen immediately. In 1962, the Supreme Court said that he was not a Jew. He might still receive Israeli citizenship by applying in the normal way allowed to non-Jews, but not under the Law of Return. The Supreme Court said that the interests of the modern State of Israel were more important than the interests of Orthodox Judaism alone. This angered the Orthodox, of course.

In the second case, the Supreme Court ruled in 1968 that children of a mixed marriage (in which the mother was Jewish) were Jewish. This time, the government called on the Knesset to pass a law stating that, for the purposes of the Law of Return, the word Jew means "one born to a Jewish mother or converted to Judaism and not a member of another religion." The Orthodox opposed this ruling, too. It was not what the law said that bothered them, but what it failed to say.

The new law did not say "converted to Judaism *by an Orthodox rabbi*," or *"according to Jewish law."* So, in effect, the law permitted Reform and Conservative converts to become Israeli citizens and be accepted as Jews in Israel. Despite their opposition, the law was passed by the Knesset. The Orthodox political parties continue their efforts to change the Law of Return so that Jews by choice who were converted by non-Orthodox rabbis would not be accepted as authentic Jews. These efforts threaten to destroy Jewish unity throughout the world. The devotion of Orthodox political leaders to *halachah* (Jewish law) is suspect, moreover, because they will not accept conversions at which Reform or Conservative rabbis officiate even when Jewish law is followed faithfully.

The debate rages on. It takes other forms: Who is and who is not a rabbi? Is a Reform rabbi to be allowed to perform marriages in Israel? Should the government support Reform and Conservative congregations as they do Orthodox congregations? Should the Reform and Conservative Jews of Israel be allowed to have their own religious courts, just as the Orthodox do?

It is obvious that the Orthodox establishment would like to be the *only* religious choice for Jews in the Jewish state. Their position stems from the belief that theirs is the only true religious life for Jews. Yet they have failed to attract any great number of Israelis; indeed, many Israelis have felt a very negative attitude toward the high-handed ways of the Orthodox establishment. As long as it seemed the only choice, Israelis mainly shunned Jewish religious life entirely.

Yet one of the great breakthroughs of modern times has been precisely in the area of religious thought and practice. Both Reform and Conservative Judaism provide alternatives to the codes of Jewish law on which Orthodoxy is based. In many ways, Reform and Conservative Judaism are like Pharisaism (see chapter six), since they allow each new generation to take part in the process of creating new meaning for the laws and the Covenant. And, if modern citizens of Israel are to find a religious way of life that is comfortable and positive for them, they are more likely to find it in the Reform and Conservative movements, or in the newer forms of Reconstructionism and Chavurah Judaism.

If Orthodoxy means the refusal to change, as it often seems in Israel, then it can hardly claim to be "true" Judaism. Even the talmudic sages understood the need for constant thinking and rethinking of the meaning of Judaism. In the Talmud, we are told that "no law shall be made which the majority of the community cannot bear." And it is obvious that Orthodox law, as dictated by the Orthodox establishment in Israel, is not by any means practical for the majority of the Jews of Israel.

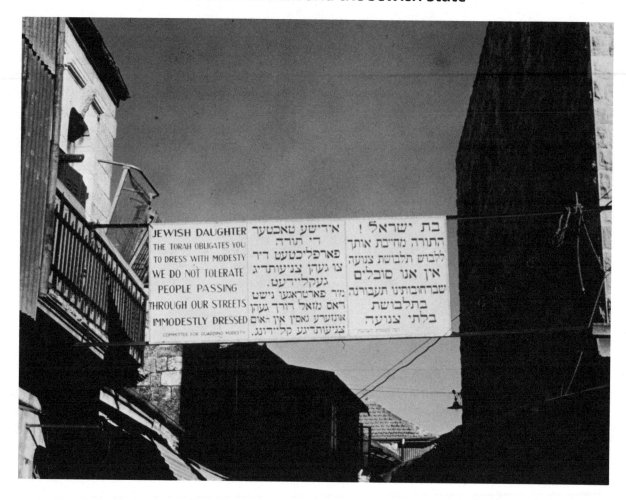

Street sign in the ultra-Orthodox Mea Shearim section of Jerusalem.

IV: CHANGES IN ISRAELI ORTHODOXY

Following the Eichmann trial (see chapter twenty-three) and the Six Day War, when Jerusalem was reunited, many young people in Israel began to think more deeply about their personal religious beliefs. New thinking *dati* Jews founded some fifteen *yeshivot* where young people could study the whole of Judaism—not just the legal concerns of Torah and Talmud—in order to "find themselves" or discover their own meanings for being Jewish.

A few of these *yeshivot* even have special departments for girls and women to attend—something almost unknown in Orthodox religious life in Israel before this. Many students come from regular universities or from high school or the army to study in these new academies for just one year. Because the *yeshivot* are Orthodox, they receive tax monies, but they also seek private contributions in Israel and among the Jews of the Diaspora to support their work. The young people studying there are called *ba'ale teshuvah* or "returnees" to Judaism.

Some of Israel's *dati'im* also feel that the Orthodox establishment has become too radical in its politics. In applying the moral values of

Judaism to political problems, they are voicing opinions different from those of the standard religious parties. Though they are a minority among the Orthodox in Israel, they are opposed to setting up new settlements in the West Bank and they object to the kind of government which the Revisionist Likud party has set up with the help of the Orthodox establishment. Some are even opposed to Israel's presence in Lebanon. More than that, there are voices that object to the division of Oriental and Ashkenazic Jews—a division that has become intensely political in recent years.

These new voices among the Orthodox tend to take Reform and Conservative Judaism more seriously, too. They do not seek the control over all Jews that the Orthodox establishment has tried to maintain. As yet, these new voices are few in number, but the fact that they are being heard at all is important to the future of Judaism as a religion in the State of Israel.

PREVIEW

The future of religion in Israel may take unexpected shape. Not all Jews who have an interest in religion are interested in new Orthodox forms of Judaism, by any means. Many are interested mainly in what is called *toda'ah yehudit*, "Jewish consciousness." They are bringing pressure on the Ministry of Education to teach more about Jewish ethics and values in the secular Israeli school system. They attend lectures and take courses in Jewish ideas and Jewish thought. Many study Bible and Talmud in a new way, asking what Jewish tradition has to say to modern Jews living in an independent Jewish state. And, as we have noted, many have turned to religious groups like the Reform and Conservative movements, which offer a different kind of Judaism from the Orthodox establishment, a Judaism that differs in three ways: (a) Judaism is perceived as a tradition which has always evolved to meet changing circumstances and needs and which must therefore continue to change; (b) Jewish religious pluralism is affirmed, meaning that more than one authentic expression of Judaism exists; (c) while ritual is accepted as indispensable, the ethical ideals of Judaism are equally important—they must be applied to all problems of business and industry, of labor, of politics, of scientific inquiry, of international relations.

The future of Israel depends on how this basic issue is resolved. Those who oppose the acceptance of non-Orthodox religious Judaism in Israel also reject modern insights regarding birth control, abortion, autopsy, archeological digs, and other issues. What is ultimately at stake here is whether Israel will be a modern, enlightened Jewish state or a narrow, parochial, almost medieval province.

Personal freedom has been a part of the Covenant from the time that our people left Egypt and settled in the Promised Land. The Covenant made Israel the homeland of the Jewish people. In some way, it must also be the Covenant which will keep Israeli Jews modern and Jewish.

Things to Consider

Jewish tradition says that "no law shall be made which the majority of the community cannot bear." In Israel, today, most Jews cannot live by Orthodox law. In what ways has Zionism made it difficult for Israelis to be Orthodox? Do you think that Reform or Conservative Judaism can become important to Israelis? Why? Why not?

After reading this chapter, do you believe that Israel should change its laws regarding religion? Which laws should be changed? How would you change them?

Some Jews say it is unnecessary for Israelis to be religious since Judaism in Israel is "in the air the Israelis breathe." Do you agree or disagree? Do you think the Jewish religion is important or not so important in the Jewish state?

REFORM AND CONSERVATIVE JUDAISM IN ISRAEL

The Orthodox have a religious monopoly on Israel. Reform and Conservative Jews who make aliyah *are welcomed officially as individuals, but their movements are very unwelcome to the Orthodox leaders. When the movements in Israel, at their very beginning, complained to Ben-Gurion about this, he said that, if enough Conservative and Reform Jews made* aliyah, *even this would change. But changes have been very slow in coming.*

The first Reform synagogue in Israel was set up in 1933 by Reform Jews who fled nazism in Germany. (Germany was the birthplace of Reform Judaism.) In 1935, a second Reform synagogue was set up in Jerusalem. The first Conservative synagogue was founded in Jerusalem in 1937. None of these synagogues asked for government money. They were built on the pattern of synagogues in the Diaspora, supporting themselves by membership and paying salaries to their rabbis. For a long while, they made few in-roads among the Israelis.

Nelson Glueck examining a vessel from Abraham's time.

By this time, Reform Jews in the Diaspora had become great supporters of Israel, and the president of the Reform rabbinical school, Dr. Nelson Glueck, who was also a biblical archeologist and spent much time in Israel, asked the government for land on which to build a Reform rabbinical college and chapel in Jerusalem. The Orthodox saw this as a great threat. When the school was opened in 1963, the great debate about non-Orthodox Judaism in Israel began in earnest.

The Sephardic chief rabbi openly announced that freedom of religion in Israel should not include the Reform Jews since "Reform is not a religion" and it might cause Judaism to be "torn asunder." Some Israeli politicians, hoping to make the Reform and Conservative Jews welcome without changing the Orthodox monopoly on Judaism in the Land, asked Reform and Conservative Jews to register officially as "religions other than Jewish." They could then receive tax monies and operate as the Orthodox do in Israel. Both the Conservative and Reform movements rejected this offer. They demand that all forms of Jewish *religion be accepted as Jewish in the Jewish state.*

After much pressure from the Jews of the Diaspora, and especially from Conservative and Reform Zionists, the government began quietly to aid the two movements in Israel. A grant was made to help build a Conservative synagogue on French Hill in Jerusalem. Land was made available in other cities for Reform and Conservative synagogues. But, so far, everything has been given un*officially, not as a matter of equal rights.*

Yet, the Conservative and Reform movements place great importance on the State of Israel and its future. By the 1980s, the movements had made great strides: fifteen Reform synagogues were members of the Israel Movement for Progressive Judaism and 39 Conservative syna-

gogues were members of the United Synagogue of Israel. Both Conservative and Reform movements have official parties in the World Zionist Organization. The Reform group is named ARZA. In Hebrew this means "to the land"; as an English acronym it stands for Association of Reform Zionists of America. ARZA is the largest component of ARZENU ("our land"), a federation of Reform Zionist parties in six countries. The Conservative parallel to ARZA is called MERCAZ ("center"), meaning the Movement to Reaffirm Conservative Zionism. The Reform movement, worldwide, has even established its main headquarters in Jerusalem. Both seek to reach out to Israelis with new kinds of Judaism, allowing for growth and change, giving the individual a greater say in all matters of religion.

The Reform movement has established two kibbutzim, Yahel and Lotan. A non-kibbutz settlement for Reform Jews is now being planned for the Galilee; the Conservative movement has started preparation for its first kibbutz. Since 1976, the Reform rabbinical college in Jerusalem, the Hebrew Union College-Jewish Institute of Religion, has been offering a year of study in Israel to all students becoming American Reform rabbis and has been graduating Sabras as rabbis to serve the needs of Reform congregations in Israel. An even deeper attachment between Reform and Conservative Jews and the Land of Israel is gained through the many study tours and summer or year-long courses offered to young people, and even to adults, from the Diaspora.

Many Israelis, used to Orthodox politics and

Planting a tree at the dedication of Kibbutz Yahel.

arguments, have little or no use for any organized Jewish religion. But, slowly, the two movements from the Diaspora are taking hold in Israel. As more Israelis join, and more Conservative and Reform Jews come to Israel, the Reform and Conservative movements will grow to be a power in the Land, and many of the Orthodox monopolies will be overthrown. Then all religious Jews in Israel—no matter what kind of Judaism they choose—will be allowed true religious freedom.

28

THE GREAT PROMISE

The Maccabiah, Israel's own Olympic Games, are about to begin. Thousands of Israelis watch the parade of athletes, ready to cheer their favorites.

An Israeli dance festival is underway. Yemenites perform the dances of their heritage. Kibbutz dance groups show a hundred different ways of doing the *horah* and other folk dances. Thousands of Israelis watch and join in the singing.

School vacation comes and the classes load on busses to take an Israeli-style *tiyul*, part "hike" and part bus ride, to visit the same places where millions of tourists come and go each year.

Thousands of new immigrants, all dark-skinned Ethiopian Jews, come to Jerusalem once a year on pilgrimage. They are celebrating a holiday mentioned in the Bible, the *Segged* day which only Ethiopian Jews celebrate.

Members of Israel's huge scouting movement, *Hatsofim,* meet with scouts from all around the world at an International Jamboree of World Scouts. It's also a chance to swap stories with Jewish scouts from America, Britain, France, and the rest of the world.

Israeli soldiers at the front pause to pray. In the midst of the Yom Kippur War, many observed Sukot by building the small temporary dwelling, the *sukah*.

In Tel Aviv, a craftsman sits behind his table, raising his hammer to strike the edge of a raw diamond delicately. A few more strikes, and the diamond takes on its wondrous emerald shape, glittering in the light, shining in its every facet beneath the magnifying glass. Israeli diamond-cutting is considered to be the finest of its kind.

The oranges hang ripe on the trees. Harvesters sort them into sizes, saving the very best for shipment to Spain, Italy, and the United States—to be known the world over as Jaffa oranges.

The wine industry of Israel, now over one hundred years old, announces that it will release for sale wines produced in the early part of this century—wines that will be prized and tasted along with the best bottles from France and California.

An Israeli scientist announces a new kind of air conditioning for automobiles, one that uses the heat of the engine to create the cool air on the inside of the car. Less gas will be needed for this new invention. The world will depend just that much less on its small reserves of petroleum.

The Weizmann Institute announces that it can produce "heavy water," for use in atomic research. Israel now supplies 90 percent of the heavy water in use around the world.

At the Technion, studies in laser beams led to the invention of the surgical laser knife which is now used around the world in open heart surgery. Israeli medical scientists have also made great strides in the study of cancer.

In the middle of the desert, wheat grows needing nothing but the small amounts of rainfall that come to the Negev each year. It's part of an experiment to discover how the ancient Nabateans who once farmed this part of the country collected their water and used it.

Off the coast of Eilat, salt water is turned into fresh drinking water in a desalinization plant.

THE GREAT PROMISE

The seventh Maccabiah, 1965, Israel's own Olympics.

The promise of enough water for everyone in the world lies in this kind of process, for the world is three-quarters ocean.

A new group of Israeli soldiers climb the "snake path" leading up to the top of Masada, where once the Zealots watched the Romans build a ramp reaching upward from the valley floor and swore they would not fall into Roman hands (see chapter six). Looking down from the heights of this desert fortress, the soldiers are sworn to defend Israel with their lives. Israel shall not fall again.

An Israeli writer receives word that an English translation of his novel has become a best seller in America. He is a kibbutznik. The money will go to the kibbutz, to make all who live there a little more comfortable. But his heart leaps with joy to know that Americans will understand Israel a little better.

A new Russian immigrant becomes Israel's most popular songwriter and singer overnight. Thousands of Israelis hum the melody of his song as they drive to work or take a shared taxi called a *sherut* ("service") from Jerusalem to Beersheba. The words to the tune are well known. They are the central prayer of Judaism, the *Shema*. Where else could the *Shema* be a popular hit song?

In South America, in the offices of the Jewish Agency, Israelis prepare lesson plans and textbooks for Spanish-speaking and Portuguese-speaking Jews of the Diaspora. They have spearheaded Jewish education in Europe, South America, and other Diaspora communities.

In a meeting of the youth group known as *Hashachar* (Young Judea) in the United States, an Israeli *shaliach,* visiting the United States for a couple of years, talks to young people about Zionism. From his lips come names like Rav Kook, Moses Hess, and Rabbi Zevi Kalischer—all religious men who spoke of Zionism and the Holy Land.

In the Ben Zevi Institute, a young Israeli who was born in Dallas, Texas, helps to research the folklore and heritage of Oriental Jews who came from Persia, Yemen, Ethiopia, Iraq, and Syria.

On the hour, *Kol Yisrael* ("The Voice of Israel"—Israel's official radio station) broadcasts the news of the day. Throughout Israel people stop and listen. On busses that belong to Egged, Israel's bus company, the radios are turned on so that passengers can hear. What has happened in the United Nations? What is the

Dancing the horah.

235

new arms that Israel needs to keep its military ahead of that of its Arab neighbors? Has the Israeli soccer team won in the international soccer competition?

Has the messiah come?

Scattered among the nations of the earth, Jews tune their television sets and listen to their radios. They feel a special surge of loyalty when the word Israel is spoken, or when Israel is in the headlines. They watch and listen with special care to what is happening in the Middle East. Many have visited Israel, some have even studied there or lived there briefly, hundreds of thousands more hope to visit Israel soon.

Many will land in the airport at Lydda, step down from the airplane, and some even bend to kiss the earth of the Holy Land. Their first stop will be the Western Wall in Jerusalem. They will stand before it and try to imagine the glory of Solomon's Temple or the Temple in the days of King Herod. They may visit Herzl's tomb, or the Museum of the Diaspora which shows the long history of the Jewish people in its years of wandering, or Yad Vashem where they will be

(Above) Mosaic plaque and grape arbor, entrance to the Carmel Winery, Rishon le-Zion. (Below) Brachish water plant, the pilot plant for saline water research.

government doing? What's happening in the West Bank? Is the economy going to get better or will inflation just keep rising? Are Israel's neighbors planning new conflicts and wars or are they thinking at long last about peace? Will the next government be formed by the Revisionists or the Labor leaders? Will the archeologists digging in Jerusalem near the ancient Temple mount be allowed to continue digging, or will the Orthodox complain that disturbing the bones and artifacts of the past is "unholy" and try to stop it? Have the Palestinian terrorists hijacked a plane or assassinated more innocent people? Or have some of them finally come to their senses and decided to seek a peaceful solution before it's too late? Has the United States decided to ship the

Underwater coral, Eilat.

reminded of the horrors of the Holocaust. In the Museum of Glass in Tel Aviv they will discover one of the world's most ancient arts, and in the Billy Rose Sculpture Garden at Hebrew University they will see the work of Jewish artists in the fresh open air of Jerusalem. They may visit ancient monuments like the Tomb of Rachel, the graves of the Sanhedrin, the desert palace of Herod at Masada, the Tower of David, the Roman amphitheater and baths at Caesarea, the mosaic floors of the synagogues near Lake Kinneret. They may stand in wonder before the colorful valley at Mitzpeh Ramon, swim effortlessly in the buoyant Dead Sea, relax in the hot mineral baths at the Dead Sea and Kinneret, take a glass-bottom boat to see the fantastic coral of the Red Sea off the coast of Eilat. They may visit the cool limestone caves of Bet Guvrin in the middle of a hot desert day or the valley where the armies of Saladin and Richard the Lion-Hearted met in battle. Most of all, they will be amazed by what the Israelis have done to this ancient land— how the desert has been forced to bloom, how a city of glass and steel and stone was raised up on barren sand dunes to become Tel Aviv, how the New City of Jerusalem with its towers and government buildings blends so easily with the Old City, how the cotton grows six feet tall and the trees give dates and pomegranates and olives as

well as peaches and oranges, how the money raised by Israel Bonds and foreign investors has grown into factories and industries throughout the Land.

Israel's problems, as great as they are, seem small compared to its great achievements. A child among the modern nations of the world, Israel is a grandparent to many of them already— their people study agriculture, business, and industry in Israel's universities and schools; they study how a new nation can rise to greatness in such a short span of years.

Some things do not change. With a little help, Moses would soon be a fine speaker of modern Hebrew. Herod might marvel at the Jewish love of building. Joseph Nasi would be pleased to see the city he loved so well, Tiberias, as it stands today. Moses Montefiore might be happy to know that the first buildings he had built outside the walls of the Old City of Jerusalem are now a section called Yemin Moshe in his honor, filled

The Dead Sea at night.

UNIT SIX: Judaism and the Jewish State

Solar energy scientist, contributing to Israeli industry.

with young artists and designers. His dream of a working windmill never came to pass, but the windmill attracts visitors and has become as much a part of the city of Jerusalem as the wall built by the Moslems. Ben Yehudah would love the street language and slang of Israel's youth— he would probably take out his notebook and begin work on a whole new dictionary of the Hebrew language.

Herzl would shake hands eagerly with the Sabras of Israel, knowing that his dream had helped shape a new kind of Jew, proud of being a Jew, ready to stand against the whole world if need be to defend the Jewish state. Achad Ha-Am would be delighted with the fact that the Reform movement's world headquarters are located in Jerusalem and that Israel sends volunteers to Jewish communities everywhere to teach and learn from them. A. D. Gordon would see the harvest of the "religion of labor." Jabotinsky would be proud of the strength and dedication of Israel's Defense Forces. Weizmann would be stunned to learn that the anti-British Israelis had fought a war together with Britain in the Sinai.

PREVIEW

What is Israel's future? Whatever the answer, it will be shaped by what Jews in Israel and Jews in the Diaspora choose to do. We, who live outside of the Jewish state, have a great stake in what happens inside the Jewish state. More and more, the people of Israel share that knowledge. Jews must stand together. As the Talmud says, "Every Jew is responsible, each for the other."

Israel has caused a revolution in modern Jewish thinking. Jews have returned to the Land, as farmers, as workers. Jews have built in the Land a society based on freedom and democracy. Jews have brought their own people home to safety in a true "ingathering of the exiles." And we must hope that the Jews who did this, the Jews of Israel, will increasingly awaken to their own Jewishness, to seek out what it can mean to them personally, spiritually, politically, and culturally.

Behind all this is the ancient Covenant with its promise and its demand. The promise has, in many ways, been fulfilled. The Jewish people and the Jewish homeland are again free to live Jewishly. The demand of the Covenant has yet to be fulfilled. The new goal of Zionism must be to shape a Jewish people on its own soil that will become the "light to the nations," that will finally be in its own terms "a kingdom of priests and a holy people." So much depends on how these words are understood—on how you understand them, and what you make of them in your own life and in your own dealings with the State of Israel. For the story of the future will be your story. The world will be the world you create.

There have always been Jews living in the Land of Israel. Now you know how they have lived, why they remained when even hope seemed lost. You know, too, the problems and perils that are faced by the young nation of Israel.

Now you shall write the next chapter. *Chazak veamats,* "Be of courage and good strength." The words you write by the way you act will be the history you give to your children to read. It will be another chapter in the story of Israel—the Covenant and the people.

Peace is Israel's top priority. (Above) "The Peaceable Kingdom," oil painting by Edward Hicks, based on peaceful biblical themes. (Below) Sun breaking through rain clouds, Old and New Jerusalem.

PHOTO CREDITS

American Jewish Archives, HUC-JIR: p. 83.

Consulate General of Israel: pp. 25, 60, 74, 104, 124, 168, 175 (top), 178, 180, 186 (photo, W. Braun), 192, 193, 205, 208, 213, 237 (top).

D. Harris and W. Braun, Jerusalem: p. 56 (top).

F. Schlesinger, Jerusalem: p. 76.

Hadassah Photo: pp. 126, 140 (top).

H. R. Abramson: pp. 39, 65, 71, 81 (bottom), 217, 220 (top), 236 (top).

Israel Government Coins and Medals Corporation: p. 163.

Israel Government Press Office: pp. 56 (bottom), 75 (top), 227 (bottom).

Israel Government Tourist Office: pp. 59, 226.

Israel Office of Information: pp. 57, 158, 164, 179, 183, 185, 227 (top), 235 (bottom).

Israel Press and Photo Agency: pp. 24, 30, 199 (bottom), 203, 207, 215.

Israel State Archives, Jerusalem: p. 151.

Joint Distribution Committee: p. 171.

JPS. *Haggadah and History,* Yosef H. Yerushalmi: p. 22.

Leo Baeck Institute, New York. Photos, Eric Pollitzer: pp. 97, 98.

New York Times Photograph: p. 214.

North Country News Service: p. 19.

Philip Hiat: p. 40 (top).

Photo Illustrations of Canada: p. 26.

Pierpont Morgan Library: p. 37.

United Nations: p. 177.

United Nations Relief and Works Agency: p. 216.

W. Braun, Jerusalem: p. 50.

White House Photographs: p. 210.

Zev Radovan, Jerusalem: p. 233.

Zionist Archives and Library: pp. 90, 91 (bottom), 92, 93, 94, 102, 103, 105, 106, 112, 113, 114, 121, 122, 127, 128, 131, 132, 133, 136, 140 (bottom), 146, 169, 175 (center & bottom), 194.

INDEX

INDEX

INDEX

INDEX

INDEX

INDEX

INDEX

INDEX